CORRECTIONS
OFFICER
EXAM

CORRECTIONS OFFICER EXAM

2nd Edition

LEARNINGEXPRESS®

NEW YORK

Library of Congress Cataloging-in-Publication Data:
Corrections officer exam.—2nd ed.
    p. cm.
  ISBN 1-57685-522-8
  1. Correctional personnel—United States—Examinations—Study guides.
  2. Correctional personnel—United States—Examinations, questions, etc.
  3. Corrections—Vocational guidance—United States.
I. LearningExpress (Organization)
HV9470.C69 2004
365'.076—dc22

                                                           2004016495

Printed in the United States of America

9 8 7 6 5 4 3 2 1

Second Edition

ISBN 1-57685-522-8

Regarding the Information in this Book
We attempt to verify the information presented in our books prior to publication. It is always a good idea, however, to double-check such important information as minimum requirements, application and testing procedures, and deadlines with your local law enforcement agency, as such information can change from time to time.

For more information or to place an order, contact LearningExpress at:
    55 Broadway
    8th Floor
    New York, NY 10006

Or visit us at:
    www.learnatest.com

Contributors

The following individuals contributed to the content of this book.

Marco A. Annunziata is a former teacher and freelance writer. He lives in New York City, New York.

Tom Ferrell is a business communications consultant and writer based in Boulder, Colorado.

Dr. Zelma W. Henriques is a Professor in the Department of Law, Police Science, and Criminal Justice Administration at John Jay College of Criminal Justice at the City University of New York.

Mary Hesalroad, a police officer for the Austin, Texas Police Department, has many years of experience as a law enforcement recruiter.

Judith N. Meyers is director of the Two Together Tutorial Program of the Jewish Child Care Association in New York City and formerly an Adult Basic Education Practitioner at City University of New York

Margaret Muirhead is a freelance writer. She has worked on LearningExpress's *TOEFL Exam Essentials* and *Praxis I, Second Edition.* She lives in Arlington, Massachusetts.

Judith F. Olson, M.A., is a chairperson of the language arts department at Valley High School in West Des Moines, Iowa where she also conducts test preparation workshops.

Judith Robinovitz is an independent educational consultant and director of Score At the Top, a comprehensive test preparation program in Vero Beach, Florida.

Jay Smith is an exercise physiologist and Director of Physical Fitness and Health Maintenance Programs for the Massachusetts Criminal Justice Training Council.

Contents

How to Use This Book ▶

So you have made the choice to become a corrections officer! You will find a career in corrections to be both challenging and rewarding. The work is interesting, pays well, and offers good benefits. However, before you land the job you want, you must face a rigorous selection process. Competition is tough, so you will need a top score on the written exam to become an attractive candidate. Through numerous practice exams and instruction chapters, this book will give you the review you need to ace the test. You will also learn about other important stages of the selection process, including the application process and interview. The hiring process can take from a few months to one year, so make sure you are ready to make a dedicated effort to your goal.

You will want to begin your preparation by reading Chapter 1, "Becoming a Corrections Officer" to find out whether a career in corrections is really right for you. This chapter describes typical duties, the fast-growing job prospects, and the nature of the work. It will also give you a basic introduction to the selection process, including all of the hurdles—from the written test to the medical exam—that you will meet on your way to getting your uniform.

Next, in Chapter 2, "The Federal Employment Process," you will read specifics about the hiring procedures for federal corrections officers—from initial application to the training academy. You will learn all about getting hired, trained, paid, and promoted in this desirable segment of the corrections field.

Chapter 3, "The State Employment Process," offers an overview of what it takes to become a state-employed corrections officer, focusing on the top-rated states with the highest employment in this profession. Read this chapter carefully to understand how to prepare yourself for each stage of the game.

Chapter 4, "The Learning Express Test Preparation System," will give you invaluable advice about how to organize your time before and during the written exam. If you have had trouble with written exams in the past (anxiety, running out of time), do not skip this chapter—it gives you great test-taking strategies, including tips about how to choose the right multiple-choice answer when you are unsure. Be sure to take advantage of the sample study plans in this chapter. The best insurance for acing your exam is good preparation, and these study schedules will help you organize your time.

After devising a study plan for yourself, jump right in and take a practice exam offered in Chapter 5. Once you have taken the exam and know the areas where you need the most work, you can begin studying the different subjects in Chapters 6–10. After substantial review of your problem subjects, you have the option of taking two more practice exams in Chapters 11 and 12 to see if your score improves. From there, you can determine how much more preparation you need and whether you want to seek help from a tutor or specific study in a subject.

Do not forget to read Chapters 13–16, which cover crucial information about the Physical Ability Test, the Personal History Statement and Background Investigation, the Oral Interview, the Psychological Assessment, and Medical Exam. These steps in the selection process may be just as important, if not more, than the written test in deciding your rank as a job candidate. This book provides information about how to best train for the physical test as well as useful strategies for completing your personal statement and for presenting yourself at the interview so that you make a strong and positive impression.

In short, this book is here to help. It covers all of the basics of what corrections departments across the country are looking for in a candidate, and it gives you examples of what typical corrections officer exams are like. You have given yourself a big advantage by choosing to use this book. However, one essential ingredient that this book does not provide is *specific* requirements for the corrections department in your city or state of interest. This book is best used in combination with the information you get from your corrections department about the details of its hiring process. Make a phone call to the department's personnel office, and clarify exactly what steps you need to take. Your success in becoming a corrections officer depends largely on your motivation and the amount of effort you are willing to make to achieve your goals.

CORRECTIONS OFFICER EXAM

CHAPTER

Becoming a Corrections Officer

CHAPTER SUMMARY

If you want to know whether a career as a corrections officer suits you, just keep reading. This chapter describes typical duties, the fast-growing job prospects, and the nature of the work. You will find information about the hiring process and tips on making yourself a top-notch candidate. You will also find plenty of facts about current trends in corrections at the federal, state, and local level.

Today's corrections officer needs to be a quick thinker, able learner, good leader, and physically and emotionally strong. These are important traits because it takes a variety of skills and knowledge—not to mention stamina—to do this job.

Officers work in stressful, sometimes dangerous, settings, where their job is to maintain security and order. This work requires training in areas such as understanding criminal behavior, knowing how to deal with groups of inmates who come from different cultural and ethnic backgrounds, and managing the tension that builds among people who are confined to a cell and cut off from the outside world. Technical knowledge also is becoming more important for this job. Where budgets allow, many facilities are putting in high-tech safety and security devices. Corrections officers are the ones who have to be able to operate these sophisticated systems.

There is also a lot to cope with in terms of the working conditions. It's a fact that many prisons are overcrowded and underfunded, that more violent offenders are behind bars than ever before, and that drug use among inmates is widespread. These and other major changes in the prison system have added strain to an already tough environment.

Sheer numbers tell more of the tale: the U.S. prison population has more than tripled since 1980. The Bureau of Justice Statistics (BJS) reported a total of 1,440,655 prisoners under state or federal jurisdiction at the end of

2001. More than 1.2 million of those are housed in state facilities and over 160,000 in federal facilities. As for local jails, the population of inmates and people awaiting trial reached a record high of 737,912 as of midyear 2002. Inmate populations grew in 2002 by 2.5% in state prison, 5.4% in local jails, and 5.8% in federal prisons.

As the number of inmates continues to climb, so does the need for corrections officers. Corrections facilities throughout the country are actively looking for qualified job candidates that will meet the challenges of this demanding position.

The Daily Routine

The fundamental responsibility of a corrections officer is to make sure that a prison, jail, or other type of correctional facility stays safe and secure. To do this, they guard, supervise, and give guidance to criminal offenders who are confined to the facility.

Corrections officers monitor the activities and behavior of inmates at all times—when they are sleeping, showering, eating, working, or exercising. They escort inmates to and from cells and other areas of the prison and, as needed, back and forth from outside areas such as courtrooms or medical facilities. They explain the institution's policies and regulations to inmates, and also may schedule the inmates' work assignments and take part in vocational training.

Search and inspection are regular duties. This includes everything from reading inmates' mail to inspecting cells to conducting body searches of inmates. These duties are aimed at finding any forbidden items or materials (such as drugs, weapons, tools, or other contraband) or uncovering any criminal activities (such as smuggling operations or plans for escape). Along with admitting and escorting authorized visitors, corrections officers also may monitor conversations between inmates and visitors.

Depending on the size and set-up of a facility, corrections officers may be assigned to specific areas such as the laundry room, mailroom, motor pool, or an on-site medical center. Certain specialized tasks may also be available, such as being part of the road crew or canine unit. Security duties include patrolling the grounds and buildings to make sure that locks, bars, and doors are secure. Corrections officers also check medical and food supply areas for possible thefts and are always on the lookout for unsanitary or unsafe conditions, especially fire hazards.

A vital role of corrections officers is to discipline and keep order among inmates. They must watch for signs of tension or conflict in order to prevent physical violence or emergency situations such as riots. At times this can require the use of force or weapons. Delivering first aid or basic medical treatment also may be necessary. However, while corrections officers must enforce the rules of a prison, they also must protect inmates and stay within the boundaries of prisoners' rights.

Preparing written reports is another part of the job. These may include keeping daily logbooks and writing conduct or progress reports about inmates. These reports must be accurate and complete because they may be used by parole boards or by the courts. Corrections officers also need to inform their supervisors in person of any fights, suspicious activity, or violations of prison rules that may occur.

What corrections officers do on the job depends to some extent on the facility where they work. Different types of facilities—federal or state prisons, city or county jails, boot camps, reformatories, detention centers—vary in scope and use different levels of security. For example, a maximum-security prison may be walled or double-fenced and have gun towers, numerous security devices, cell housing for inmates, and a large staff to supervise inmates. A boot camp, on the other hand, may have patrol guards (instead of being fenced or walled), dormitory housing (instead of cells), and a lower staff-to-inmate ratio. Because of these differences, the duties you perform and the danger you face on a daily basis can vary depending on the institution where you are employed.

Communication Skills

Good communication skills are one of the most important traits you can bring to the job. Some officers work a cellblock alone, overseeing from 50 to 100 prisoners and relying mostly on person-to-person communication skills to enforce prison rules. Officers must be tough disciplinarians who can keep inmates in line—one way they accomplish this is to suspend privileges if an inmate violates regulations. Officers must also be fair—they cannot display favoritism and are required to report any prisoner who breaks the rules.

Corrections officers sometimes act as part of a team that includes social workers, psychologists, parole and probation officers, and teachers, who counsel, guide, or educate inmates. That could mean helping to develop inmates' reading and writing skills, counseling them about drug and alcohol abuse, preparing them for employment upon their release, or helping to sort through personal problems. Many prisons offer advanced training in the skills corrections officers need to conduct one-on-one or group counseling sessions.

Your ability to communicate matters in other ways as well. As a corrections officer, you are responsible for instructing inmates about prison regulations, explaining their work assignments, and supervising them in their daily routine. You will need to understand prison policies and follow orders yourself. Open and clear communication with other officers and your supervisors is essential, as is using concise, correct writing skills in your daily reports.

Jobs on the Rise

According to the U.S. Bureau of Labor Statistics (BLS), job opportunities for corrections officers are expected to be excellent throughout the decade. Job openings for corrections officers will likely increase faster than the average for all occupations through 2012. A growing inmate population, in combination with the need to replace corrections officers who retire or change jobs, will create thousands of job positions each year. Expansion of corrections facilities and the construction of new facilities will also increase the need for corrections officers—although jail and prison construction may slow somewhat in states and localities where budgets are tight. A recent trend toward giving longer sentences and reducing parole for criminal offenders means that inmates will be held for longer periods of time, thus generating the need for more corrections officers to supervise them. Job security for corrections officers is high and layoffs are rare in this field, due to the increasing inmate population. As the numbers of prisoners increase, so does the demand for corrections officers. Another trend in corrections work is for government agencies to contract with private companies to staff corrections facilities. For example, in 2000, more than 260 privately run corrections facilities were under contract with state or federal governments—an increase of 140% from 1995. Because of this trend, private companies will be another source of employment for corrections officers.

The BLS reports that corrections officers held about 476,000 jobs in 2002—up from 282,000 jobs in 1992. About 16,000 of these officers worked at federal prisons, while about 60% worked at state facilities, including prisons, prison camps, and youth correctional institutions. Prisons owned and operated by private companies accounted for another 16,000 jobs. City and county jails or other local facilities provided most of the remaining jobs. Although a total of 118 urban jail systems exists across the nation, the majority of corrections officers work in larger institutions located in rural areas.

JUST THE FACTS
Federal Inmates by Security Level

Minimum	28,576
Low	57,152
Medium	36,825
High	15,761

(Source: Federal Bureau of Prisons automated information systems, February 2004)

Hours and Earnings

On average, corrections officers work eight-hour shifts, five days a week. Some institutions use other work schedules, such as four work days followed by two days off. Because correctional facilities require 24-hour protection, every work schedule includes some nights, weekends, and holidays. As a corrections officer, you can expect to work paid overtime and some double shifts, plus you may be called in during emergencies. Depending on your assignments, you may be working either indoors or outdoors. Conditions in correctional institutions vary. Some newly constructed facilities are well-lit and temperature-controlled, whereas older prisons can be overcrowded, dark, and noisy.

The average annual income of corrections officers was $35,090 in 2003, with the lowest ten percent earning $22,390 and the highest ten percent earning $52,880. As with most jobs, the salary you earn as a corrections officer depends on where you work and for whom you work. Corrections officers who work for the federal government earn more on average than those who work for state or local governments or for a private contractor. This pay difference exists in part because the Federal Bureau of Prisons (BOP) requires that new hires have a college education or related work experience. Median yearly salaries in 2003 ranged from $42,700 at a federal facility, $35,980 at a state-run institution, and $34,080 at a local prison or jail..

JUST THE FACTS
The federal inmate population in 2004 was made up of:

> 56% Whites
> 40% African Americans
> 1.6% Asian
> 1.6% Native Americans

(Source: Federal Bureau of Prisons automated information systems, February 2004)

Level of experience and time on the job can also influence a corrections officer's earnings. On the federal level, a starting salary for a corrections officer in 2003 was about $23,000, according to the Federal Bureau of Prisons. The geographical location of the facility can affect pay rates as well. For example, incomes for federal corrections officers were slightly higher in areas where local earning levels were higher. Gaining more on-the-job experience and additional education or training can lead to both salary increases and promotions. Corrections officers may be promoted to positions that involve supervising other officers, administrative duties, or counseling. They also may use their experience to move into related areas such as probation and parole.

This job typically offers standard benefit packages, including major medical, hospital, disability, and life insurance; paid vacation days, holidays, and sick leave; and a retirement plan. Many institutions offer extra benefits such as dental coverage, vision care plans, and credit unions. Uniforms and equipment are usually provided by the institution. Educational benefits are becoming more common, with institutions paying for corrections officers to attend college or special training courses, or offering salary increases for those who take courses or earn degrees on their own. Institutions also may offer various "employee assistance programs" (EAPs), which may include financial or legal aid, stress management classes, substance abuse counseling, and personal or family counseling. In federal positions and most state jobs, the retirement coverage allows officers to retire at age 50 after completing 20 years of service or at any age following 25 years on the job.

JUST THE FACTS
In 1999, 7 states held about half of all jail inmates:

California	77,142
Texas	57,930
Florida	51,080
New York	34,411
Georgia	32,835
Pennsylvania	26,996
Louisiana	25,631

(Source: Bureau of Justice Statistics, Census of Jails, 1999)

Reality Check

Going into this job, it is important to be realistic about your working environment. Working in a correctional facility is often stressful, and at times, dangerous. Every year, prisons and jails report a number of inmate assaults on staff members. While both jails and prisons can be dangerous places to work, the constantly changing nature of the jail population creates hazards that are less likely in prisons where the inmate population is more stable. In 1999, a third of jail systems reported that staff members were physically confronted by inmates. In jails, the population fluctuates as individuals enter or leave the system through arrest, transfer to prison, or release. The time between when a person is arrested and when the jail staff learns about that person's identity or criminal record is a critical, and dangerous, phase. Corrections officers may place a violent offender with the general population of detainees because the staff is not yet aware of the person's criminal record. Here are some statistics provided by the Bureau of Justice Statistics (BJS) that describe some of the characteristics of today's inmates:

- Violent offenders accounted for the largest percentage (49.3%) of the state prison population.
- Drug law violators comprised the largest percentage (54.7%) of the federal prison population.
- Nearly half (45%) of the inmates in state and federal prisons combined have been in prison three or more times before.

These figures tell you something about the inmates you will encounter on the job. Besides drug and violent offenders, prison populations also include property offenders, public-order offenders, and others.

JUST THE FACTS
Although men are 15 times more likely than women to be incarcerated in a state or federal prison, the female inmate population is increasing at a faster rate than the male prisoner population. Since 1995, the number of female prisoners has increased annually by an average 5.4%, whereas the number of male inmates has increased by an average 3.6%.
(Source: Bureau of Justice Statistics Bulletin)

Overcrowded prisons are another job factor to consider. According to BJS findings, by the end of 2002, state prisons were operating 1% and 17% above capacity, and federal prisons were 33% above their rate capacity. (The "intended capacity" is the highest number of prisoners a facility was built to hold.) These are key figures because tension tends to mount in these conditions, which can lead to violence, escape attempts, or riots.

JUST THE FACTS
By mid-year 2002, the nation's prisons and jails held more than 2 million inmates for the first time. State and federal prisons housed more than 1.3 million prisoners, and municipal and county jails held more than 665,000 inmates.
(Source: Bureau of Justice Statistics)

As you consider whether you are right for the job, ask yourself some tough questions. How will you:

- cope with being around convicted criminals on a daily basis?
- handle the built-in level of potential violence?
- give fair and decent treatment to a prisoner whose attitudes and views are offensive to you?
- put up with verbal and possibly physical abuse?
- put aside any prejudices or stereotypes in dealing with inmates whose racial, ethnic, religious, or cultural background are different from your own?
- keep an open mind about the chance that some inmates will serve their time and go on to lead law-abiding lives after being released?

- Emotionally mature and stable
- Good communication and interpersonal skills
- Alert, able to think and act quickly
- Good leadership and supervisory skills
- Diplomatic, patient, and a good listener
- Reliable and honest
- Ethical and fair

- Accepting of racial, ethnic, cultural, and religious differences
- Sympathetic but realistic understanding of human behavior
- Strong sense of self, not easily manipulated or offended
- Physical strength and stamina

Keep in mind that many correctional facilities are active in training and counseling corrections officers to help manage the daily pressures of this important job. Although the job can be a test of your mettle, corrections work is a part of a vital system that aims to protect society from harm.

▶ Getting the Job: The Selection Process

Now that you know about the everyday duties of a corrections officer, the hiring prospects, salary and benefits, and the working environment, the next step is to begin the process of applying for the job. The selection process for corrections officers differs depending on whether you are applying to federal, state, or local institutions. Chapters 2 and 3 of this book provide more detailed information about the requirements for state and federal institutions. Although there is no one set of standard qualifications or hiring procedures for the job, the following overview will provide you with *typical* aspects of the selection process.

Because the job requires a high level of responsibility, you can expect that the selection process will be time-consuming. It may take you several months to a year to land the job. Local, state, and federal facilities across the nation are looking for applicants who can think and act quickly, and who can handle the challenges of becoming an authority figure. Public safety

agencies do not want to rush through the process of determining whether you have these qualities.

Competition for entry-level positions in the corrections field can also be intense. The remainder of this chapter will guide you through the hiring process—the written exam, the physical ability test, the background investigation, the interview, and the medical or psychological exam—so that you will be prepared and have an edge over your competitors.

The Eligibility List

Most departments—whether local, state, or federal—hire entry-level corrections officers from a list that ranks eligible candidates from highest to lowest. They hire the applicant who ranked number one in their hiring process and work their way down the list. How rank is determined varies from agency to agency. Some departments emphasize written test scores whereas others rely more on the interview portion of the hiring process. Other agencies look at a combination of factors to rank applicants, including written, verbal, and physical ability test scores. In some rare instances, departments have a hiring process that consists of only a background investigation and an interview.

In order to make sure that your name will be at the top of your agency's eligibility list, you need to commit to preparing for a rigorous selection process. The following summary will outline the basic features of the hiring procedure for corrections officers and will give you the information you need to begin the process.

Basic Qualifications

Most agencies agree on the same basic list of qualifications that you will need to become a corrections officer. The list of minimum requirements includes:

- a minimum age—some agencies require applicants to be 18 years old; more often, agencies set the minimum at 20 or 21 years old. Maximum ages have been challenged in the courts, with the result that most agencies no longer list a maximum age.
- U.S. citizenship or, in some agencies, resident alien status
- a high school diploma or a General Equivalency Degree (GED) and, increasingly, some college hours or even a college degree
- no criminal record, although some agencies do accept a limited history of misdemeanor offenses
- sound physical and mental health, including good vision and hearing and an appropriate weight-to-height ratio
- A valid driver's license and a satisfactory driving record (for some positions)

Some institutions also include a local residency requirement. Fluency in languages other than English that are common to the inmate population is another advantage. Many corrections agencies give special consideration to qualified veterans over civilians. This may take the form of a policy, sometimes called a "Veteran's Preference" policy, whereby points are automatically added to the passing score of an applicant's written exam. Some agencies use this policy because they consider military personnel to be qualified with skills—such as use of firearms—that are important on the job.

Disqualifying Factors

Automatic disqualifiers include a felony record. In most cases, agencies will not consider convicted felons for any correctional employment. Some misdemeanors can also disqualify an applicant, depending on the agency.

In addition, corrections officers must be able to physically perform basic job-related tasks. Disabilities that would not be a problem in other occupations might become disqualifying conditions for corrections officers. For instance, many departments ask that applicants have a certain level of hearing. Being overweight can also be a disqualifying factor. For more information about applicants with disabilities, see the section about Medical Exams later in this chapter. To find out the basic qualifications required by the agency of your choice, contact the recruiting or personnel office directly. It will send you a list of qualifications and let you in on the steps you will need to follow to apply.

The Exam Announcement

When agencies are in a hiring mode, the first step they usually take is to post a job announcement for the position of corrections officer (sometimes called *detention officer* in the jail system). The announcement will outline the basic qualifications for the corrections officer position and the all-important details of the selection process. Most agencies have some form of written exam requirement. You should see a date when the written exam will be given and a location for the testing site.

Get a copy of this announcement. Often your public library will have a copy, or the recruiting/personnel department of the hiring agency will have copies. You should also check the agency Internet website for openings since many agencies now post job listings online.

Depending on how often the agency gives exams, the notice may simply tell you when and where to show up to take the next exam. Most agencies give a written exam at least once every year, if not more often. Carefully read the exam announcement and any other materials the agency sends, like brochures. Be sure to double-check any fine print and be clear about test times, directions, or other crucial details.

The Application

Although rare, some departments do not ask applicants to take a written test. In this instance, the first step you may take in the hiring process is to fill out a multi-paged application to detail your education, employment experience, and personal data. If this is the case, treat the written application as your Personal History Statement, which you will read about later in this chapter and in Chapter 14. Other agencies require only a short application in order to take the written exam; the lengthy Personal History Statement comes later, once you pass the exam.

When you call an agency to ask for an exam announcement or application, the person who answers the phone may conduct a brief prescreening to make sure that you meet the basic qualifications. This person on the other end of the line is not likely to be the one who conducts your background investigation, so being direct and concise is your best strategy.

The Written Exam

The written exam, if one is required, is your first opportunity to show that you have what it takes to be a corrections officer. As such, it's extremely important. People who don't pass the written exam don't go any farther in the selection process. Furthermore, the written exam score often figures into applicants' rank on the eligibility list; in some cases, this score by itself determines your rank, whereas in others it is combined with other scores, such as physical ability or interview scores. As a result, a person who merely passes the exam with a score of, say, 70, is unlikely to be hired when there are plenty of applicants with scores in the 90s. The exam bulletin may specify what your rank will be based on.

An excellent way to boost your score on the exam is to study and complete the practice exams in this book that correspond to the corrections exam for which you're studying.

What the Written Exam Is Like

Although there is no standard, national corrections exam, most written exams required by corrections agencies share many similarities. They test fundamental skills and aptitudes: how well you understand what you read, your ability to follow directions, your

judgment and reasoning skills, your ability to read and understand maps and floor plans, and sometimes your memory or your math skills. In this preliminary written exam, you will not be tested on your knowledge of corrections behavior, corrections policies and procedures, or any other specific body of knowledge. This test is designed only to see if you can read, reason, and do basic math.

Corrections officers have to be able to read, understand, and act on complex written materials such as laws, policy handbooks, and regulations. They have to write incident reports and other materials in clear and correct language. The basic skills that the written exam measures are skills corrections officers use every day.

Most exams are multiple-choice tests of the sort you've probably encountered in school. You get an exam book and an answer sheet where you select an answer choice, by filling in circles (bubbles) or squares with a number 2 pencil.

Increasingly, agencies are supplementing multiple-choice tests with other test formats. Because writing is an important part of a corrections officer's job, some agencies ask applicants to write an essay or mock report. You might be asked to write two or three paragraphs about a general topic (topics are designed so that you can answer them without having any specialized knowledge). Or you might be shown videotape or slides and asked to write about what you see. In this case, the agency can assess both your writing skills and your short-term memory.

How to Prepare for the Written Exam

Pay close attention to any study or informational material the recruiting unit or personnel department provides about the exam. Ask if the agency has a test study guide. If it does, be sure to allow yourself time to read it and complete any practice questions.

If the hiring agency does not have a study guide, you can prepare for the test by getting a basic, standardized test preparation book at your local library or

- Ask for and *use* any material the personnel department provides about the test. Some agencies have study guides; some even conduct study sessions. Give yourself an advantage by using them.
- Practice. Review the material in the instructional chapters in this book, which offer tips on how to improve in each skill area on the exam. Take the practice corrections exams in chapters 5, 11, and 12.
- Try to find some people who have taken the exam recently, and ask them about what was on the exam. Their hindsight—"I wish I had . . ."—can be your foresight.

bookstore. Any test prep book that has basic skills questions in it, including reading comprehension, writing, and math, will help. For focused, specific preparation, based on corrections exams actually given throughout the United States, work through the practice corrections exams, sample exercises, and test instruction in this book.

Kinds of Questions You Can Expect

Exams usually cover such subjects as reading, writing, math, memory, and judgment. Sometimes your ability to read a map or graph is also tested. The exam bulletin or position announcement, available from your recruitment office, should tell you what subjects are on your exam. All of these subjects are covered in detail in later chapters.

▶ Finding Out How You Did

Applicants are generally notified in writing about their performance on the exam. The notification may simply say whether or not you passed, or it may inform you of your score. It may also say when you should show up for the next step in the process, which is often a physical ability test.

▶ The Physical Ability Test

The physical ability test (or PAT) is usually the next step in the process after the written exam. You may have to get a note from your doctor saying that you are in good enough shape to undertake this test before you will be allowed to participate. A few agencies give the medical exam before the physical ability test. They want to make sure that candidates are not taking any health risks by completing the physical test. See Chapter 13 for an in-depth look at what to expect and how to prepare for the PAT.

▶ The Personal History Statement and Background Investigation

Very early in the application process, the hiring agency will have you fill out a long form about your personal history. You will usually be interviewed about this material by a member of the corrections department or the personnel department. As the department begins to get serious about considering you, it will conduct an investigation into your background, using your personal history statement as a starting point.

This step may be the most important in the whole process, even though the results may not be reflected in your rank on the eligibility list. This is where the agency checks not only your experience and education, but also, and perhaps more importantly, your character. Do you have the integrity, honesty, commitment, and respect for authority that a corrections officer must have? Corrections departments go to a lot of trouble and expense to find out. Every important aspect of filling out and submitting your statement is covered in Detail in Chapter 14.

▶ The Interview and Oral Board

The selection process in your chosen jurisdiction may include one or more interviews. There may be an interview connected with your personal history statement, in which the interviewer simply tries to confirm or clarify what you've written. Most agencies also conduct another interview before an "oral board" that continues the process of determining whether candidates will make good corrections officers. The oral board typically assesses qualities such as interpersonal skills, communication skills, judgment and decision-making abilities, respect for diversity, and adaptability. The board itself consists of two to five people, who may be corrections officers or civilians. Read Chapter 15, "The Oral Interview," to learn more about the interview process and the oral board.

▶ The Psychological Assessment

Because corrections work is a stressful occupation that demands a high level of responsibility, many corrections and law enforcement departments use psychological evaluation to identify candidates with underlying instabilities. They may also want to see if candidates have healthy ways to cope with pressure. Sometimes, too, the real purpose of the psychological evaluation is not so much to disclose instabilities as to determine applicants' honesty, habits, and other such factors. More often than not, the psychological evaluation consists of one or more written tests and an interview with a psychologist or psychiatrist. The

tests, interview, and other important aspects of the psychological assessment are covered in detail in Chapter 16.

▶ The Medical Examination

Every corrections officer candidate must undergo a full medical examination at some point in the application process. The medical exam is not much different than the annual physical that you take at your physician's office, and in almost all cases, you'll be asked to supply a blood and urine sample for mandatory drug testing. For more detailed information on the medical exam, see Chapter 16.

▶ Future Trends

Changing trends in corrections, law enforcement, and the criminal justice system will influence your on-the-job experience as a corrections officer. After dramatic increases in the inmate population during the 1980s and 1990s, the incarceration rate has begun to level off to a degree, but it remains high. In fact, with 1.3 million adults in prison, the United States has the highest recorded rate of imprisonment per capita of any country in the world. And the incarcerated population continues to grow—between 1995 and 2002, the number of prisoners nationwide increased an average 3.6% each year.

At the federal level, a major factor in the growth of the prison population in the past decades was the "truth in sentencing" guidelines that stemmed from the Sentencing Reform Act of 1984. These guidelines take into account how serious a crime is and the criminal record of the offender when sentences are made. Because this raised the odds of federal offenders being convicted, the number of offenders sent to federal prisons rose in turn.

In state prisons, growth in the inmate population resulted mostly from a larger number of adult arrests for serious offenses, leading to more offenders being put into prison. Like the federal system, the states have experienced a huge rise in prison admissions over the last decade. Current experiments with "Three Strikes and You're Out" and "Life Without Parole" laws stand to raise new admissions even higher if the legislation sticks.

Local jails have also seen more new admissions due to more arrests. Added to that are more felons being sentenced to local jails. Then, there is the larger role that local jails now play as the caretakers for state and federal prisoners.

The population increase in prisons and jails throughout the country, in combination with tougher sentencing laws, will generate a growing need for corrections staff, but these changes will also affect working conditions. Although prison expansion and construction of new prisons will help to house the influx of inmates, invariably some facilities will become overcrowded. Crowded conditions can exacerbate fighting and rioting among inmates—increasing the need for corrections officers who are knowledgeable and well-trained to deal with potentially volatile situations.

The sharp increase among drug law offenders contributes to another problem faced by today's prisons. Inmates do not necessarily leave their drug problems outside prison walls, with the result that drugs are sold, bought, and used inside correctional facilities. Job training for corrections officers involves learning strategies to handle special issues such as substance abuse or drug-related violence between inmates and against officers.

Ethnic and racial diversity among inmates poses another challenge for today's corrections staff. Agencies have increased training among corrections officers to manage inmates who come from different backgrounds and may have strong ties, for instance, to a street gang or a radical religious organization.

Experts in the field are constantly at work developing new methods to manage the current inmate population. Correctional boot camps for nonviolent offenders are one experiment to deal with offenders. These camps focus on rehabilitation, most often through education, job training, and substance abuse counseling or treatment. At the same time, some institutions have gone in the opposite direction by reinstating work groups or "chain gangs." Another current movement is to get rid of recreational equipment, television, and other inmate privileges and programs. Experts who oppose this approach believe that these privileges can help to reduce tensions and encourage better behavior. Yet another trend involves private companies owning and operating prisons under contract with government agencies—a trend that may be considered controversial by some policy makers.

Your future as a corrections officer will be affected by trends like these—everything from higher rates of arrest and imprisonment to different philosophies about how to handle inmates. As you prepare for the selection process of becoming a corrections officer, pay special attention to newspaper or magazine accounts about today's prison and legal systems. Changing approaches to law enforcement and corrections will have "real world" effects on the individuals guarding the country's jail and prisons—and soon, that could mean you.

▶ Make the Commitment

Now that you know the basics about what to expect from the selection process, how can you give yourself a competitive edge over other applicants? To land the job of your choice, you need to make a dedicated effort to the application and selection process *now*. Along with the tips and practical guidance that you will find in this book, following are five steps to getting the job you want.

1. **Get fit.** Commit to a physical fitness program today. Preparation will not only help you ace the physical ability test, it will prepare you for the everyday physical demands of corrections work. Consider learning stress management techniques or martial arts as a way to train yourself physically and mentally. Demonstrating that you have healthy ways to cope with work pressures will go a long way to showing that you are ready for the job.

2. **Do some research.** Spend time at a local or college library or search online to find out any relevant information about corrections work and your job search. Find out the application requirements and procedures at state, federal, or local correctional facilities in your region. (For more detailed information about the hiring procedures specific to state corrections officers or those employed by the federal government, read Chapters 2 and 3 of this book carefully.)

3. **Create a study plan.** Allot adequate time to get ready for the written examination. Start studying and taking the practice exams in this book now. Your goal is to earn a score that puts you in a good position against the competition.

4. **Prepare for the interview.** Give yourself plenty of time to create an accurate, detailed personal history statement and to practice interviewing strategies before you meet the oral board. Think about why you want to become a corrections officer and get a good sense of your talents and long-term goals. If you are uncomfortable about talking before a group, consider taking a public-speaking course or stage a mock interview with family and friends.

5. **Get smart.** Look into formal education in corrections. Take a college class or two, or aim yourself toward a full degree.

The Federal Employment Process

CHAPTER SUMMARY

Federal corrections officer jobs pay well and have excellent job security. How can you go about landing one of these sought-after positions? This chapter outlines the basic requirements you need for the job, salary and benefit information, plus all you need to know about the federal hiring process.

I f you are interested in becoming a corrections officer in a federal prison, you will quickly become familiar with the Federal Bureau of Prisons (BOP), with headquarters in Washington, D.C. As part of the U.S. Department of Justice, the BOP is responsible for hiring all corrections officers who work at federal prison institutions nationwide. Federal penal and correctional facilities are for people who have violated federal laws or are awaiting trial for violations. The Bureau oversees a total of 104 institutions and has more than 180,000 prisoners under its jurisdiction. More than 153,000 of these prisoners are confined in federal facilities, with the remaining population housed in privately managed institutions under contract with the government, and in some cases in state or local jails in agreement with federal authorities.

The need for federal corrections officers at new institutions combined with a high turnover rate make the BOP one of the hot spots for employment opportunities with the federal government. The Bureau of Labor Statistics reports that federal correctional facilities accounted for 16,000 corrections officer positions in 2002.

The federal government offers the highest average salary for corrections officers compared with state, local, or privately run facilities, but the requirements for the job are also more competitive than most state or county institutions. To be hired as an entry-level federal corrections officer, you must have either a bachelor's degree, three

According to a 2002 report by the Bureau of Justice Statistics, more than half (57%) of federal inmates are serving a sentence for a drug offense and about 10% are in prison for a violent offense. According to findings in 1997, federal prisoners were more likely than state inmates to be:

- women (7% vs. 6%)
- Hispanic (27% vs. 17%)
- age 45 or older (24% vs. 13%)
- with some college education (18% vs. 11%)
- noncitizens (18% vs. 5%)

or more years of general work experience, or a combination of undergraduate education and general experience that is equivalent to three years of full-time work. "General work experience" means jobs that include duties such as assisting or guiding others, counseling, responding to emergency situations, supervising or managing, teaching, or on-commission sales positions. The requirements for schooling and work experience also reflect the fact that the BOP is looking to attract applicants who are interested in federal law enforcement as a life career. The agency seeks job candidates who have the aptitude to advance within its ranks to positions of greater responsibility. Having a bachelor's degree in psychology, criminology, or counseling is also highly desirable because of BOP's emphasis on inmate rehabilitation.

When you are applying for a corrections officer position with the federal government, you may notice a reference in the job description that indicates the facility's security level. The federal government operates institutions with five different levels of security to deal with a diverse inmate population. These levels depend on such factors as the ratio of inmates to guards, type of inmate housing, and type of security systems:

- **Minimum security:** dormitory housing, no fences, low staff to inmate ratio
- **Low security:** dormitory housing, double-fenced perimeters, higher staff to inmate ratio
- **Medium security:** cell-type housing, double-fenced perimeters reinforced with electronic detection systems, even higher staff to inmate ratio
- **High security:** single or multiple cell housing, double fenced and walled perimeters, close staff supervision
- **Administrative:** inmates with chronic mental or physical conditions or escape-prone inmates of all security levels held here

As of February 2004, most federal inmates (38.8%) were in low-security facilities, followed by medium security (25%) and minimum security (19.4%). More than 10% of federal inmates were in a high-security institution, and 6.1% had not been assigned a security level.

Important Addresses and Phone Numbers

General Information
www.bop.gov
202-307-3198

Request an application:
Career Information Service Line
800-347-7744 or 202-307-3175
or contact nearest regional office

Mid-Atlantic Region
Delaware
Indiana
Kentucky
Maryland
Michigan
North Carolina
Ohio
Tennessee
Virginia
District of Columbia
Call: 301-317-3211

North Central Region
Colorado
Illinois
Iowa
Kansas
Minnesota
Missouri
Montana
Nebraska
North Dakota
South Dakota
Wisconsin
Wyoming
Call: 888-251-5458

Northeast Region
Connecticut
Maine
Massachusetts
New Hampshire
New Jersey
New York
Pennsylvania
Rhode Island
Vermont
Call: 800-787-2749

South Central Region
Arkansas
Louisiana
New Mexico
Oklahoma
Texas
Call: 800-726-4473

Southeast Region
Alabama
Florida
Georgia
Mississippi
South Carolina
Puerto Rico
Call: 888-789-1022

Western Region
Alaska
Arizona
California
Hawaii
Idaho
Nevada
Oregon
Utah
Washington
Call: 925-803-4700

Return completed applications:
Federal Bureau of Prisons
Examining Section
Room 460
320 First Street, NW
Washington, D.C. 20534

Minimum Requirements

These are the minimum qualifications for an entry-level or grade 5 federal corrections officer position:

- You must be a U.S. citizen (waivers may be available for positions that are difficult to fill when no qualified U.S. citizens are available)
- You must be under 37 years old.
- You must have a four-year college degree; or at least three years of previous experience in law enforcement, corrections, or an area of general experience; or a combination of undergraduate schooling and general work experience that equals three years of full-time work.

Examples of General Work Experience

The following are examples of occupations that fulfill the general work experience required by the BOP:

- teacher
- counselor
- worker with juvenile delinquents
- parole/probation worker
- welfare/social worker
- firefighter
- nurse
- clergyman
- emergency medical technician
- air traffic controller
- supervisor or manager
- commissioned sales person
- security guard
- children's day care worker

In the federal staffing system, jobs are graded to correspond with the position's pay rate, level of responsibility, and job requirements—as you are promoted, your grade level increases. Entry-level corrections officer positions are at grade 5 (listed in job descriptions as GS-05) and grade 6 (listed as GS-06). To qualify for a corrections officer job at grade 6, the requirements are higher. You must finish nine semester hours of 14 quarter hours of graduate study in criminal justice, criminology, social science, or another related field, or at least one year of full-time specialized work experience. Qualifying work experience includes enforcing rules in a corrections or mental health institution, dealing with domestic disturbances, or apprehending or arresting law violators.

Examples of Specialized Work Experience

The following are examples of occupations that would fulfill the requirement for specialized work experience for corrections officer GS-06 positions:

- corrections officer
- detention officer
- police officer
- border patrol agent
- state trooper
- sheriff
- park ranger
- deputy sheriff who supervises jail inmates
- worker at a mental health residential institution

Volunteer or part-time work can count toward fulfilling the necessary work experience. You can also combine your schooling and on-the-job experience as long as it is equivalent to the requirement.

Age Limit

There is no minimum age limit, but candidates must fulfill the education or work experience requirements. If you are 37 years old and are already holding a civilian federal law enforcement position, you may still be eligible to become a corrections officer as long as at the time of your initial appointment you were not yet at the maximum age. The BOP requires that you provide paperwork to show when you first started work in federal law enforcement.

Military Service

Military time does not count as federal service, so it will not satisfy the age requirement if you are over 37 years old. However, military service is credited toward your annual vacation time if you become a corrections officer. You may also be entitled to "Veteran's Preference," which gives special consideration to qualified veterans over civilians in the hiring process. If you make a claim for veteran's preference, the hiring staff will either accept or reject your claim at the time of the interview. Some positions are filled under the Veteran's Readjustment Appointment (VRA) Authority and only qualifying veterans are eligible.

Disability

Federal law prohibits discrimination against hiring a disabled person who is qualified for the job and who can perform the essential functions of the job with or without reasonable accommodations. If you have a disability but can meet the medical and physical requirements of the job, you can work as a corrections officer. A medical exam and the physical abilities test (PAT) will determine whether you meet the physical standards of the work. The physical requirements of corrections work include some of the following functions: walking or standing for up to an hour; viewing a human figure at a distance of one quarter mile or a target at 250 yards; hearing and detecting motion; smelling smoke or drugs; performing self-defense; using firearms; running; climbing stairs; lifting, dragging, and carrying objects. For more about what is involved in the federal physical abilities test read on in this chapter.

Job Disqualifiers

A criminal record may disqualify you from a federal corrections officer position. If you have been convicted of a misdemeanor crime of domestic violence, you need to provide evidence that the conviction has been set aside, expunged, or pardoned. Convicted felons must have proof that they have been granted authorization from the government to carry a firearm.

The background investigation will perform a criminal check and contact your former employers and personal references to determine whether you are suitable for the job of corrections officer. Be honest about your background in the application and interview. Negative information about your past that surfaces after you have been hired will most likely lead to your immediate removal from the job.

Past drug use can also affect your chances of getting hired. However, in some circumstances, the hiring staff may be flexible about past drug behavior. The BOP has a zero tolerance policy about illegal drug use among employees. Again, be sure to be forthright about your background during the hiring process.

A bad credit record can also influence your suitability as a job candidate. If you think your credit record is not the best, get a copy of your credit report now. If you have overdue bills, consider making a payment arrangement with your creditors. Bring all documentation with you to the interview.

▶ Selection Process

To begin the selection process, you must first get that all-important application form. To do so, go to the BOP website at www.bop.gov. The online application system for federal corrections jobs, called BOP-HIRES, gives you detailed information about job requirements, benefits, and openings on a continuous basis. You can update your online application at any time. You can also find federal corrections jobs listed at the government-operated website USAJobs, at www.usajobs.opm.gov.

If you do not have access to the Internet, the BOP prefers that you call the Career Information Service Line or contact the nearest regional office for applications. (See the "Important Addresses and Phone Numbers" section of this chapter.) Veterans have yet another option. They may apply directly to the federal correctional facility in the area where they would prefer to work.

To fill out an online application or resume, you must have an e-mail address. To access the job listings on the BOP-HIRES system, sign in first as a "new user." Register by entering your current e-mail address and selecting an eight-character password. The website is protected and your information is case sensitive, so you need to re-enter your password once you become a registered user.

If you forget your password, don't worry. Select the "Forgot your password" option from the menu. It will prompt you to enter your e-mail, date of birth, and ZIP code. You can then log in and assign yourself a new password by selecting the "Change password" option.

If you don't have an e-mail account, consider signing up for an address with a free service such as Hotmail or Yahoo. If you change your e-mail address, simply select the "Edit personal information" option under registered users and log-in. Make the necessary changes to your registration, and click on "Next" to save your edits.

If you are not applying directly online, you will need to complete and submit an OF-612 (Optional Application for Federal Employment), SF-171 (Standard Form 171), or a copy of your resume. You can request these forms from the office that you are applying to or you can download a form from the BOP website using Adobe Acrobat software. Make sure to photocopy your original application or resume before you turn it in—you will need a copy to review if you are contacted for an interview. Remember to sign and date your application before mailing it—the BOP only accepts applications with original signatures and dates.

If you are applying through the online BOP-HIRES system, work through the application form first without submitting it. Jot down any questions that would benefit from some research and preparation. You will be asked to provide general information, give information pertaining to your work experience and education, and answer multiple-choice questions describing your knowledge, skills, and abilities. You may want to draft a response or look up an accurate date before you enter it in final form. Proofread and make sure your information is complete and accurate before submitting your application online. You can also go back and edit or update your online application.

Resume Checklist

If you choose to submit a resume instead of an application form, be certain to include the following information:

- **Job announcement number, title, and grade.**
- **Personal information** including your full name, mailing address, day and evening phone numbers (with area code), Social Security Number, your citizenship status, and veteran's preference.
- **Education** including the names of the high schools, colleges, or universities you attended, with city and state, subject major, and the year you received your degree. (If you didn't receive a degree, include your total credits earned.)
- **Work experience** including job titles, duties and accomplishments, name and address of your employer, name and phone number of your supervisors, start and end dates, your hours per week, and salary. List each job as a separate entry. Note whether your current supervisor can be contacted.
- **Job-related qualifications** including related course work, skills, certificates, licenses, honors, and awards.

If you have held a civilian federal job, list the highest grade level that you have attained on your resume.

Knowledge, Skills, and Abilities (KSAs)

After you have filled out your application form, your next step in the process is to list your Knowledge, Skills, and Abilities (KSAs). KSAs are qualities that the agency considers necessary to perform a given job. Federal job announcements will normally list three to six criteria, or KSAs, that you must fulfill to be considered for the position. If you are working online, you will fill out a multiple-choice questionnaire about your KSAs as part of the online application. The KSAs necessary for a starting corrections officer position are the following:

- ability to supervise
- ability to communicate verbally
- ability to react to a crisis situation

This phase of the application process is extremely important. The first person to review your application, a human resources reader, will verify that you have *thoroughly* completed your application package and met the minimum qualifications for the job. Then the human resources staff determines if you meet the announcement's qualifications and are QUALIFIED or HIGHLY QUALIFIED. At that point, the staff will review your KSA responses and grade them (grades range from 5 to 20 points). Finally, it rates your application and ranks you against all of the applicants—those with the highest scores form a "best qualified list." When your name reaches this list, your application moves forward to the hiring manager or hiring panel for consideration. If you do not adequately respond to the required KSAs, you will not be selected for this top group of applicants, and may not be considered for the job. Be sure to respond to the KSA questionnaire carefully and honestly—the hiring staff will probably ask

you to back up any claims you make with evidence during your interview. Be sure that you have the name, address, and phone number of a supervisor or other contact that can verify your experience. Here is the type of inquiry you will encounter on the KSA portion of your online application:

Select one response that most accurately describes your level of experience and ability to supervise:

1. I have ensured that individuals confined in a correctional or mental health facility adhere to the rules and regulations.
2. I have supervised or managed coworkers, subordinates, or detainees in a non-correctional environment.
3. I have led work teams or work crews.
4. I have no experience supervising, managing, or leading individuals.

Some federal jobs require that you respond to KSAs in a written worksheet. However, for most corrections officer positions, this is not necessary unless you have already held a federal corrections position and are applying to a higher position of authority. If this is the case, closely study the job description and the KSA requirements, so that you can craft responses that mirror back to the hiring officials the very traits and talents that they have defined as essential to the job. Your challenge is to capture in writing how your experiences match the knowledge, skills, and abilities required for corrections work.

Important Documents

Your last step in the application procedure is to include any documents or additional forms that are required and mail your completed application packet. The job vacancy announcement will specify which documents or forms to include. The following are examples of forms you may need to gather before sending in your application packet:

- Applicant Availability Statement
- college transcripts (if applicable)
- DD-214, military release form, if applicable
- Form SF-15 (Claim for ten-Point Veterans Preference), along with a letter from the Veterans Administration or the branch of service in which you served, dated within the past 12 months

You will be asked to fill out two forms to bring with you to the interview: the Declaration of Federal Employment (OF-306) and Questionnaire for Public Trust Positions (SF-85P). You can download these forms from the BOP website. Do **not** mail these forms with your application packet.

If you are not applying online, mail your packet to the BOP Examining Section in Washington, D.C., or, if different, the address specified by the vacancy announcement. When the BOP receives your application packet, they will use an automated rating system to process your application. You will be assigned a rating based on the results. The rating takes place about two weeks from the date your application is received and a Notice of Results will be mailed directly to you, or you can view your ranking online. Your rating is based on a scale of 70 to 99. Applicants with veteran's preference may receive an additional five or ten points.

If the BOP rates you as an eligible applicant, you will take your place on a list of eligibles for one year. After ten months, if you have not been contacted for an interview, you can extend your eligibility by submitting updated information. If you wait more than twelve months to update your application, you will have to start over with the application process.

Also, if changes occur in your life that will qualify you for a position at a higher grade, you do not need to wait until the end of the tenth month to let the BOP hear the news. Submit that information immediately.

If an institution in your area has vacancies, they will get approximately three names for each open position from the BOP eligibility list. For instance, if two

corrections officer positions are available, the BOP will send the hiring prison six names. The names will be ranked in order, with the highest scoring applicant listed first. If an institution receives your name from the BOP, you will receive an "Inquiry as to Availability" and instructions for scheduling pre-employment procedures.

Depending on your rank as well as the needs and hiring policies of the facility, you may be scheduled to take a psychological exam; no written exam is required. All federal corrections officer applicants will be subject to an oral interview as well as a medical examination performed by a federal medical officer. The physical will be arranged by the hiring institution at no charge to you. In addition, the facility will conduct a security investigation to ensure your qualifications as a federal prison employee. If you are not selected for employment, your name will be returned to the BOP for possible future consideration.

After your name is on the BOP eligibility list, you also have the option to contact the personnel office at the prison facility where you want to work and inquire about job availability. Chances are that a personnel office staff member will ask you about your BOP rank. Obviously, if you rank high on the eligibility list, the facility will be more interested in recruiting you. However, remember that all hiring depends on job vacancies at the facility.

▶ Background Investigation and Interview

Before you become a federal corrections officer, the BOP will perform a background investigation. The investigation includes a criminal check and credit check as well as interviews with your former employers, personal references, and other sources. The goal of the background check is to determine how your character and behavior will affect your job performance.

The BOP interviews all applicants before it makes a final selection. You will not have to travel far for your interview—the hiring agency will arrange for an interview in your general area. For more information about what to expect at your interview, read Chapter 15, "The Oral Interview."

▶ Training

For one year following your appointment, you will be considered a probationary employee. During your first year, you must undergo 200 hours of formal training. When you report for work, you will receive 80 hours of orientation training that familiarizes you with the institutional policies and procedures specific to the facility that hired you. You will learn about the institution's regulations and security procedures, and techniques for supervising and communicating with inmates.

Within the first 60 days of your appointment as a corrections officer, you will also attend a three-week, 120-hour training program at the federal training facility in Glynco, Georgia. Federal corrections officers are trained according to guidelines established by the American Correctional Association (the same organization responsible for accrediting prison facilities). The federal government will pay for your transportation to Georgia and your room and board during the training program. Training classes begin at 7:30 A.M. and end at 4:30 P.M. Topics you will cover include classroom work in legal issues and communications and skills training in self-defense and firearms proficiency. There are three written exams covering the lectures as well as various practical tests. The average federal corrections officer class consists of 48 people. To complete the course, you must achieve an acceptable performance level in the use of firearms and on the written academic tests. You will also be expected to pass a Physical Abilities Test (PAT) consisting of:

- **Dummy Drag**—Drag a 75-pound dummy a minimum of 694 feet continuously within three minutes.
- **Climb and Grasp**—maximum time limit of seven seconds
- **Obstacle Course**—maximum time limit of 58 seconds
- **Run and Cuff**—Run one-quarter of a mile and apply handcuffs within two minutes and 35 seconds.
- **Stair Climb**—Wearing a 20-pound weight belt, climb up and down 108 steps in 45 seconds.

During your one-year probationary period, your supervisor will work with you to provide you with training and closely monitor you to judge whether you are suitable and competent for the job. During this time period, you will also see if your abilities and career goals are compatible with corrections work. If you are interested in transferring to a new location, you can apply for a transfer after you complete your one-year trial period. Transfer opportunities are available throughout the United States, including Hawaii and Puerto Rico.

You will continue to receive yearly on-the-job training after your probationary period to keep you up-to-date with new developments in the field. Depending on your position, you may also take advantage of career development opportunities through a range of specialty training courses offered by the BOP.

▶ Salary and Benefits

Federal corrections officers receive a predetermined salary and benefits just like other federal employees. You are paid according to a federal personnel pay rate scale referred to as the General Schedule (GS). The base rate or GS-level is the same everywhere, but depending on the location of the facility you are assigned to work at, you may receive extra compensation called "locality pay." The following are examples of the low-end of salary ranges for federal corrections officers:

U.S. Penitentiary, McCreary, KY	$31,690
U.S. Penitentiary, Atwater, CA	$32,306
Federal Correctional Center, Manchester, KY	$32,933
Federal Correctional Institution, Littleton, CO	$33,882
Camden and Burlington Counties, NJ	$34,245

Note: Figures are from job vacancy announcements listed at USAJobs

Federal penal institutions operate 24 hours a day, every day of the year. You can expect to work eight-hour shifts. You will rotate through different sets of days off, shifts, and posts. If you are assigned to a night shift, you will be paid a percentage of your basic hourly rate above regular pay. Officers assigned to work Sunday will be paid 25% above regular pay.

Health and Life Insurance

One benefit available for federal corrections officers is health insurance. Most institutions offer plans in which the government will pay up to 70% of the insurance premiums. Basic life insurance may also be available; the federal government will pay up to one-third of the cost for this coverage.

Retirement

As a federal law enforcement employee, you will qualify for a retirement plan in which you may retire at age 50 after 20 years of service in a federal correctional facility. After 25 years of service you may retire at any age.

Vacation and Sick Leave

All new full-time corrections officers accrue 13 days of sick leave annually. You will also receive 13 days of vacation or annual leave. After three years of federal service, your vacation time increases to 20 days each year. After 15 years of service, you earn 26 days of annual leave.

Other Benefits

Federal employees can participate in a voluntary retirement savings and investment plan. Federal workers can contribute up to 12% of their basic pay to the plan in pre-tax dollars. The BOP automatically contributes an amount equal to 1% of an employee's salary to the plan, even if the employee does not participate in this option. The government will also match a portion of employee contributions.

The government also helps defray the cost of public transportation for employees who commute to work in urban areas. Employees can be reimbursed up to $100 per month.

The State Employment Process

CHAPTER SUMMARY

Throughout the nation, state corrections departments use a number of different ways to assess corrections officer candidates. This chapter gives you an overview of the process of selecting recruits, from initial application to the training academy.

About three out of every five corrections officers are employed by state governments, making states the top employer in this field, over local governments, federal agencies, and private companies. State governments also offer the second highest pay levels for corrections officers, behind only federal positions.

As in the federal system, state prisons experienced a sharp increase in the growth of the inmate population since the 1980s. Today, the rate of incarceration in state prisons continues to rise, although not as dramatically. In 2002, the number of prisoners in state institutions increased by 2.5% compared with larger increases (over 5%) in federal facilities and local jails. However, state prisons house the highest number of prisoners compared with any other type of corrections institution—more than 1.2 million prisoners are confined in state prisons.

As a result of this burgeoning inmate population, added to other trends in the field such as mandatory sentencing guidelines and reduced parole for inmates, the demand for corrections officers in state prisons is growing. Coupled with high turnover and difficulty attracting qualified job candidates to rural locations, job prospects for state corrections officers are excellent. And with the increasing offender population, layoffs in the profession are rare.

According to the Bureau of Justice Statistics, state prison inmates are racially diverse, young, and most have a high-school diploma. The latest summary findings showed that of state prison inmates:

- 64% belonged to racial or ethnic minorities
- about 57% were under age 35
- about 57% had a high school diploma or its equivalent
- nearly half were sentenced for a violent crime
- 20% were convicted of a property crime
- 21% were convicted of a drug crime

If you are interested in a challenging job with great benefits, excellent job security, and advancement opportunities, a state corrections officer position might be right for you. This chapter will give you an overview of the selection process in states throughout the country and important contact information for state corrections departments.

Employment Hot Spots and Job Criteria

Your job prospects will vary by jurisdiction. Some states are experiencing budget cuts that may affect the rate of employment in the corrections field. However, most states are looking for qualified candidates and are trying to fill positions on a continuous basis. Although you may not be interested in or able to relocate to a new state in order to become a corrections officer, you can increase your chances of employment in states with the highest concentration of officers. The five states with the highest concentration of corrections officers—meaning that this occupation makes up more than 4.5% of all jobs in the state—are Louisiana, Mississippi, New Mexico, New York, and Texas, according to the Bureau of Labor Statistics. Here is the breakdown of the concentration of corrections officers per state and the annual mean wage earned by corrections officers in each of these five states:

STATE	NUMBER OF CORRECTIONS OFFICERS AND JAILERS	YEARLY AVERAGE INCOME
Texas	41,430	$28,190
New York	37,490	$47,030
Louisiana	11,130	$24,180
Mississippi	5,360	$22,150
New Mexico	3,340	$24,450

Basic requirements for corrections officers depend on each state's guidelines. Use the state Web resources in this chapter or telephone the human resources division of your state agency to find out exactly what are the eligibility criteria for the job. The requirements for state corrections officers are usually less rigorous than those for federal positions, but this is changing in some jurisdictions. For example, while many state departments require that applicants have only a high school diploma, some agencies are adopting higher education requirements for entry-level corrections officers. Usually this means some completed college course work. The following are some **typical standards** for state corrections officers:

- You must be at least 18 years old (in some states, 20 or 21 years old).
- You must be a U.S. citizen, or in some states, have resident alien status.
- You must have a high school diploma or a General Equivalency Degree (GED).
- You must be able to perform the essential functions of the job, with or without reasonable accommodation.

Disqualifying factors often include some of the following:

- You have a record of a felony or offense involving domestic violence.
- You have a drug-related conviction.
- You are on probation for a crime, or have pending criminal charges.

▶ Selection Process

State corrections departments often share basic components of the hiring process. Many state corrections departments or state-run job networks allow you to apply online. If not, call the personnel office of your state agency to request an application and to find out the steps you need to take in the hiring process. Some common selection procedures include the following:

- written examination measuring areas such as reading comprehension, observation, memory, situational reasoning, and communication skills
- background investigation
- medical exam
- physical performance tests
- drug screening
- polygraph (lie detector) test
- interview
- psychological testing

These procedures are discussed in Chapter 1, and many elements of the hiring process are covered in detail in later chapters of this book. Familiarize yourself with what is involved with each component and be sure to prepare for each hiring stage so that you can become a top candidate for the job.

No one standard corrections officer exam applies to state agencies across the nation. Each state has different hiring procedures and uses different written tests. Some, like Washington State, no longer require an exam. Instead, that state asks questions that relate to a candidate's job suitability on its application. Other states, like Oklahoma, give a written exam only after a candidate attends a training program or academy. Candidates take an "exit exam" on topics covered by the training course.

Written exams for corrections officers are often general knowledge tests that measure reading comprehension and basic math skills. Increasingly, corrections exams look at an applicant's "situational reasoning"—in other words, how an applicant makes judgments about real job scenarios. Some situational-reasoning tests require candidates to watch a simulated incident on video or review photographs and text about a corrections situation and then answer questions pertaining to what they observed and how they interpreted the event. The following are some examples of testing requirements of several state corrections departments. Note some of the similarities and differences between the testing requirements: most use multiple-choice formats, but some measure only general knowledge, whereas others emphasize on-the-job reasoning skills or memory and observational abilities.

STATE	WRITTEN TEST FORMAT
California	Pass/fail multiple-choice exam that measures knowledge of basic grammar, spelling, punctuation, reading comprehension, and math.
Georgia	Multiple-choice exam with a total of 132 questions. The test includes three parts: a video exam, a reading section, and a counting exam.
Illinois	Two written exams: the Test of Adult Basic Education (TABE) and the Inmate Disciplinary Report (IDR). The TABE measures reading comprehension and vocabulary skills. The IDR is a video test that evaluates observation and judgment about real-life corrections situations.
Kansas	Video test used to determine candidates' job suitability.
Minnesota	Pass/fail exam that consists of reading comprehension and a video exam.
Oregon	Pass/fail work compatibility exam, followed by a multiple-choice exam that measures responses to situations that candidates may experience on the job.
Texas	100-question general knowledge test consisting of five sections: memory and observation, situational reasoning, reading comprehension, vocabulary, and arithmetic.

To find out the testing requirements for the job you are interested in, contact the personnel department in your state.

▶ Salary and Benefits

Corrections officers receive a range of salaries and benefits, depending on the state institution where they are employed. Job listings at state institutions provide a salary range for corrections positions—if you are hired, your pay level will fall somewhere in the range, depending on your experience and skill level. Salaries for entry-level corrections officers will most likely begin at the lower end of the range. The following are examples of salary ranges for various state corrections officers:

Maryland Department of Public Safety & Correctional Services	$26,500–$44,000
Texas Department of Criminal Justice	$20,500–$31,000
California Department of Corrections	$33,500–$55,000
Nevada Department of Corrections, Ely State Prison	$30,500–$47,000
Arkansas Department of Correction	$22,000–$27,481

Note: Figures are from recent job vacancy announcements listed at www.corrections.com.

The states with the highest pay levels for corrections officers are New Jersey, California, Massachusetts, New York, and Nevada. The following outlines the annual mean wage of corrections officers per state and the number of corrections officers employed in each of these five states.

TOP DOLLAR STATE	NUMBER OF CORRECTIONS OFFICERS AND JAILERS	YEARLY AVERAGE INCOME
New Jersey	13,530	$50,330
California	32,220	$48,150
Massachusetts	8,100	$47,830
New York	37,490	$47,030
Nevada	37,490	$43,330

Again, there is no nationwide standard for benefit packages for state employees. To find out what kind of benefits corrections officers receive in your state, you need to contact the human resources office of the state corrections department or the personnel division of the state government. You can also research benefits information online. Although employee benefit packages vary from state to state, they tend to be substantial. Common benefits include the following:

- medical, disability, and life insurance
- sick leave, vacation, and holiday pay
- educational incentives
- pension plan

State corrections departments often supply uniforms and personal equipment you use on the job. Some benefits packages include dental care, or fringe benefits like free meals while you are working.

▶ Training

Most likely, you will initially be considered a probationary employee and then will begin training. Most state departments use training guidelines set by certain professional organizations, including the American Correctional Association and American Jail Association. What varies the most from place to place is whether you will receive mostly on-the-job training or first go through a formal training program, such as an academy.

Many state corrections facilities send new officers to special academies or regional training centers. These formal programs are also used by many local facilities, such as county or city jails. In some cases, this training is required as part of a statewide certification process. Academy training can last for several weeks or a few months. Classroom instruction may cover some of the following topics:

- understanding inmate behavior
- counseling inmates
- handling conflicts among inmates
- contraband control
- inmate rights
- custody and security procedures
- fire and safety techniques
- written and oral communications

You may also undergo physical fitness training and develop certain technical skills. These include the use of firearms and chemical weapons, self-defense, restraint tactics, first aid, and emergency procedures.

Any formal training you receive will be followed by on-the-job training, which takes place under the supervision of experienced corrections officers. This is when you will put your knowledge and skills into practice, and find out more about your institution's rules and policies. Even if the facility you work for does not send you to an academy or training center, you will be taught the basic skills and knowledge you need through on-the-job training and you may attend formal courses as needed.

It is also common for corrections officers to attend formal training courses once they have been on the job for a while. This is known as in-service training. These courses are usually designed to teach officers new ideas and techniques or certain specialized skills, often for advancement in the job.

Learning the Ropes

Training requirements vary among state corrections departments. The following are examples of the training programs for corrections officers at several state departments.

▶ When You Do Succeed

Congratulations! You have received the letter or phone call asking you to accept a position at the facility where you applied. You are on the road to your law enforcement career.

In most cases, you will start work as an entry-level corrections officer. You may go through some formal training at an academy, followed by hours of on-the-job training or you may work at your job for several weeks before going through formal state-sanctioned training. At the end of your training, you may also be expected to pass a certification exam. The certification exam is usually directly related to the training curriculum, so you will know exactly what you need to study. And you will need to study; these exams can be tough. But if you pass, your reward is the job you have been working and waiting for all this time.

STATE	TRAINING PROGRAM
Alabama	400 hours of formal training in skills and custody and rehabilitation techniques. Must pass physical agility test upon completion. Probationary employment period lasts six months.
Arizona	seven-week academy training; upon passing, earn a certificate and 18 college credits.
California	16-week formal academy training and 2-year apprenticeship program for beginning corrections officers.
New York	one-year training program with eight weeks formal academy training. Formal training includes academic courses that can be used as 16 college credits. Must pass physical test at completion of training.
North Carolina	four-week (160 hours) basic training program. Course includes training in firearms, unarmed self-defense, and other psychomotor skills. Must pass written test, physical test, and show proficiency in firearms at completion of program.
Pennsylvania	four- to five-week basic training program at academy. Course covers communication skills, inmate behavior, self-defense, ethics, CPR/first aid, report writing, and search procedures.

► State Web Resources

These web resources link to state corrections departments or state human resources divisions and job hotlines. Because job requirements and hiring procedures differ from state to state, be sure to research what exactly is involved in the corrections selection process in the jurisdiction of your choice. Many state websites provide information about current state-level corrections officer openings and allow you to apply for positions online. They also list important department phone numbers and addresses, if you wish to request an application by phone or mail.

Alabama Department of Corrections
www.doc.state.al.us

Alaska Department of Corrections
www.correct.state.ak.us

Arizona Department of Correction
www.adc.state.az.us

Arkansas Department of Corrections
www.state.ar.us/doc

California Department of Corrections
www.corr.ca.gov

Colorado Department of Corrections
www.doc.state.co.us

Connecticut Department of Correction
www.ct.gov/doc

Delaware Department of Correction
www.state.de.us/correct

Florida Department of Corrections
www.dc.state.fl.us

Georgia Department of Corrections
www.dcor.state.ga.us

State of Hawaii Department of Public Safety
www.hawaii.gov/psd

Idaho Department of Correction
www.corr.state.id.us

Illinois Department of Corrections
www.idoc.state.il.us

Indiana Department of Correction
www.in.gov/indcorrection

Iowa Department of Corrections
www.doc.state.ia.us

Kansas Department of Corrections
www.docnet.dc.state.ks.us

Kentucky Department of Corrections
www.corrections.ky.gov

Louisiana Department of Public Safety and Corrections
www.corrections.state.la.us

Maine Department of Corrections
www.state.me.us.corrections

Maryland Department of Public Safety and Correctional Services
www.dpscs.state.md.us

Massachusetts Department of Correction
www.mass.gov/doc

Michigan Department of Corrections
www.michigan.gov/corrections

Minnesota Department of Corrections
www.doc.state.mn.us

Mississippi Department of Corrections
www.mdoc.state.ms.us

Missouri Department of Corrections
www.doc.missouri.gov

Montana Department of Corrections
www.corr.state.mt.us

Nebraska Department of Correctional Services
www.corrections.state.ne.us

Nevada Department of Corrections
www.doc.nv.gov

New Hampshire Department of Corrections
www.state.nh.us.doc

New Jersey Department of Corrections
www.state.nj.us/corrections

New Mexico Corrections Department
www.corrections.state.nm.us

New York State Department of Correctional Services
www.docs.state.ny.us

North Carolina Department of Correction
www.doc.state.nc.us

North Dakota Department of Corrections and Rehabilitation
www.state.nd.us/docr/

Ohio Department of Rehabilitation and Correction
www.drc.state.oh.us

Oklahoma Department of Corrections
www.doc.state.ok.us

Oregon Department of Corrections
www.doc.state.or.us

Pennsylvania Department of Corrections
www.cor.state.pa.us

Rhode Island Department of Corrections
www.doc.state.ri.us

South Carolina Department of Corrections
www.state.sc.us/scdc

South Dakota Department of Corrections
www.state.sd.us/corrections/corrections.html

Tennessee Department of Correction
www.state.tn.us/correction

Texas Department of Criminal Justice
www.tdcj.state.tx.us

Utah Department of Corrections
www.udc.state.ut.us

Vermont Department of Corrections
www.doc.state.vt.us

Virginia Department of Corrections
www.vadoc.state.va.us

Washington Department of Corrections
www.doc.wa.gov

West Virginia Division of Corrections
www.wvf.state.wv.us/wvdoc

Wisconsin Department of Corrections
www.wi-doc.com

Wyoming Department of Corrections
www.doc.state.wy.us/corrections.asp

▶ Corrections Organizations

These web resources offer links to current state and local job openings throughout the United States and provide information about topics relevant to the corrections field today.

American Correctional Association
www.aca.org—This website offers a job bank with employment listings across the nation. It also provides information about training and courses offered by the ACA and includes articles about corrections events and issues in *Corrections Today,* a magazine published by the association.

American Jail Association
www.corrections.com/aja—Features articles from *American Jails Magazine* as well as training and education opportunities sponsored by the AJA.

American Probation and Parole Association
www.appa-net.org—gives information about membership, training opportunities, and links to publications focusing on issues in the field of community-based corrections.

The Corrections Connection
www.corrections.com—Includes news articles about current issues in the industry as well as links to leading organizations in the field, training opportunities, and federal, state, and county job resources. You can access job announcements through this site and post your own web page or resume.

National Institute of Corrections
www.nicic.org—A United States Department of Justice website that provides corrections-related links and information about up-to-date topics in the field.

National Association of Blacks in Criminal Justice
www.nabcj.org—provides information about the group's conferences as well as training and networking opportunities.

LearningExpress Test Preparation System

CHAPTER SUMMARY

Taking the corrections officer written exam can be tough. It demands a lot of preparation if you want to achieve a top score. Your rank on the eligibility list is often determined largely by this score. The Learning-Express Test Preparation System, developed by leading test experts, gives you the discipline and attitude you need to be a winner.

This chapter can help you take control of the entire test preparation process. It clearly explains the steps you need to take to achieve a top score on the written exam. Do not underestimate the importance of doing well on the written exam. Your future career in corrections depends on it. This chapter will help you to:

- Become familiar with the format of the exam
- Overcome excessive test anxiety
- Prepare gradually for the exam instead of cramming
- Understand and use vital test-taking skills
- Know how to pace yourself through the exam
- Know how to use the process of elimination
- Know when and how to guess
- Be in tip-top mental and physical shape on the day of the exam

Thus, the entire purpose of this chapter is to ensure that you are in control of the test-prep process. You do not want the exam to control you.

The LearningExpress Test Preparation System puts you in control. In just nine easy-to-follow steps, you will learn everything you need to know to make sure that you are in charge of your preparation and your performance on the exam. Other test-takers may let the test get the better of them; other test-takers may be unprepared or out of shape, but not you. You will have taken all the steps you need to take to get a high score on the corrections officer exam.

Here's how the LearningExpress Test Preparation System works: Nine easy steps lead you through everything you need to know and do to get ready to master your exam. The time listed next to each of the steps listed below includes both reading about the step and one or more activities. It's important that you do the activities along with the reading, or you won't be getting the full benefit of the system. Each step tells you approximately how much time that step will take you to complete.

Nine Steps to Success	Time
1. Get Information	30 minutes
2. Conquer Test Anxiety	20 minutes
3. Make a Plan	50 minutes
4. Learn to Manage Your Time	10 minutes
5. Learn to Use the Process of Elimination	20 minutes
6. Know When to Guess	20 minutes
7. Reach Your Peak Performance Zone	10 minutes
8. Get Your Act Together	10 minutes
9. Do It!	10 minutes
Total	**3 hours**

We estimate that working through the entire system will take you approximately three hours, though it's perfectly OK if you work faster or slower than the time estimates assume. If you can take a whole afternoon or evening, you can work through the whole Learning-Express Test Preparation System in one sitting. Otherwise, you can break it up, and do just one or two steps a day for the next several days. It's up to you—remember, *you* are in control.

► Step 1: Get Information

Time to complete: 30 minutes
Activity: Read Chapter 1, "Becoming a Corrections Officer"

Knowledge is power. The first step in the Learning-Express Test Preparation System is finding out everything you can about your corrections officer written exam. If you have access to the Internet, you can perform a search on any basic search engine, such as www.yahoo.com, www.excite.com, or www.google.com to find out if the department of corrections you want to apply to has a website. If you find that your targeted department of corrections has a website, review it carefully to see if it contains any information about the written exam. If not, contact the department of corrections you want to apply to and ask for the personnel office. Request a position announcement, find out if an exam bulletin is available, and ask when the next written exam is scheduled. If the department issues an exam bulletin, then you'll get a brief outline of what skills will be tested on the written exam.

What You Should Find Out

The more details you can find out about the written exam, either from the bulletin online, or from speaking with a recruiter, the more efficiently you'll be able to study. Here's a list of some things you might want to find out about your exam:

- What skills are tested?
- How many sections are on the exam?
- How many questions does each section have?
- Are the questions ordered from easy to hard, or is the sequence random?
- How much time is allotted for each section?
- Are there breaks in between sections?
- What is the passing score and how many questions do you have to answer right in order to get that score?
- Does a higher score give you any advantages, like a better rank on the eligibility list?
- How is the test scored: Is there a penalty for wrong answers?
- Are you permitted to go back to a prior section or move on to the next section if you finish early?
- Can you write in the test booklet or will you be given scratch paper?
- What should you bring with you on exam day?

If you haven't already done so, stop here and read Chapter 1 of this book, which gives you a brief overview of the entire corrections officer selection process. Then move on to the next step to find out how you can get a handle on test anxiety.

▶ Step 2: Conquer Test Anxiety

Time to complete: 20 minutes
Activity: Take the Test Stress Test
Having as much information as possible about the exam is the first step in getting control of the exam. Next, you have to overcome one of the biggest obstacles to test success: test anxiety. Test anxiety cannot only impair your performance on the exam itself; it can even keep you from preparing! In Step 2, you'll learn stress management techniques that will help you succeed on your exam. Learn these strategies now, and practice them as you work through the exams in this book, so they will be second nature to you by exam day.

Combating Test Anxiety

The first thing you need to know is that a little test anxiety is a good thing. Everyone gets nervous before a big exam—and if that nervousness motivates you to prepare thoroughly, so much the better. It's said that Sir Laurence Olivier, one of the foremost British actors of this century, threw up before every performance. His stage fright didn't impair his performance; in fact, it probably gave him a little extra edge—just the kind of edge you need to do well, whether on a stage or in an examination room.

Stress Management Before the Test

If you feel your level of anxiety getting the best of you in the weeks before your test, here is what you can do to bring the level down again:

- **Get prepared.** There's nothing like knowing what to expect and being prepared for it to put you in control of test anxiety. That's why you are reading this book. Use it faithfully, and remind yourself that you are better prepared than most of the people who will be taking the test.

- **Practice self-confidence.** A positive attitude is a great way to combat test anxiety. This is no time to be humble or shy. Stand in front of the mirror and say to your reflection, "I'm prepared. I'm full of self-confidence. I'm going to ace this test. I know I can do it." If you hear it often enough, you will believe it.

- **Fight negative messages.** Every time someone starts telling you how hard the exam is or how it's almost impossible to get a high score, fight back by telling them your self-confidence messages above. If the someone with the negative messages is *you*, telling yourself *you don't do well on exams, you just can't do this,* don't listen. Listen to your self-confidence messages instead.

- **Visualize.** Imagine yourself reporting for duty on your first day of corrections officer training. Think of yourself wearing your uniform with pride and learning the skills you will use for the rest of your life. Visualizing success can help make it happen— and it reminds you of why you are doing all this work in preparing for the exam.

- **Exercise.** Physical activity helps calm your body down and focus your mind. Being in good physical shape can actually help you do well on the exam, as well as prepare you for the physical ability test. So, go for a run, lift weights, go swimming—and do it regularly.

Stress Management on Test Day

There are several ways you can bring down your level of test anxiety on test day. They will work best if you practice them in the weeks before the test, so you know which ones work best for you.

- **Deep breathing.** Take a deep breath while you count to five. Hold it for a count of one, then let it out on a count of five. Repeat several times.

- **Move your body.** Try rolling your head in a circle. Rotate your shoulders. Shake your hands from the wrist. Many people find these movements very relaxing.

- **Visualize again.** Think of the place where you are most relaxed: lying on the beach in the sun, walking through the park, or wherever is most comforting to you. Now close your eyes and imagine you are actually there. If you practice in advance, you'll find that you only need a few seconds of this exercise to experience a significant increase in your sense of well-being.

When anxiety threatens to overwhelm you right there during the exam, there are still things you can do to manage the stress level:

- **Repeat your self-confidence messages.** You should have them memorized by now. Say them quietly to yourself, and believe them!

- **Visualize one more time.** This time, visualize yourself moving smoothly and quickly through the test answering every question right and finishing just before time is up. Like most visualization techniques, this one works best if you have practiced it ahead of time.

- **Find an easy question.** Skim over the test until you find an easy question, and answer it. Getting even one circle filled in can get you into the test-taking groove.

- **Take a mental break.** Everyone loses concentration once in a while during a long test. It's normal, so you shouldn't worry about it. Instead, accept what has happened. Say to yourself, "Hey, I lost it there for a minute. My brain is taking a break." Put down your pencil, close your eyes, and do some deep breathing for a few seconds. Then you'll be ready to go back to work.

On the next page is the Test Stress Test. Answer the questions on that page to learn more about your level of test anxiety.

Test Stress Test

You only need to worry about test anxiety if it is extreme enough to impair your performance. The following questionnaire will provide a diagnosis of your level of test anxiety. In the blank before each statement, write the number that most accurately describes your experience.

0 = Never   1 = Once or twice   2 = Sometimes   3 = Often

_____ I have gotten so nervous before an exam that I simply put down my books and didn't study for it.

_____ I have experienced disabling physical symptoms such as vomiting and severe headaches because I was nervous about an exam.

_____ I have neglected to show up for an exam because I was too scared to take it.

_____ I have experienced dizziness and disorientation while taking an exam.

_____ I have had trouble filling in the little circles because my hands were shaking so hard.

_____ I have failed an exam because I was too nervous to complete it.

_____ **Total: Add up the numbers in the blanks above.**

Understanding Your Test Stress Score

Here are the steps you should take, depending on your score. If you scored:

■ Below 3, your level of test anxiety is nothing to worry about; it's probably just enough to give you that little extra edge.

■ Between 3 and 6, your test anxiety may be enough to impair your performance, so you should practice the stress management techniques listed in this section regularly to try to bring your test anxiety down to manageable levels.

■ Above 6, your level of test anxiety is a serious concern. In addition to practicing the stress management techniques listed in this section, you may want to seek additional, personal help. Call your local high school or community college and ask for the academic counselor. Tell the counselor that you have a level of test anxiety that sometimes keeps you from being able to take exams. The counselor may be willing to help you or may suggest someone else you should talk to.

▶ Step 3: Make a Plan

Time to complete: 50 minutes
Activity: Construct a study plan
Maybe the most important thing you can do to get control of yourself and your exam is to make a study plan. Too many people fail to prepare simply because they fail to plan. Spending hours the day before the exam poring over sample test questions not only raises your level of test anxiety, it also is simply no substitute for careful preparation and practice over time.

Don't fall into the cram trap. Take control of your preparation time by mapping out a study schedule. There are four sample schedules on the following pages, based on the amount of time you have before the exam. If you are the kind of person who needs deadlines and assignments to motivate you for a project, here they are. If you are the kind of person who doesn't like to follow other people's plans, you can use the suggested schedules here to construct your own.

An important aspect of a study plan is flexibility. Your plan should help you, not hinder you, so be prepared to alter your study schedule once you get started, if necessary. You will probably find that one or more steps will take longer to complete than you had anticipated, while others will go more quickly.

In constructing your study plan, you should take into account how much work you need to do. If your score on the first practice test wasn't what you had hoped, consider taking some of the steps from Schedule A and getting them into Schedule D some-

how, even if you do have only three weeks before the exam.

Even more important than making a plan is making a commitment. You can't improve your skills in reading, writing, and judgment overnight. You have to set aside some time every day for study and practice. Try for at least 20 minutes a day. Twenty minutes daily will do you much more good than two hours on Saturday.

If you have months before the exam, you are lucky. Don't put off your study until the week before the exam! Start now. Even ten minutes a day, with half an hour or more on weekends, can make a big difference in your score—and in your chances of getting hired!

Schedule A: The Leisure Plan

If no test is announced near your city, you may have a year or more in which to get ready. This schedule gives you six months to sharpen your skills. If an exam is announced in the middle of your preparation, you can use one of the later schedules to help you compress your study program. Study only the chapters that are relevant to the type of exam you will be taking.

TIME	PREPARATION
6 months before the test	Take Exam 1 from Chapter 5. Then study the explanations for the answers until you know you could answer all the questions right. Start going to the library once every two weeks to read books or magazines about law enforcement, or browse through corrections officer–related websites on the Internet.
5 months before the test	Read Chapter 6 and work through the exercises. If possible, find other people who are preparing for the test and form a study group.
4 months before the test	Read Chapter 7 and work through the exercises. Start making flash cards of vocabulary and spelling words.
3 months before the test	Read Chapter 8 and work through the exercises. Practice your math by making up problems out of everyday events.
2 months before the test	Read Chapters 9 and 10 and work through the exercises. Exercise your memory by making note of people and places you see each day. Continue to read and work with your flash cards.

1 month before the test	Take one of the sample tests in either Chapter 11 or 12. Use your score to help you decide where to concentrate your efforts this month. Go back to the relevant chapters or get the help of a friend or teacher.
1 week before the test	Review both of the sample tests you took. See how much you've learned in the past months. Concentrate on what you have done well and decide not to let any areas where you still feel uncertain bother you.
1 day before the test	Relax. Do something unrelated to corrections officer exams. Eat a good meal and go to bed at your usual time.

Schedule B: The Just-Enough-Time Plan

If you have three to six months before your exam, that should be enough time to prepare for the written test, especially if you score above 70 on the first sample test you take. This schedule assumes four months; stretch it out or compress it if you have more or less time, and only study the chapters that are relevant to the type of exam you will be taking.

TIME	PREPARATION
4 months before the test	Take one practice exam from Chapters 5 or 11 to determine where you need the most work. Read Chapters 6 and 7 and work through the exercises. Start going to the library once every two weeks to read books about the corrections field, or visit corrections officer–related websites online. Also, make flash cards of vocabulary and spelling words.
3 months before the test	Read Chapter 8 and work through the exercises. Practice your math by making up problems from everyday events.
2 months before the test	Read Chapters 9 and 10 and work through the exercises. Exercise your memory by making note of people and places you see each day. Continue to read and work with your flash cards.
1 month before the test	Take one of the sample tests in Chapters 11 or 12. Use your score to help you decide where to concentrate your efforts this month. Go back to the relevant chapters and use the extra resources listed there, or get the help of a friend or teacher.
1 week before the test	Review both of the sample tests you took. See how much you have learned in the past months. Concentrate on what you have done well, and decide not to let any areas where you still feel uncertain bother you.
1 day before the test	Relax. Do something unrelated to corrections officer exams. Eat a good meal and go to bed at your usual time.

Schedule C: More Study in Less Time

If you have one to three months before the exam, you still have enough time for some concentrated study that will help you improve your score. This schedule is built around a two-month time frame. If you have only one month, spend an extra couple of hours a week to get all these steps in. If you have three months, take some of the steps from Schedule B and fit them in. Only study the chapters that are relevant to the type of exam you will be taking.

TIME	PREPARATION
8 weeks before the test	Take one sample test from Chapter 5 to find your weakest subjects. Choose the appropriate chapter(s) from among Chapters 6–8 to read in these two weeks.
6 weeks before the test	Read Chapters 6–8 and work through the exercises.
4 weeks before the test	Read Chapters 9 and 10 and work through the exercises.
2 weeks before the test	Take one of the second sample tests in either Chapter 11 or 12. Then score it and read the answer explanations until you are sure you understand them. Review the areas where your score is lowest.
1 week before the test	Review Chapters 6–10, concentrating on the areas where a little work can help the most.
1 day before the test	Relax. Do something unrelated to corrections officer exams. Eat a good meal and go to bed at your usual time.

Schedule D: The Fast Track

If you have three weeks or less before the exam, you really have your work cut out for you. Carve half an hour out of your day, *every day,* for study. This schedule assumes you have the whole three weeks to prepare in; if you have less time, you'll have to compress the schedule accordingly. Only study the chapters that are relevant to the type of exam you will be taking.

TIME	PREPARATION
3 weeks before the test	Take one practice exam from Chapter 5. Then read the material in Chapters 6–8 and work through the exercises.
2 weeks before the test	Read the material in Chapters 9–10 and work through the exercises. Take one of the sample tests in either Chapters 11 or 12.
1 week before the test	Evaluate your performance on the second sample test. Review the parts of Chapters 6–10 where you had the most trouble. Get a friend or teacher to help you with the section you found to be the most difficult.

2 days before the test	Review both of the sample tests you took. Make sure you understand all of the answer explanations.
1 day before the test	Relax. Do something unrelated to corrections officer exams. Eat a good meal and go to bed at your usual time.

► Step 4: Learn to Manage Your Time

Time to complete: 10 minutes to read, many hours of practice!
Activities: Practice these strategies as you take the sample tests in this book

Steps 4, 5, and 6 of the LearningExpress Test Preparation System put you in charge of your exam by showing you test-taking strategies that work. Practice these strategies as you take the sample tests in this book, and then you will be ready to use them on test day.

First, you will take control of your time on the exam. The first step in achieving this control is to find out the format of the exam you're going to take. Some corrections officer exams have different sections that are each timed separately. If this is true of the exam you'll be taking, you'll want to practice using your time wisely on the practice exams and trying to avoid mistakes while working quickly. Other types of exams don't have separately timed sections. If this is the case, just practice pacing yourself on the practice exams, so you don't spend too much time on difficult questions.

- **Listen carefully to directions.** By the time you get to the exam, you should be familiar with how all the subtests work, but listen to the person who is administering the exam just in case something has changed.
- **Pace yourself.** Glance at your watch every few minutes, and compare the time to how far you've

gotten in the subtest. When one-quarter of the time has elapsed, you should be a quarter of the way through the subtest and so on. If you're falling behind, pick up the pace a bit.

- **Keep moving.** Don't dither around on one question. If you don't know the answer, skip the question and move on. Circle the number of the question in your test booklet in case you have time to come back to it later.
- **Keep track of your place on the answer sheet.** If you skip a question, make sure you skip that space on the answer sheet too. Check yourself every 5–10 questions to make sure the question number and the answer sheet number are still the same.
- **Don't rush.** Though you should keep moving steadily through the test, rushing won't help. Try to keep calm and work methodically and quickly.

► Step 5: Learn to Use the Process of Elimination

Time to complete: 20 minutes
Activity: Complete worksheet on Using the Process of Elimination

After time management, your next most important tool for taking control of your exam is using the process of elimination wisely. It's standard test-taking wisdom that you should always read all the answer choices before choosing your answer. This practice helps you find the right answer by eliminating wrong answer choices. And, sure enough, that standard wisdom applies to your exam, too.

Let's say you're facing a vocabulary question that goes like this:

13. "Biology uses a <u>binomial</u> system of classification." In this sentence, the word <u>binomial</u> most nearly means
   a. understanding the law.
   b. having two names.
   c. scientifically sound.
   d. having a double meaning.

If you happen to know what *binomial* means, of course, you don't need to use the process of elimination, but let's assume that, like many people, you don't. So you look at the answer choices. "Understanding the law" sure doesn't sound very likely for something having to do with biology. So you eliminate choice **a**—and now you only have three answer choices to deal with. Mark an ✕ next to choice **a** so you never have to read it again.

On to the other answer choices. If you know that the prefix *bi-* means *two,* as in *bicycle,* flag answer **b** as a possible answer. Mark a check mark beside it, meaning "good answer, I might use this one."

Choice **c,** "scientifically sound," is a possibility. At least it's about science, not law. It could work here, though, when you think about it, having a "scientifically sound" classification system in a scientific field is kind of redundant. You remember the *bi* thing in *binomial,* and probably continue to like answer **b** better. But you are not sure, so you put a question mark next to **c,** meaning "well, maybe."

Now, choice **d,** "having a double meaning." You are still keeping in mind that *bi-* means *two,* so this one looks possible at first. But then you look again at the sentence the word belongs in, and you think, "Why would biology want a system of classification that has two meanings? That wouldn't work very well!" If you are really taken with the idea that *bi* means *two,* you

might put a question mark here. But if you are feeling a little more confident, you'll put an ✕. You have already got a better answer picked out.

Now your question looks like this:

13. "Biology uses a <u>binomial</u> system of classification." In this sentence, the word <u>binomial</u> most nearly means
   ✕ **a.** understanding the law
   ✔ **b.** having two names
   ? **c.** scientifically sound
   ? **d.** having a double meaning

You have got just one check mark, for a good answer. If you are pressed for time, you should simply mark answer **b** on your answer sheet. If you have got the time to be extra careful, you could compare your checkmark answer to your question-mark answers to make sure that it's better. (It is: the *binomial* system in biology is the one that gives a two-part genus and species name like *homo sapiens.*)

It's good to have a system for marking good, bad, and maybe answers. We're recommending this one:

   ✕ = bad
   ✔ = good
   ? = maybe

If you don't like these marks, devise your own system. Just make sure you do it long before test day—while you are working through the practice exams in this book—so you won't have to worry about it during the test.

Even when you think you're absolutely clueless about a question, you can often use the process of elimination to get rid of at least one answer choice. If so, you're better prepared to make an educated guess, as you will see in Step 6. More often, the process of elimination allows you to get down to only *two* possibly right answers. Then you're in a strong position to guess. And sometimes, even though you don't know the right answer, you can find it simply by getting rid of the wrong ones, as you did in the example above.

Using the Process of Elimination

Use the process of elimination to answer the following questions.

1. Ilsa is as old as Meghan will be in five years. The difference between Ed's age and Meghan's age is twice the difference between Ilsa's age and Meghan's age. Ed is 29. How old is Ilsa?
   a. 4
   b. 10
   c. 19
   d. 24

2. "All drivers of commercial vehicles must carry a valid commercial driver's license whenever operating a commercial vehicle."

   According to this sentence, which of the following people need **NOT** carry a commercial driver's license?
   a. a truck driver idling his engine while waiting to be directed to a loading dock
   b. a bus operator backing her bus out of the way of another bus in the bus lot

   c. a taxi driver driving his personal car to the grocery store
   d. a limousine driver taking the limousine to her home after dropping off her last passenger of the evening

3. Smoking tobacco has been linked to
   a. increased risk of stroke and heart attack.
   b. all forms of respiratory disease.
   c. increasing mortality rates over the past ten years.
   d. juvenile delinquency.

4. Which of the following words is spelled correctly?
   a. incorrigible
   b. outragous
   c. domestickated
   d. understandible

Answers

Here are the answers, as well as some suggestions as to how you might have used the process of elimination to find them.

1. **d.** You should have eliminated answer **a** right off the bat. Ilsa can't be four years old if Meghan is going to be Ilsa's age in five years. The best way to eliminate other answer choices is to try plugging them in to the information given in the problem. For instance, for choice **b**, if Ilsa is 10, then Meghan must be 5. The difference between their ages is 5. The difference between Ed's age, 29, and Meghan's age, 5, is 24. Is 24 two times 5? No. Then choice **b** is wrong. You could eliminate choice **c** in the same way and be left with choice **d**.

2. **c.** Note the word *not* in the question, and go through the answers one by one. Is the truck driver in choice **a** "operating a commercial vehicle?" Yes, idling counts as "operating," so he needs to have a commercial driver's license.

Likewise, the bus operator in choice **b** is operating a commercial vehicle; the question doesn't say the operator has to be on the street. The limo driver in choice **d** is operating a commercial vehicle, even if it doesn't have a passenger in it. However, the cabbie in choice **c** is not operating a commercial vehicle, but his own private car.

3. **a.** You could eliminate answer **b** simply because of the presence of the word *all*. Such absolutes hardly ever appear in correct answer choices. Choice **c** looks attractive until you think a little about what you know—aren't fewer people smoking these days, rather than more? So how could smoking be responsible for a higher mortality rate?

   (If you didn't know that mortality rate means the rate at which people die, you might keep this choice as a possibility, but you would still be able to eliminate two answers and have only two to choose from.) And choice d is plain silly, so you could eliminate that one too. You are left with the correct choice, **a.**

4. a. How you used the process of elimination here depends on which words you recognized as being spelled incorrectly. If you knew that the correct spellings were outrageous, domesticated, and understandable, then you were home free. Surely you knew that at least one of those words was wrong!

Try using your powers of elimination on the questions in the worksheet entitled Using the Process of Elimination that begins on the previous page. The answer explanations there show one possible way you might use the process to arrive at the right answer.

The process of elimination is your tool for the next step, which is knowing when to guess.

▶ Step 6: Know When to Guess

Time to complete: 20 minutes
Activity: Complete worksheet on Your
    Guessing Ability

Armed with the process of elimination, you're ready to take control of one of the big questions in test-taking: Should I guess? The first and main answer is Yes. Unless the exam has a so-called "guessing penalty," you have nothing to lose and everything to gain from guessing. The more complicated answer depends both on the exam and on you—your personality and your "guessing intuition."

Most corrections officer written exams don't use a guessing penalty. The number of questions you answer correctly yields your score, and there's no penalty for wrong answers. So most of the time, you don't have to worry—simply go ahead and guess. But if you find that your exam does have a "guessing

penalty," you should read the section below to find out what that means to you.

How the "Guessing Penalty" Works

A "guessing penalty" really only works against random guessing—filling in the little circles to make a nice pattern on your answer sheet. If you can eliminate one or more answer choices, as outlined above, you're better off taking a guess than leaving the answer blank, even on the sections that have a penalty.

Here's how a "guessing penalty" works: depending on the number of answer choices in a given exam, some proportion of the number of questions you get wrong is subtracted from the total number of questions you got right. For instance, if there are four answer choices, typically the "guessing penalty" is one-third of your wrong answers. Suppose you took a test of 100 questions. You answered 88 of them right and 12 wrong.

If there's no guessing penalty, your score is simply 88. But if there's a one-third point guessing penalty, the scorers take your 12 wrong answers and divide by 3 to come up with 4. Then they *subtract* that 4 from your correct-answer score of 88 to leave you with a score of 84. Thus, you would have been better off if you had simply not answered those 12 questions that you weren't sure of. Then your total score would still be 88, because there wouldn't be anything to subtract.

Your Guessing Ability

The following are ten really hard questions. You're not supposed to know the answers. Rather, this is an assessment of your ability to guess when you don't have a clue. Read each question carefully, just as if you did expect to answer it. If you have any knowledge at all of the subject of the question, use that knowledge to help you eliminate wrong answer choices. Use this answer grid to fill in your answers to the questions.

ANSWER GRID

1. (a) (b) (c) (d)
2. (a) (b) (c) (d)
3. (a) (b) (c) (d)
4. (a) (b) (c) (d)

5. (a) (b) (c) (d)
6. (a) (b) (c) (d)
7. (a) (b) (c) (d)
8. (a) (b) (c) (d)

9. (a) (b) (c) (d)
10. (a) (b) (c) (d)

1. September 7 is Independence Day in
   a. India
   b. Costa Rica
   c. Brazil
   d. Australia

2. Which of the following is the formula for determining the momentum of an object?
   a. $p = MV$
   b. $F = ma$
   c. $P = IV$
   d. $E = mc^2$

3. Because of the expansion of the universe, the stars and other celestial bodies are all moving away from each other. This phenomenon is known as
   a. Newton's first law
   b. the big bang
   c. gravitational collapse
   d. Hubble flow

4. American author Gertrude Stein was born in
   a. 1713
   b. 1830
   c. 1874
   d. 1901

5. Which of the following is NOT one of the Five Classics attributed to Confucius?
   a. the I Ching
   b. the Book of Holiness
   c. the Spring and Autumn Annals
   d. the Book of History

6. The religious and philosophical doctrine that holds that the universe is constantly in a struggle between good and evil is known as
   a. Pelagianism
   b. Manichaeanism
   c. neo-Hegelianism
   d. Epicureanism

7. The third Chief Justice of the U.S. Supreme Court was
   a. John Blair
   b. William Cushing
   c. James Wilson
   d. John Jay

8. Which of the following is the poisonous portion of a daffodil?
   a. the bulb
   b. the leaves
   c. the stem
   d. the flowers

9. The winner of the Masters golf tournament in 1953 was
  a. Sam Snead.
  b. Cary Middlecoff.
  c. Arnold Palmer.
  d. Ben Hogan.

10. The state with the highest per capita personal income in 1980 was
  a. Alaska.
  b. Connecticut.
  c. New York.
  d. Texas.

Answers

Check your answers against the correct answers below.

1. c
2. a
3. d
4. c
5. b
6. b
7. b
8. a
9. d
10. a

How Did You Do?

You may have simply gotten lucky and actually known the answer to one or two questions. In addition, your guessing was probably more successful if you were able to use the process of elimination on any of the questions. Maybe you didn't know who the third Chief Justice was (question 7), but you knew that John Jay was the first. In that case, you would have eliminated choice d and, therefore, improved your odds of guessing right from one in four to one in three.

According to probability, you should get $2\frac{1}{2}$ answers correct, so getting either two or three right would be average. If you got four or more right, you may be a really terrific guesser. If you got one or none right, you may be a really bad guesser.

Keep in mind, though, that this is only a small sample. You should continue to keep track of your guessing ability as you work through the sample questions in this book. Circle the numbers of questions you guess on as you make your guess; or, if you don't have time while you take the practice tests, go back afterward and try to remember which questions you guessed at. Remember, on a test with four answer choices, your chance of guessing correctly is one in four. So keep a separate "guessing" score for each exam. How many questions did you guess on? How many did you get right? If the number you got right is at least one-fourth of the number of questions you guessed on, you are at least an average guesser—maybe better—and you should always go ahead and guess on the real exam. If the number you got right is significantly lower than one-fourth of the number you guessed on, you need to improve your guessing skills.

What You Should Do About the Guessing Penalty

That's how a guessing penalty works. The first thing this means for you is that marking your answer sheet at random doesn't pay. If you're running out of time on an exam that has a guessing penalty, you should not use your remaining seconds to mark a pretty pattern on your answer sheet. Take those few seconds to try to answer one more question right.

But as soon as you get out of the realm of random guessing, the "guessing penalty" no longer works against you. If you can use the process of elimination to get rid of even one wrong answer choice, the odds stop being against you and start working in your favor.

Sticking with our example of an exam that has four answer choices, eliminating just one wrong answer makes your odds of choosing the correct answer one in three. That's the same as the one-out-of-three guessing penalty—even odds. If you eliminate two answer choices, your odds are one in two—better than the guessing penalty. In either case, you should go ahead and choose one of the remaining answer choices.

But what if you're not much of a risk-taker, and you think of yourself as the world's worst guesser? Complete the Your Guessing Ability worksheet on pages 45–46 to get an idea of how good your intuition is.

▶ Step 7: Reach Your Peak Performance Zone

Time to complete: 10 minutes to read; weeks to complete!
Activity: Complete the Physical Preparation Checklist

To get ready for a challenge like a big exam, you have to take control of your physical, as well as your mental, state. Exercise, proper diet, and rest will ensure that your body works with, rather than against, your mind on test day, as well as during your preparation.

Exercise

If you don't already have a regular exercise program, the time during which you're preparing for your written exam is an excellent time to start one. You'll have to be in shape to pass the physical ability test, and to make it through the first weeks of basic training anyway. And if you're already keeping fit—or trying to get that way—don't let the pressure of preparing for the written exam be an excuse for quitting now. Exercise helps reduce stress by pumping wonderful good-feeling hormones called endorphins into your system. It also

increases the oxygen supply throughout your body, including your brain, so you'll be at peak performance on test day.

A half hour of vigorous activity—enough to raise a sweat—every day should be your aim. If you're really pressed for time, every other day is OK. Choose an activity you like and get out there and do it. Jogging with a friend always makes the time go faster, or take a radio.

But don't overdo it. You don't want to exhaust yourself so much that you can't study. Moderation is the key.

Diet

First of all, cut out the junk food. Go easy on caffeine and nicotine, and eliminate alcohol from your system at least two weeks before the exam. Promise yourself a celebration the night after the exam, if need be.

What your body needs for peak performance is simply a balanced diet. Eat plenty of fruits and vegetables, along with protein and carbohydrates. Foods that are high in lecithin (an amino acid), such as fish and beans, are especially good "brain foods."

Rest

You probably know how much sleep you need every night to be at your best, even if you don't always get it. Make sure you do get that much sleep, though, for at least a week before the exam. Moderation is important here, as well. Too much extra sleep could just make you groggy.

If you're not a morning person and your exam will be given in the morning, you should reset your internal clock so that your body doesn't think you're taking an exam at 3 A.M. You have to start this process well before the exam. The way it works is to get up half an hour earlier each morning, and then go to bed half an hour earlier that night. Don't try it the other way around; you'll just toss and turn if you go to bed early without having gotten up early. The next morning, get up another half an hour earlier, and so on. How long you will have to do this depends on how late you're used to getting up.

Physical Preparation

For the week before the test, write down 1) what physical exercise you engaged in and for how long and 2) what you ate for each meal. Remember, you're trying for at least half an hour of exercise every other day (preferably every day) and a balanced diet that's light on junk food.

7 Days Before the Exam

Exercise: _____ for _____ minutes

Breakfast: _____

Lunch: _____

Dinner: _____

Snacks: _____

6 Days Before the Exam

Exercise: _____ for _____ minutes

Breakfast: _____

Lunch: _____

Dinner: _____

Snacks: _____

5 Days Before the Exam

Exercise: _____ for _____ minutes

Breakfast: _____

Lunch: _____

Dinner: _____

Snacks: _____

4 Days Before the Exam

Exercise: _____ for _____ minutes

Breakfast: _____

Lunch: _____

Dinner: _____

Snacks: _____

3 Days Before the Exam

Exercise: _____ for _____ minutes

Breakfast: _____

Lunch: _____

Dinner: _____

Snacks: _____

2 Days Before the Exam

Exercise: _____ for _____ minutes

Breakfast: _____

Lunch: _____

Dinner: _____

Snacks: _____

1 Day Before the Exam

Exercise: _____ for _____ minutes

Breakfast: _____

Lunch: _____

Dinner: _____

Snacks: _____

▶ Step 8: Get Your Act Together

Time to complete: 10 minutes to read; time to complete will vary

Activity: Complete Final Preparations worksheet

You're in control of your mind and body; you're in charge of test anxiety, your preparation, and your test-taking strategies. Now it's time to take charge of external factors, like the testing site and the materials you need to take the exam.

Find Out Where the Test Is and Make a Trial Run

The exam bulletin or notice the recruiting office sent you will tell you when and where your exam is being held. Do you know how to get to the testing site? Do you know how long it will take you to get there? If not, make a trial run, preferably on the same day of the week at the same time of day. Make note, on the Final Preparations worksheet, of the amount of time it will take you to get to the exam site. Plan on arriving 10–15 minutes early so you can get the lay of the land, use the bathroom, and calm down. Then figure out how early you will have to get up that morning, and make sure you get up that early every day for a week before the exam.

Gather Your Materials

The night before the exam, lay out the clothes you will wear and the materials you have to bring with you to the exam. Plan on dressing in layers; you won't have any control over the temperature of the examination room. Have a sweater or jacket you can take off if it's warm or put on if the air conditioning is on full blast. Use the checklist on the Final Preparations worksheet on page 50 to help you pull together what you will need.

Don't Skip Breakfast

Even if you don't usually eat breakfast, do so on exam morning. A cup of coffee doesn't count. Don't eat doughnuts or other sweet foods, either. A sugar high will leave you with a sugar low in the middle of the exam. A mix of protein and carbohydrates is best: cereal with milk and just a little sugar, or eggs with toast will do your body a world of good.

▶ Step 9: Do It!

Time to complete: 10 minutes, plus test-taking time

Activity: Ace the Corrections Officer Written Exam!

Fast forward to exam day. You're ready. You made a study plan and followed through. You practiced your test-taking strategies while working through this book. You're in control of your physical, mental, and emotional state. You know when and where to show up and what to bring with you. In other words, you're better prepared than most of the other people taking the exam with you. You're psyched.

Just one more thing. When you're done with the corrections officer written exam, you will have earned a reward. Plan a celebration. Call up your friends and plan a party, or have a nice dinner for two—whatever your heart desires. Give yourself something to look forward to.

And then do it. Go into the exam, full of confidence, armed with the test-taking strategies you've practiced till they're second nature. You're in control of yourself, your environment, and your performance on the exam. You're ready to succeed. So do it. Go in there and ace the exam. And look forward to your future career in corrections!

Final Preparations

Getting to the Exam Site

Location of exam: _____

Date of exam: _____

Time of exam: _____

Do I know how to get to the exam site?   Yes___   No ___   (If no, make a trial run.)

Time it will take to get to exam site: _____

Things to Lay Out the Night Before

Clothes I will wear   ____

Sweater/jacket   ____

Watch   ____

Photo ID   ____

Admission card   ____

4 #2 pencils   ____

_____   ____

_____   ____

CHAPTER

5 ▶ Corrections Officer Exam I

CHAPTER SUMMARY

This is the first of three practice exams in this book based on exams used by departments of correction around the country to assess candidates applying for positions as corrections officers. This exam focuses on job-related skills. Use it to see how you would do if you had to take the exam today.

Though written examinations for corrections officers vary depending on the state, county, or municipal corrections agency, most exams test just a few basic skills, like the ones covered in this exam.

This test consists of one hundred questions in six areas. In Part One, Reading Comprehension, consists of reading passages and questions about them. Part Two, Preparing Written Material, includes questions on how to express given information in writing. Part Three, Math, includes simple arithmetic problems. For Part Four, Memory and Observation, you will read a passage and look at a drawing for ten minutes, and then answer questions about them without looking back. Also included in this part is a section on Counting, wherein you will have to time yourself and answer five simple counting questions in one minute. For Part Five, Situational Reasoning, you will choose the best answer to the questions, using your good judgment and common sense. Part Six, Applying Written Material, will ask you to apply the corrections rules and procedures it gives you to specific situations.

1.	ⓐ	ⓑ	ⓒ	ⓓ
2.	ⓐ	ⓑ	ⓒ	ⓓ
3.	ⓐ	ⓑ	ⓒ	ⓓ
4.	ⓐ	ⓑ	ⓒ	ⓓ
5.	ⓐ	ⓑ	ⓒ	ⓓ
6.	ⓐ	ⓑ	ⓒ	ⓓ
7.	ⓐ	ⓑ	ⓒ	ⓓ
8.	ⓐ	ⓑ	ⓒ	ⓓ
9.	ⓐ	ⓑ	ⓒ	ⓓ
10.	ⓐ	ⓑ	ⓒ	ⓓ
11.	ⓐ	ⓑ	ⓒ	ⓓ
12.	ⓐ	ⓑ	ⓒ	ⓓ
13.	ⓐ	ⓑ	ⓒ	ⓓ
14.	ⓐ	ⓑ	ⓒ	ⓓ
15.	ⓐ	ⓑ	ⓒ	ⓓ
16.	ⓐ	ⓑ	ⓒ	ⓓ
17.	ⓐ	ⓑ	ⓒ	ⓓ
18.	ⓐ	ⓑ	ⓒ	ⓓ
19.	ⓐ	ⓑ	ⓒ	ⓓ
20.	ⓐ	ⓑ	ⓒ	ⓓ
21.	ⓐ	ⓑ	ⓒ	ⓓ
22.	ⓐ	ⓑ	ⓒ	ⓓ
23.	ⓐ	ⓑ	ⓒ	ⓓ
24.	ⓐ	ⓑ	ⓒ	ⓓ
25.	ⓐ	ⓑ	ⓒ	ⓓ
26.	ⓐ	ⓑ	ⓒ	ⓓ
27.	ⓐ	ⓑ	ⓒ	ⓓ
28.	ⓐ	ⓑ	ⓒ	ⓓ
29.	ⓐ	ⓑ	ⓒ	ⓓ
30.	ⓐ	ⓑ	ⓒ	ⓓ
31.	ⓐ	ⓑ	ⓒ	ⓓ
32.	ⓐ	ⓑ	ⓒ	ⓓ
33.	ⓐ	ⓑ	ⓒ	ⓓ
34.	ⓐ	ⓑ	ⓒ	ⓓ

35.	ⓐ	ⓑ	ⓒ	ⓓ
36.	ⓐ	ⓑ	ⓒ	ⓓ
37.	ⓐ	ⓑ	ⓒ	ⓓ
38.	ⓐ	ⓑ	ⓒ	ⓓ
39.	ⓐ	ⓑ	ⓒ	ⓓ
40.	ⓐ	ⓑ	ⓒ	ⓓ
41.	ⓐ	ⓑ	ⓒ	ⓓ
42.	ⓐ	ⓑ	ⓒ	ⓓ
43.	ⓐ	ⓑ	ⓒ	ⓓ
44.	ⓐ	ⓑ	ⓒ	ⓓ
45.	ⓐ	ⓑ	ⓒ	ⓓ
46.	ⓐ	ⓑ	ⓒ	ⓓ
47.	ⓐ	ⓑ	ⓒ	ⓓ
48.	ⓐ	ⓑ	ⓒ	ⓓ
49.	ⓐ	ⓑ	ⓒ	ⓓ
50.	ⓐ	ⓑ	ⓒ	ⓓ
51.	ⓐ	ⓑ	ⓒ	ⓓ
52.	ⓐ	ⓑ	ⓒ	ⓓ
53.	ⓐ	ⓑ	ⓒ	ⓓ
54.	ⓐ	ⓑ	ⓒ	ⓓ
55.	ⓐ	ⓑ	ⓒ	ⓓ
56.	ⓐ	ⓑ	ⓒ	ⓓ
57.	ⓐ	ⓑ	ⓒ	ⓓ
58.	ⓐ	ⓑ	ⓒ	ⓓ
59.	ⓐ	ⓑ	ⓒ	ⓓ
60.	ⓐ	ⓑ	ⓒ	ⓓ
61.	ⓐ	ⓑ	ⓒ	ⓓ
62.	ⓐ	ⓑ	ⓒ	ⓓ
63.	ⓐ	ⓑ	ⓒ	ⓓ
64.	ⓐ	ⓑ	ⓒ	ⓓ
65.	ⓐ	ⓑ	ⓒ	ⓓ
66.	ⓐ	ⓑ	ⓒ	ⓓ
67.	ⓐ	ⓑ	ⓒ	ⓓ
68.	ⓐ	ⓑ	ⓒ	ⓓ

69.	ⓐ	ⓑ	ⓒ	ⓓ
70.	ⓐ	ⓑ	ⓒ	ⓓ
71.	ⓐ	ⓑ	ⓒ	ⓓ
72.	ⓐ	ⓑ	ⓒ	ⓓ
73.	ⓐ	ⓑ	ⓒ	ⓓ
74.	ⓐ	ⓑ	ⓒ	ⓓ
75.	ⓐ	ⓑ	ⓒ	ⓓ
76.	ⓐ	ⓑ	ⓒ	ⓓ
77.	ⓐ	ⓑ	ⓒ	ⓓ
78.	ⓐ	ⓑ	ⓒ	ⓓ
79.	ⓐ	ⓑ	ⓒ	ⓓ
80.	ⓐ	ⓑ	ⓒ	ⓓ
81.	ⓐ	ⓑ	ⓒ	ⓓ
82.	ⓐ	ⓑ	ⓒ	ⓓ
83.	ⓐ	ⓑ	ⓒ	ⓓ
84.	ⓐ	ⓑ	ⓒ	ⓓ
85.	ⓐ	ⓑ	ⓒ	ⓓ
86.	ⓐ	ⓑ	ⓒ	ⓓ
87.	ⓐ	ⓑ	ⓒ	ⓓ
88.	ⓐ	ⓑ	ⓒ	ⓓ
89.	ⓐ	ⓑ	ⓒ	ⓓ
90.	ⓐ	ⓑ	ⓒ	ⓓ
91.	ⓐ	ⓑ	ⓒ	ⓓ
92.	ⓐ	ⓑ	ⓒ	ⓓ
93.	ⓐ	ⓑ	ⓒ	ⓓ
94.	ⓐ	ⓑ	ⓒ	ⓓ
95.	ⓐ	ⓑ	ⓒ	ⓓ
96.	ⓐ	ⓑ	ⓒ	ⓓ
97.	ⓐ	ⓑ	ⓒ	ⓓ
98.	ⓐ	ⓑ	ⓒ	ⓓ
99.	ⓐ	ⓑ	ⓒ	ⓓ
100.	ⓐ	ⓑ	ⓒ	ⓓ

PART ONE: READING COMPREHENSION

Following are several reading passages. Answer the questions that come after each, based solely on the information in the passages.

Stalking is defined as the "willful, malicious, and repeated following and harassing of another person." The act of stalking can probably be traced back to the earliest episodes of human history, but in the United States no substantive law existed to protect the victims of stalkers in until 1990. Prior to this, the most that police officials could do was arrest the stalker for a minor offense or suggest the victim obtain a restraining order, a civil remedy often ignored by the offender. Frightened victims had their worst fears confirmed: they would have to be harmed—or killed—before anything could be done.

Stalking was brought into the public eye in 1989 by the stalker-murder of television star Rebecca Schaeffer and then the 1990 stalker-murders of four Orange County women in a single six-week period. When it was discovered that one of the Orange County victims had a restraining order in her purse when her stalker murdered her, California reacted by drafting the first anti-stalking law. Now most states have similar laws.

The solution is not perfect: Some stalkers are too mentally deranged or obsessed to fear a prison term, and on the flip side, there is the danger, however small, of abuse of the law, particularly in marital disputes. Most importantly, law enforcement officials and general society need to be better educated about stalking, especially about its often sexist underpinnings. (The majority of stalking victims are women terrorized by former husbands or boyfriends.)

But the laws are a vast improvement, and they carry the threat of felony penalties of up to ten years in prison for those who would attempt to control or possess others through intimidation and terror.

1. Which of the following best expresses the main idea of the passage?
   a. More education is needed about sexism, because sexism is the most important element in the crime of stalking.
   b. Stalking is thought of as a new kind of crime, but has probably existed throughout human history.
   c. The new anti-stalking legislation is an important weapon against the crime of stalking, though it is not the complete answer.
   d. Today almost every state in the United States has a very effective, if not perfect, anti-stalking law.

2. Which of the following is NOT mentioned in the passage as a weakness in the new anti-stalking legislation?
   a. The laws alone might not deter some stalkers.
   b. A person might be wrongly accused of being a stalker.
   c. The police and public do not completely understand the crime.
   d. Victims do not yet have adequate knowledge about anti-stalking laws.

3. Based on the passage, why are restraining orders ineffective in preventing stalking?
   a. Only civil charges can be leveled against the violator.
   b. Prior to 1990, restraining orders could not be issued against stalkers.
   c. Law enforcement officials do not take such orders seriously.
   d. Restraining orders apply only to married couples.

4. Which of the following is NOT a stated or implied motive for stalking?
   a. to own the victim
   b. to terrify the victim
   c. o rob the victim
   d. to badger the victim

On occasion, corrections officers may be involved in receiving a confession from an inmate under their care. Sometimes, one inmate may confess to another inmate, who may be motivated to pass the information on to corrections officers. Often, however, these confessions are obtained by placing an undercover agent, posing as an inmate, in a cell with the prisoner. On the surface, this may appear to violate the principles of the constitutional Fifth Amendment privilege against self-incrimination. However, the courts have found that the Fifth Amendment is intended to protect suspects from coercive interrogation, which is present when a person is in custody and is subject to official questioning. In the case of an undercover officer posing as an inmate, the questioning does not appear to be official; therefore, confessions obtained in this manner are not considered coercive.

5. According to the passage, the Fifth Amendment privilege against self-incrimination applies to which of the following situations?
   a. One inmate is motivated to pass a fellow inmate's confession onto a corrections officer.
   b. A uniformed officer badgers a suspect in custody until he or she confesses to a crime.
   c. A corrections officer overhears one inmate confessing to another inmate.
   d. An inmate voluntarily confesses his or her crime to a corrections officer.

6. The privilege against self-incrimination can be found in
   a. an opinion of the Supreme Court.
   b. prison rules and regulations.
   c. state law governing prisons.
   d. the Bill of Rights.

7. The privilege against self-incrimination does not apply to inmates who
   a. were read their rights when they were arrested.
   b. have already been convicted.
   c. believe they are talking to a fellow inmate.
   d. have received life sentences.

In recent years, issues of public and personal safety have become a major concern to many Americans. Violent incidents in fast food restaurants, libraries, hospitals, schools, and offices have led many to seek greater security inside and outside of their homes. Sales of burglar alarms and high tech security devices such as motion detectors and video monitors have skyrocketed in the last decade. Convenience stores and post offices have joined banks and jewelry stores in barricading staff behind iron bars and safety glass enclosures. Communities employ private security forces and encourage homeowners to keep trained attack dogs on their premises. While some people have sympathy for the impetus behind these efforts, there is also a concern that these measures will create a siege mentality leading to distrust among people that could foster a dangerous isolationism within neighborhoods and among neighbors.

8. The passage suggests which of the following about community security?

   a. Communities are more dangerous today than they were ten years ago.

   b. Too much concern for security can destroy trust among neighbors.

   c. Poor security has led to an increase in public violence.

   d. Isolated neighborhoods are safe neighborhoods.

9. The word *foster* in the last sentence of the passage most nearly means

   a. adopt.

   b. encourage.

   c. prevent.

   d. secure.

10. The author believes that

   a. more security is needed to make neighborhoods safer.

   b. people should spend more money on home security.

   c. people should not ignore the problems created by excessive safety concerns.

   d. attack dogs and high-tech devices are the best protection against violent crime.

11. In the last sentence, the phrase *siege mentality* means

   a. hostility.

   b. defensiveness.

   c. fear.

   d. corruption.

Hearsay evidence, which is the secondhand reporting of a statement, is allowed in court only when the truth of the statement is irrelevant. Hearsay that depends on the statement's truthfulness is inadmissible because the witness does not appear in court and swear an oath to tell the truth, his or her demeanor when making the statement is not visible to the jury, the accuracy of the statement cannot be tested under cross-examination, and to introduce it would be to deprive the accused of the constitutional right to confront the accuser. Hearsay is admissible, however, when the truth of the statement is unimportant. If, for example, a defendant claims to have been unconscious at a certain time, and a witness claims that the defendant actually spoke to her at that time, this evidence would be admissible because the truth of what the defendant actually said is irrelevant.

12. The main purpose of the passage is to

   a. explain why hearsay evidence abridges the rights of the accused.

   b. question the truth of hearsay evidence.

   c. argue that rules about the admissibility of hearsay evidence should be changed.

   d. specify which use of hearsay evidence is inadmissible and why.

13. Which of the following is NOT a reason given in the passage for the inadmissibility of hearsay evidence?

   a. Rumors are not necessarily credible.

   b. The person making the original statement was not under oath.

   c. The jury should be able to watch the gestures and facial expressions of the person making the statement.

   d. The person making the statement cannot be cross-examined.

14. How does the passage explain the proper use of hearsay evidence?

   a. by listing a set of criteria

   b. by providing a hypothetical example

   c. by referring to the Constitution

   d. by citing case law

15. The passage suggests that the criterion used for deciding that most hearsay evidence is inadmissible is most likely
   a. the unreliability of most hearsay witnesses.
   b. the importance of physical evidence to corroborate witness testimony.
   c. concern for discerning the truth in a fair manner.
   d. doubt about the relevance of hearsay testimony.

In order for our society to make decisions about the kinds of punishments we will impose on convicted criminals, we must understand why we punish criminals. Some people argue that retribution is the purpose of punishment and that, therefore, the punishment must in some direct way fit the crime. This view is based on the belief that a person who commits a crime deserves to be punished. Because the punishment must fit the specific crime, the *theory of retribution* allows a sentencing judge to consider the circumstances of each crime, criminal, and victim in imposing a sentence.

   Another view, the *deterrence theory,* promotes punishment in order to discourage commission of future crimes. In this view, punishment need not relate directly to the crime committed, because the point is to deter both a specific criminal and the general public from committing crimes in the future. However, punishment must necessarily be uniform and consistently applied, in order for the members of the public to understand how they would be punished if they committed a crime. Laws setting sentencing guidelines are based on the deterrence theory and do not allow a judge to consider the specifics of a particular crime in sentencing a convicted criminal.

16. The *retribution theory* of punishment
   a. is no longer considered valid.
   b. holds that punishment must fit the crime committed.
   c. applies only to violent crimes.
   d. allows a jury to recommend the sentence that should be imposed.

17. The passage suggests that a person who believes that the death penalty results in fewer murders would most likely believe in
   a. the deterrence theory.
   b. the retribution theory.
   c. giving judges considerable discretion in imposing sentences.
   d. the integrity of the criminal justice system.

18. A good title for this passage would be
   a. Sentencing Reform: A Modest Proposal.
   b. More Criminals Are Doing Time.
   c. Punishment: Deterrent or Retribution?
   d. Why I Favor Uniform Sentencing Guidelines.

19. A person who believes in the deterrence theory would probably also support
   a. non-unanimous jury verdicts.
   b. early release of prisoners because of prison overcrowding.
   c. a broad definition of the insanity defense.
   d. allowing television broadcasts of court proceedings.

20. The theories described in the passage differ in
   a. the amount of leeway they would allow judges in determining sentences.
   b. the number of law enforcement professionals who espouse them.
   c. their concern for the rights of the accused.
   d. their concern for protecting society from crime.

PART TWO: PREPARING WRITTEN MATERIAL

Questions 21–29 consist of four numbered sentences. Choose the sentence order that would result in the best paragraph.

21. 1) There is a need for rehabilitation because the system's current emphasis on imprisonment is a failure. 2) Without rehabilitation before and after their discharge from prison, offenders are more likely to commit more crimes. 3) A common example of rehabilitation is prison labor, such as assembling electronic components. 4) Rehabilitation is a constructive way to improve the criminal justice system.
   a. 4, 1, 3, 2
   b. 3, 4, 2, 1
   c. 3, 2, 4, 1
   d. 2, 3, 1, 4

22. 1) Criminal laws are usually written by state legislatures. 2) In addition, there is a third kind of criminal law. 3) Recognized Native American tribes have jurisdiction over some crimes that are committed on their reservations. 4) However, some crimes, such as racketeering, are federal.
   a. 3, 2, 4, 1
   b. 3, 4, 1, 2
   c. 1, 4, 2, 3
   d. 1, 3, 2, 4

23. 1) Although these mechanical alarms are fairly recent, the idea of a security system is not new. 2) Anyone who lives in a large, modern city has heard the familiar sound of electronic security alarms. 3) The oldest alarm system was probably a few strategically placed dogs that could discourage intruders with a loud warning cry. 4) Most alarms are just loud noises, but more sophisticated alarms have the ability to alert the proper authorities.
   a. 2, 3, 4, 1
   b. 1, 3, 4, 2
   c. 1, 4, 2, 3
   d. 2, 4, 1, 3

24. 1) During the parole period, he or she is supervised by a parole officer. 2) The parole officer must also be concerned, however, about the safety of the community. 3) After a prisoner has served his or her sentence, he or she may be paroled to the county where he or she was tried. 4) A parole officer has a certain amount of latitude in supervising a parolees' transition from prison life.
   a. 3, 1, 4, 2
   b. 2, 4, 3, 1
   c. 4, 3, 1, 2
   d. 3, 2, 4, 1

25. 1) For elimination purposes, major case prints should be obtained from all persons who may have touched areas associated with a crime scene. 2) In criminal cases, the availability of readable fingerprints is often critical in establishing evidence of a major crime. 3) It is necessary, therefore, to follow proper procedures when taking fingerprints. 4) Major case prints are more thorough than standard fingerprints; they include prints made of all parts of the hand from the tips to the palm, the sides of the fingers, and sides of the palm.
  a. 4, 3, 1, 2
  b. 3, 2, 4, 1
  c. 2, 3, 1, 4
  d. 2, 4, 3, 1

26. 1) This concept is used effectively in Japan. 2) Tokyo has thousands of *Kobans*; the system has made the Japanese feel safe while walking around the city. 3) A recent idea in law enforcement is community-oriented policing. 4) In every Japanese neighborhood there are *Kobans,* or guard shacks, where a local police officer sits.
  a. 3, 2, 1, 4
  b. 3, 1, 4, 2
  c. 1, 3, 2, 4
  d. 1, 2, 4, 3

27. 1) The Fifth Amendment of the United States Constitution guarantees citizens freedom from double jeopardy in criminal proceedings. 2) It also means that a person cannot be tried for a crime for which he has already been convicted; that is to say, a person convicted by a state court cannot be tried for the same offense in, for example, federal court. 3) Finally, a person cannot be punished more than once for the same crime. 4) This means that a person cannot be tried for a crime for which he has already been acquitted.
  a. 1, 4, 2, 3
  b. 1, 2, 4, 3
  c. 3, 2, 1, 4
  d. 3, 4, 2, 1

28. 1) The officer finds this behavior suspicious; there may be a burglary in progress, so she pulls over to better observe the house. 2) This happens several times in different parts of the house. 3) An officer in a squad car is patrolling a wealthy residential neighborhood. 4) She notices one house in which a light will come on in one part of the house for a few minutes, and then go off.
  a. 4, 2, 1, 3
  b. 3, 4, 2, 1
  c. 2, 4, 3, 1
  d. 1, 2, 3, 4

29. 1) Rutherford B. Hayes, president of the United States from 1876 to 1880, was a staunch advocate of prison reform for most of his life.

2) When he was elected president of the United States, however, he had to relinquish his position in the NPA, but prison reform remained an important issue to him throughout his term.

3) After he completed his term as president of the United States, he returned to his position as the National Prison Association's president, serving from 1883 until his death in 1893.

4) He was elected the first president of the National Prison Association (NPA) while serving as governor of Ohio in 1870.

   a. 3, 2, 1, 4
   b. 3, 1, 4, 2
   c. 1, 4, 2, 3
   d. 1, 2, 4, 3

For questions 30–33, choose the sentence that best combines the underlined sentences into one.

30. The economy is improving.
There are still many people who are unemployed.

   a. Because the economy is improving, there are still many people who are unemployed.
   b. Improving the economy, because there are still many people who are unemployed.
   c. Whether there are still many people who are unemployed; because the economy is improving.
   d. Although the economy is improving, there are still many people who are unemployed.

31. Sheila did not return from her fishing trip until 9:00 P.M.
We were all frantic with worry.

   a. Sheila did not return from her fishing trip until 9:00 P.M.; however, we were all frantic with worry.
   b. While we were all frantic with worry, Sheila did not return from her fishing trip until 9:00 P.M.
   c. Sheila did not return from her fishing trip until 9:00 P.M., whether we were all frantic with worry.
   d. Because Sheila did not return from her fishing trip until 9:00 P.M., we were all frantic with worry.

32. Ronaldo can hardly wait for Election Day.
He is very curious to see who will be elected the next President

   a. Ronaldo can hardly wait for Election Day; he is very curious to see who will be elected the next President.
   b. Ronaldo can hardly wait for Election Day: he is very curious to see who will be elected the next President.
   c. Ronaldo can hardly wait for Election Day—he is very curious to see who will be elected the next President.
   d. Ronaldo can hardly wait for Election Day, he is very curious to see who will be elected the next President.

33. <u>The Brown Bear looks like a ferocious predator.</u>
<u>The Brown Bear feeds on vegetable matter.</u>
   a. Looking like a ferocious predator, the Brown
      Bear feeds on vegetable matter.
   b. Feeding on vegetable matter, the Brown Bear
      looks like a ferocious predator.
   c. The Brown Bear looks like a ferocious preda-
      tor; however, it feeds on vegetable matter.
   d. The Brown Bear feeds on vegetable matter,
      and it looks like a ferocious predator.

In questions 34–40, a portion of the sentence is underlined. Under each section there are four ways of phrasing the underlined option. Choice **a** repeats the original
underlined portion; the other three provide alternative
choices. Select the choice that best expresses the
meaning of the original sentence. If the original sentence is better than any of the alternatives, choose
option **a**.

34. Corrections Officer Williams <u>reiterated</u> that the
   prisoner was planning to escape, because of the
   bed sheets tied together in the cell.
   a. reiterated
   b. imagined
   c. implied
   d. inferred

35. Shortly after landing upon the Red Planet, the
   Mars Rover took a picture of <u>some own tire</u>
   <u>tracks.</u>
   a. some own tire tracks.
   b. it's own tire tracks.
   c. their own tire tracks.
   d. its own tire tracks.

36. General George <u>Washington born</u> in Virginia on
   February 22, 1732, was the first President of the
   United States.
   a. Washington born
   b. Washington—born
   c. Washington, born
   d. Washington. Born

37. It was either Rodolfo or Randy who <u>brought</u>
   <u>their</u> Frisbee to the park.
   a. brought their
   b. brought his
   c. brought there
   d. brang his

38. Many people believe in <u>UFOs however I've</u> never
   seen one.
   a. UFOs however I've
   b. UFOs, however, I've
   c. UFOs however, I've
   d. UFOs; however, I've

39. The <u>principle objective of the documentary is to</u>
   <u>show you how global warming will effect</u> tem-
   peratures around the world.
   a. principle objective of the documentary is to
      show you how global warming will effect
   b. principle objective of the documentary is to
      show you how global warming will affect
   c. principal objective of the documentary is to
      show you how global warming will affect
   d. principal objective of the documentary is to
      show you how global warming will effect

40. In the early 1900s, the prison used a horse-drawn <u>cariage</u> to transport inmates.
  a. cariage
  b. carrage
  c. carriage
  d. carriage

PART THREE: MATH

Questions 41–50 are followed by four answer choices. Select the choice that best answers the question.

41. $0.49 \times 0.07 =$
  a. 34.3
  b. 0.0343
  c. 3.43
  d. 0.343

42. Five people in Sonja's office are planning a party. Sonja will buy a loaf of French bread ($3 a loaf) and a platter of cold cuts ($23). Barbara will buy the soda ($1 per person) and two boxes of crackers ($2 per box). Mario and Rick will split the cost of two packages of Cheese Doodles™ ($1 per package). Danica will supply a package of five paper plates ($4 per package). How much more will Sonja spend than the rest of the office put together?
  a. $14
  b. $13
  c. $12
  d. $11

43. $7,777 - 3,443 + 1,173 =$
  a. 5,507
  b. 5,407
  c. 5,307
  d. 5,207

Use the table below to answer questions 44–45.

The table below shows the typical work schedule for a prison.

44. How many corrections officers work at the prison?
  a. 225
  b. 335
  c. 426
  d. 626

45. Which shift has to perform more tasks per officer?
  a. day shift
  b. evening shift
  c. graveyard shift
  d. They are all the same.

	DAY SHIFT	EVENING SHIFT	GRAVEYARD SHIFT
Number of Corrections Officers	154	122	59
Tasks to Complete	385	164	155

46. Scott, an electrician, charges an initial fee of $35 plus the cost of materials, plus his hourly rate of $65/hour for labor. Scott worked on Tuesday from 9:30 A.M. until 2:45 P.M. with a half an hour lunch break. On Wednesday, he worked from 9:00 A.M. until 4:30 P.M. with a 45-minute lunch break. How much will Scott charge for this job with materials costing $47.35?
   a. $794.85
   b. $782.50
   c. $829.85
   d. $911.10

47. What is another way to write 3^4?
   a. 12
   b. 24
   c. 27
   d. 81

48. The manager of the prison cafeteria uses algebraic expressions to calculate the number of servings she can prepare with the amount of food she has in stock. If each can of spaghetti sauce contains 20 servings, which expression below represents the number of servings in n cans of spaghetti sauce?
   a. $20 + n$
   b. $20 - n$
   c. $20 \times n$
   d. $20 \div n$

49. 0.80 is equal to which of the following?
   a. $\frac{3}{5}$
   b. $\frac{8}{11}$
   c. $\frac{4}{50}$
   d. $\frac{4}{5}$

50. To calculate his weekly earnings (E), a salesperson uses the formula $E = 0.22s + 150$, where s is his total sales. What did he earn last week if his sales were $2,200?
   a. $590
   b. $634
   c. $980
   d. $2,350

PART FOUR: MEMORY, OBSERVATION, AND COUNTING

Following are a drawing of a street scene, and a short reading passage. Study these for 10 minutes. At the end of 10 minutes, turn the page and answer the 20 questions without referring back to the study material. You have 5 minutes to answer the questions. If you refer back to the study material after the 10 minutes are up, you will be disqualified. When the 5 minutes are up, you may continue with the rest of the test.

Officer Virginia Giordano is one of 12 drill instructors in Rockland Prison's voluntary boot camp program. She is a 15-year veteran and has the third longest tenure of all the instructors. Every morning at 3:45 A.M., she enters Dormitory 5, which houses 20 female inmates. She turns on the light and yells that they have 15 minutes to meet her in front of the dormitory dressed in running shorts, t-shirts, and running shoes for their morning roll call and exercises.

At the end of 15 minutes, any inmate who is not in line and standing at attention is required to drop to the ground and do 75 pushups. One inmate is required to count out loud for the inmate doing the pushups; the other inmates must march in place. After everyone is properly in line, Officer Giordano leads the inmates through ten minutes of stretching exercises and 15 minutes of calisthenics, and then marches them to the track and runs with the inmates in military formation for five miles.

At the end of the five miles, Officer Giordano leads the inmates through another ten minutes of stretching exercises, and then marches the 20 inmates to the cafeteria for breakfast. The inmates in the boot camp program are the second group of inmates in the prison to eat breakfast. They have 20 minutes to eat and clean up the cafeteria in preparation for the next group. When they are done, they march back to their dormitories, shower, and prepare to spend the rest of the morning in the classroom studying for their GED.

At 10:30 A.M., Officer Giordano marches the inmates from the classroom back to their dormitory, where they have one hour to relax. At 11:30 A.M., the inmates return to the cafeteria for lunch. Like breakfast, they have 20 minutes to eat and clean up the cafeteria. After lunch they again return to the dormitory, where they spend an hour cleaning the dormitory until it meets Officer Giordano's standards of spotlessness.

At 1:00 P.M., the inmates from Dormitory 5 split into four separate groups, each group with a different chore around Rockland Prison. The different groups split up maintenance chores such as groundskeeping and laundry. At 4:30 P.M., Officer Giordano musters the four groups together and marches the inmates back to the cafeteria, where they have 30 minutes to eat and clean up after themselves. After dinner, they return to the dormitory to clean up and face the evening's duties.

51. What is the name of the officer who is in charge of the inmates in Dormitory 5?
    a. Gordamo
    b. Girolamo
    c. Giorgio
    d. Giordano

52. How many miles do the inmates in the boot camp program run?
    a. two
    b. three
    c. four
    d. five

53. Where do the voluntary boot camp inmates run?
    a. cross country
    b. around the recreation yard
    c. on a track
    d. around the perimeter of the fence

54. How many minutes do the boot camp inmates stretch after running?
    a. 10
    b. 15
    c. 20
    d. 25

55. Why are the inmates in the voluntary boot camp spending time in a classroom?
a. to study life skills to re-enter society
b. to learn prison rules
c. to study for their GEDs
d. to earn good time for early release

56. If an inmate in the voluntary boot camp program is late getting in line with the other inmates before their run, how many pushups will he have to do?
a. 65
b. 75
c. 85
d. 95

57. Where do the inmates in the voluntary boot camp program sleep?
a. in a dormitory
b. in a cellblock
c. in maximum security cells
d. in metal bunks

58. At 1:00 P.M., the inmates split into how many groups?
a. 2
b. 3
c. 4
d. 5

59. At what time do the inmates eat their lunch?
a. 10:30 A.M.
b. 11:30 A.M.
c. 10:00 A.M.
d. 11:00 A.M.

60. At what time does the officer wake up the inmates in the voluntary boot camp program?
a. 3:15 A.M.
b. 3:45 A.M.
c. 4:30 A.M.
d. 4:45 A.M.

61. The bearded man coming out of the store with "Dollar Days" on the window is carrying
a. a gun in his left hand.
b. a gun in his right hand.
c. a gun in his waistband.
d. a wallet.

62. The telephone number on the Rent-A-Van truck is
a. 222-7712.
b. 222-2177.
c. 555-7712.
d. 555-2177.

63. The entrance to the subway leads to which line?
a. downtown Q and W
b. downtown N and R
c. uptown Q and W
d. uptown N and R

64. The elderly woman near the subway entrance is
a. walking two dogs on leashes.
b. looking through her purse.
c. walking toward the subway entrance.
d. feeding pigeons.

65. Near the entrance to the Moon Bar, there is a man playing
a. the guitar.
b. cards.
c. the violin.
d. the drums.

66. Gotham Savings is located at
a. 83 9th Ave.
b. 84 7th Ave.
c. 85 7th Ave.
d. 86 7th Ave.

67. The number on the taxicab's license plate is
   a. X78-987.
   b. 989-BAC.
   c. G22475.
   d. MB13678.

68. The subway entrance is at the corner of
   a. W. 1 St. and 7 Ave.
   b. 2 St. and 9 Ave.
   c. W. 2 St. and 7 Ave.
   d. W. 3 St and 7 Ave.

69. The sign below the one-way arrow on the traffic light pole reads
   a. No Parking.
   b. No U Turn.
   c. No Left Turn.
   d. No Passing.

70. What is written on the shopping bag carried by light-haired woman in pants?
   a. nothing
   b. 10
   c. 11
   d. 13

You have 1 minute to answer questions 71–75. When the minute is up, you may continue with the rest of the test.

71. How many hearts are needed to complete this pattern?

   a. two
   b. three
   c. four
   d. five

72. How many lower case letters are there in this set?

D D D d D D d
E E E E E E e
F F f F f F f f
G g g G g g G g
H h H h H h H H

   a. 13
   b. 14
   c. 15
   d. 16

73. How many letter *o*'s are there in the following sentence?
   It took the rookie only a week to realize that there is never a dull day at the office for a corrections officer.
   a. 9
   b. 10
   c. 11
   d. 12

74. How many 3s are in the following set?

3 7 4 9 3 8 2 7 4
4 8 3 2 9 8 4 6 7
0 9 7 4 3 0 9 7 3
3 3 2 9 8 6 3 4 7
6 3 6 3 6 3 6 3 8

   a. 11
   b. 12
   c. 13
   d. 14

75. How many circled tens (⑩) are in the following set?

a. 9
b. 10
c. 11
d. 12

PART FIVE: SITUATIONAL REASONING

Choose the best answer to the following questions, based on good judgment and common sense.

76. During dinner an obviously agitated Jewish inmate who has recently entered the prison requests to speak to a corrections officer. Officer Crane responds and asks him why he is so agitated. The inmate demands that he be served a strictly kosher diet according to his religious beliefs. What should Officer Crane do?

a. The officer should be exceptionally responsive to the problem and make an immediate request for a special diet for the inmate.
b. The officer should inform the inmate that he cannot be afforded any privileges and must eat what is offered to everyone.
c. Make a compromise and request that he be given a kosher meal once a week.
d. Tell the inmate that it is not his responsibility and that he must take it up with the cafeteria staff.

77. An inmate who is currently being treated for mental illness approaches Officer Lewis. He complains that the treatment staff is mistreating him. He pleads that the officer intervene. What should Officer Lewis do?

a. He should confront the treatment staff with the allegations.
b. He should record the complaint and refer it to his superior for investigation.
c. He should disregard the complaint as unimportant.
d. Before proceeding, he should find out what mental disorder the inmate is suffering from in order to gauge the veracity of his complaint.

78. A wheelchair-bound inmate has been a low-grade recurrent disciplinary problem. What is an appropriate response?

a. Refer the inmate for evaluation by Mental Health services.
b. Place him in isolation for 24 hours after each violation.
c. Revoke his visiting privileges until his behavior improves.
d. Revoke his access to his GED classes until his behavior improves.

79. A female inmate accuses Officer McBride of sexual assault but refuses medical attention. What should the response to this allegation be?

a. Order the inmate to a medical examiner and give her an infraction.
b. Suspend the officer immediately.
c. Investigate the allegation but do not transfer the officer unless proven guilty.
d. Transfer the officer to administrative duty and initiate an immediate and swift investigation.

80. Upon entering a correctional facility, a homosexual inmate requests to be separated from the main population. How should the intake officer respond to this request?

   a. The officer should inform the inmate that until he is at minimal risk of being assaulted he must be placed with the general population.

   b. The officer is legally obligated to honor this request.

   c. Inform the officers of the cellblock where the inmate is to be placed of the inmate's sexual orientation.

   d. Record the inmate's request and place him in isolation pending a final decision.

81. On visiting day, an inmate is observed receiving contraband from her visitor. Upon observing this activity the officer should

   a. wait for the conclusion of the visit to strip search the inmate.

   b. immediately terminate the visit and escort the visitor out of the facility with a reprimand.

   c. immediately terminate the visit and detain both the inmate and the visitor for search and possible arrest.

   d. call the police and have them arrest the visitor because corrections officers have no jurisdiction.

82. A female inmate commits a moderate infraction in the hours preceding a scheduled contact visit with her three children who are coming to visit from out of state. What actions should the corrections officer undertake? The officer should

   a. allow the visit.

   b. issue the inmate an infraction.

   c. counsel the inmate.

   d. all of the above.

83. An inmate shows signs of physical abuse and beatings. Officer Grant suspects a group of inmates is inflicting the beatings. The inmate with bruises and injuries refuses to give up his abusers. What should the officer do?

   a. Transfer the inmate to another housing area.

   b. Punish the suspected individuals.

   c. The officer cannot take action until the inmate identifies the aggressors.

   d. Punish the inmate in the hope of gaining his cooperation.

84. A new inmate charged with blackmail approaches Officers Kramer and Claus and informs them that he has connections to a terrorist organization. In return for information regarding an impending terrorist attack he demands a reduction in his sentence. The officers' response should be to

   a. immediately inform their supervisor.

   b. call the FBI immediately.

   c. wait and investigate the situation more thoroughly independently.

   d. ignore the situation since the inmate is charged with blackmail and is not a credible source of information.

85. An inmate volunteers to be a snitch in order to gain privileges. He approaches a particular corrections officer with his request with the stipulation that he remain anonymous to the rest of the staff. In this situation the officer should

   a. agree to the terms despite any objections of fellow corrections officers.

   b. report this matter to the immediate supervisor and stress the need for confidentiality.

   c. file an infraction against the inmate for attempted bribery.

   d. take credit for the information.

86. A newly assigned corrections officer realizes at the end of his shift that his keys to the cellblock are missing. He should
1. Immediately retrace his steps before filing an official report.
2. Discreetly ask officers if they have found the set of keys before filing a report.
3. Immediately notify a supervisor.
4. Ask a co-worker if he/she can make another set of keys.
   a. 1 and 2
   b. 1 and 3
   c. none of the above
   d. all of the above

87. Officer Daniels is assigned to the clinic and she overhears the doctor inform inmate Bradley that his HIV test is positive. Officer Daniels notifies fellow officers of the HIV status of inmate Bradley by memos in locker rooms and group conversations. Officer Daniels's actions are
   a. correct, because officers need to know who is infected.
   b. correct, because officers need to know the medical history of all inmates.
   c. incorrect, because the medical history of an inmate is confidential.
   d. incorrect, because the officer failed to ask permission to relay information regarding the inmate's medical condition.

88. Valerie Johnson comes to visit her brother, Roger Johnson, and brings him clothing items. While the officer is searching the clothing, he finds a quantity of marijuana sewn into the waistband of the garment. When confronted, visitor Johnson denies knowing about the drugs in the clothing. The officer should
   a. immediately notify the supervisor.
   b. flush the contraband down the toilet.
   c. order Ms. Johnson to leave the facility.
   d. let Ms. Johnson visit her brother.

89. Inmate Smith is new in the facility. He has been there for eight days and had no visits. The inmate tells the officer he needs underwear. What should the officer do?
   a. Tell the inmate to get underwear from another inmate.
   b. Tell the inmate to call home to have family bring him underwear.
   c. Tell the inmate to continue to wash the underwear he has.
   d. Obtain underwear for the inmate from the clothes box.

90. Inmate John Nash has been charged with murder. Inmate Nash tells Officer Smith that he must go to the law library every day to prepare for his case. Officer Smith denies inmate Nash entrance to the library stating that he can't go every day. In this case the officer's action is
   a. correct, because inmates are not permitted to go to the law library everyday.
   b. correct, because the inmate is not defending himself.
   c. incorrect, because the officer can't deny inmate Nash entrance to the law library.
   d. incorrect, because Officer Smith did not have inmate Nash submit his request in writing.

PART SIX: APPLYING WRITTEN MATERIAL

Following is a set of rules and procedures for corrections officers. Based on these, answer the questions that follow them. You may refer back to the rules and procedures as often as needed.

One of the duties corrections officers are expected to perform is standing guard duty at gate entrances, both outside and inside the facility. When assigned to gate duty:

1. The officer must ensure that an inmate who approaches the gate is carrying a pass.
2. The officer must read each pass and check to see that the inmate who is carrying the pass is the same inmate whose name is on the pass.
3. The pass must also be checked to see if the date, time, and nature of the inmate's errand is listed.
4. The gate officer must look to see if the pass is signed by a corrections officer who has the authority to allow the errand.
5. The gate officer must check the pass to see how much time has been allotted for the inmate to walk to the destination listed on the pass.
6. The gate officer will confiscate all forged passes and write a report detailing this offense.
7. The inmate attempting to enter or exit a gate with a forged pass will be escorted back to his or her cell by an officer.

At mealtimes, corrections officers are responsible for ensuring that inmates enter and leave the cafeteria in an orderly and safe fashion. To do so:

1. Two officers escort inmates to the cafeteria at their cellblock's designated time.
2. One officer must stand in the doorway of the cafeteria and check each inmate's card on entry.
3. A second officer seats four inmates per table.
4. The officer in charge of seating allows each table 20 minutes to eat.

5. When time is up, the officer signals the inmates at that table to stand up.
6. The seating officer will direct those inmates who are standing to leave the room through the exit.

In the event of an inmate's death, corrections officers are required to conduct an investigation, file a report, and include in the report all details known or discovered during the investigation. Failure to do so is a misdemeanor offense, and failure to do so in a timely manner is a violation of prison policy.

Corrections officers periodically check inmate cells for contraband and weapons. To execute this procedure (commonly called a *shakedown*), the officer should:

1. Make certain two officers are present to perform the search of the cell and each inmate's belongings.
2. If the inmate shares a cell with another inmate, have each person point out what property he or she owns before the search begins.
3. Have the occupants of the cell wait in the day room for the shakedown to be completed.
4. Confiscate any unauthorized items discovered in the shakedown.
5. Make notes for a report detailing what the item is and in whose property it was found.
6. Have the inmates return to the cell.
7. If contraband was found and confiscated, interview the inmate about the incident and then write a report.

When inmates need clothing items, one officer will be assigned to escort the inmates to the proper location. The officer must:

1. Line up inmates who need clothing in the hallway of their cellblock.
2. After ensuring that no more than 20 inmates are in line, the officer then escorts them to the clothing center.

3. The officer will make sure that each inmate walks along the line painted on the floor nearest to the right-hand side of the wall.

4. At the door of the clothing center, the officer will check off the name of each inmate and record the items distributed to that inmate.

5. After the inmate receives the clothing, the officer must check through each article of clothing before allowing the inmate to leave the room.

6. The officer will place each inmate in line in the hall and escort the inmates back to their cellblock after all inmates have received their clothing.

Anyone who provides a dangerous drug to the inmate of a prison facility can be charged with a felony offense.

Certain posts in prison facilities must be staffed at all times in order to fully guarantee the security of the facility. Under no circumstances is a corrections officer assigned to such a post permitted to leave it unattended unless ordered to do so by an immediate supervisor.

Inmates are allowed visitors at designated times. Visitation officers are required to comply with the following procedure:

1. Have the visitors entering the facility sign a log with their name, date, and time of visit.

2. Have visitors show photo identification to establish their identity.

3. Search the visitation area before the visitor is seated.

4. Search the visitation area after the visitor leaves.

5. Have the visitor sign out on the log when exiting the facility.

Corrections officers must not create exceptions to the rules for individual inmates, or in any way show favoritism for any inmates in their care and custody.

91. Just before lights out one evening, Officers Rios and Judd conduct a shakedown of inmate Reynolds's cell. He does not have a cellmate. Officer Rios finds a shank (a homemade knife) in a pair of inmate Reynolds's socks. The knife is so crude that Officer Rios just laughs, breaks it in two, and throws away the pieces. Officer Rios acted
   a. properly; what the officer found did not seem very dangerous in his professional opinion.
   b. improperly; an officer should be courteous to inmates, no matter what the offense.
   c. improperly; a weapon is contraband and should be reported.
   d. properly; now inmate Reynolds owes him a favor and will perhaps be better behaved.

92. Just before "lights out," inmate Murphy approaches Gate 2 and shows Officer Williams a pass. The signature on the pass is not readable. Officer Williams finds out that the pass is forged. What should she do with the pass?
   a. Throw it away and tell inmate Murphy to not try it again.
   b. Call the supervisor and have someone escort inmate Murphy through the gate to where she wanted to go.
   c. Have inmate Murphy go back to the supervisor's desk and get a valid pass.
   d. Confiscate the forged pass and write a report.

93. Officers Bertrand and Ramirez decide to shake-down inmate Tropiano's cell. Officer Bertrand tells Officer Ramirez not to bother sending the inmate to the day room, since there is only one inmate to watch. Officer Ramirez sends inmate Tropiano to the day room anyway, and they conduct the shakedown. Officer Ramirez acted

   a. improperly; he should have done what the other officer wanted, because this was a cooperative effort.

   b. properly; the inmate could have been hard to control if he decided to fight the officers.

   c. improperly; the day room was too far to send the inmate.

   d. properly; all inmates are to be sent to the day room before officers search a cell.

94. Twenty-three inmates need new clothing items from the clothing center. Officer Millwood lines all of them up in the hallway of their cellblock and then escorts them to the clothing center, having them walk along the painted line. After all the clothing is issued and checked for contraband or weapons, Officer Millwood lines up the inmates and escorts them back to their cellblock. Officer Millwood acted

   a. properly; the inmates needed clothing, and he made sure everyone was outfitted properly.

   b. improperly; he is to escort only twenty inmates at a time.

   c. properly; he made certain no contraband or weapons were hidden in the newly issued clothing.

   d. improperly; two officers should have been involved in the escort.

95. An explosion in the welding shed killed inmate Soprano and injured two other inmates. Officer Riggs was in charge of the investigation. Officer Barbera told Officer Riggs that he did not have to file a report since the death was an accident. Officer Riggs filed a report anyway. Officer Riggs acted

   a. improperly; he is not required to file a report when the cause of death is obvious.

   b. properly; failing to do so would have been a misdemeanor offense.

   c. improperly; his only responsibility was to investigate the death.

   d. properly; the insurance company will need the information.

96. While watching inmates in the recreation yard, Officer Crowley sees Inmate Winters pass what looks like a piece of folded aluminum foil to inmate Foley. Officer Crowley searches inmate Foley and finds two rocks of what appears to be crack cocaine inside the aluminum foil. He charges inmate Foley with possession of a dangerous drug, and he charges Winters with a felony also. Officer Crowley acted

   a. properly; it wouldn't be fair to file charges on one man without filing on the other.

   b. improperly; inmate Winters shouldn't be charged with anything because Inmate Foley had actual physical possession of the drug.

   c. properly; inmate Winters provided the drug to an inmate and can therefore be charged with a felony.

   d. improperly; inmates already in prison cannot be charged with more crimes.

97. Fifteen minutes before Officer Riley was due to get off duty, inmate Slattery was found dead in his bunk. Inmate Slattery was known to have a heart condition, and he most likely died from a heart attack. Officer Riley was already late for an important appointment, so he turned the body over to the medical unit and decided to write the report the next day. Officer Riley acted

a. properly; since the inmate was known to have a heart condition there was no urgency in turning in the report.

b. improperly; according to prison policy the report should be completed in a timely manner.

c. improperly; he should have turned the body over to morgue personnel.

d. properly; the officer who relieved him could write and turn in the report in his place.

98. For two days in a row inmate Langer volunteered for a work detail no one else wanted. Officer Stalin told inmate Langer that he appreciated his cooperativeness. Inmate Langer told him what he really wanted in return for his volunteering was extra dessert at mealtime. Officer Stalin told him he could not arrange this for him. Officer Stalin acted

a. improperly; he should reward the inmate for cooperating.

b. properly; Officer Stalin can arrange for a better reward than extra desserts.

c. improperly; if he doesn't do what the inmate wants, then the inmate could start trouble.

d. properly; officers must not bend the rules for an inmate.

99. Inmate Billups is in the clothing center. Officer Kory is writing down the items issued to inmate Billups, when the inmate asks her to write down that she was issued three pairs of socks rather than the four that were actually issued. Inmate Billups says she wants Officer Kory to do this because she has one more pair than she should have back in her cell, and this would correct the inventory problem. What should Officer Kory do?

a. Write down that three pairs of socks were issued instead of four.

b. Record the proper number of socks issued, and handle the extra sock problem another way.

c. Do a shakedown of the entire cellblock to see how many other inmates have extra socks.

d. Write down three pairs and put a check next to inmate Billups's name.

100. Gate 8 is staffed 24 hours per day. Officer Kittles is standing guard at Gate 8 when his supervisor calls him at 4:00 A.M. and tells him to secure the gate and report to his office immediately. Officer Kittles should

a. remind his supervisor that he is working a gate that is supposed to be staffed at all times.

b. secure the gate and report to his supervisor.

c. check his procedures manual to see what he is supposed to do.

d. stay where he is and wait for the supervisor to come to him.

ANSWERS

Use the answers below not only to see how you did but also to understand why the correct answers are correct. For Memory and Observation questions, refer to the memory material to see why the answers are right.

1. c. The last two paragraphs of the passage discuss why modern anti-stalking laws are more effective than previous methods, but also how they are flawed. The other answer choices are mentioned in the passage but are not the central argument.

2. d. The victim's knowledge or lack of knowledge about anti-stalking laws is not discussed anywhere in the passage. All of the other choices are mentioned in the third paragraph.

3. a. The first passage states that a restraining order is a *civil remedy often ignored by the offender*.

4. c. Nowhere in the passage does it state that a stalker's motive is to rob or steal from his or her victim. All the other choices are mentioned in the final paragraph.

5. b. The passage states that the *Fifth Amendment is intended to protect suspects from coercive interrogation, which is present when a person is in custody and is subject to official questioning*. The only scenario that contains an example of official questioning is found in choice **b.**

6. d. The fourth sentence of the passage refers to the *constitutional Fifth Amendment privilege against self-incrimination*. The Bill of Rights contains the first ten amendments to the United States Constitution.

7. c. The last sentence of the passage states that *In the case of an undercover officer posing as an inmate, the questioning does not appear to be official; therefore, confessions obtained in this manner are not considered coercive*. Therefore, if an inmate unknowingly confesses to an undercover officer, the privilege against self-incrimination does not apply.

8. b. The key word here is *distrust*, which implies that neighbors become suspicious of each other if they are worried about safety.

9. b. The first answer choice is meant to confuse you if you associate the word *foster* with *foster care*, and by extension, *adoption*. *Foster* means to *nurture* or *help to grow*. Look again at the sentence. What could a *general distrust*—the thing that fosters—do to a *dangerous isolationism*—the thing being fostered? A general distrust could *encourage* a dangerous isolationism.

10. c. By using phrases like *dangerous isolationism*, the author suggests that he or she doesn't approve of the move toward more security devices. The other answer choices all indicate the author's approval of the trend being discussed.

11. b. The key word here is *siege*. People who perceive themselves to be under attack tend to stick together in the face of a common enemy. They become quick to defend themselves against that enemy.

12. d. Although the last sentence expands on the main idea of the passage, the rest of the passage explains why hearsay evidence is only admissible when it doesn't matter whether or not the statement is true.

13. a. While this statement may be true, it isn't stated anywhere in the passage.

14. b. The proper use of hearsay evidence is explained by the hypothetical example found in the final sentence of the passage.

15. c. The passage mentions discerning *the truth* and *the truth of a statement* several times.

16. b. The main purpose of the first paragraph is to explain retribution theory of punishment—a theory *based on the belief that a person who commits a crime deserves to be punished.*

17. a. This is an application of the main idea of the second paragraph to a specific crime.

18. c. The passage as a whole is about two separate punishment theories: The retribution theory and the deterrence theory. The title that best sums up the content of the passage is found in choice **c.**

19. d. The second sentence of the second paragraph notes that one principle of the deterrence theory is the effect of deterring not only criminals, but also the general public. So a believer in the deterrence theory would probably support televised court proceedings, to demonstrate to the public the end-result of committing a crime.

20. a. The last sentence of both paragraphs details the effect of each theory on the amount of discretion allowed to judges in sentencing.

21. a. Sentence 4 introduces the topic of rehabilitation in the criminal justice system. Sentence 1 further expands upon the topic sentence. Sentence 3 provides an example of the topic discussed in the first two sentences. Sentence 2 provides a conclusion to the paragraph.

22. c. Sentence 1 is the topic sentence and states the general situation. Sentence 4, with the word *however*, indicates an additional situation. Sentence 2, beginning with the phrase *in addition*, signals a third situation; sentence 3 explains the third situation.

23. d. Sentence 2 introduces the topic of security alarms. Sentence 4 details different types of modern security alarms. Sentence 1 transitions from the topic of modern electronic alarms to the origins of security systems. Sentence 3 builds off of sentence 1, wrapping up the paragraph with an example of the oldest security alarm known to man, the dog.

24. a. Sentence 3 is the topic sentence. Sentence 1 provides detailed information about the topic, which is parole; sentence 4 provides further detail about the information in sentence 1. Sentence 2, with the word *however*, adds to the information.

25. c. Sentence 2 introduces the topic of the importance of fingerprinting in criminal cases. *It is necessary, therefore* in Sentence 3 refers to procedures that are vital to obtaining fingerprints, and should logically follow the topic sentence. Sentence 1 should follow sentence 3 because it details a procedure for fingerprinting, *obtaining major case prints.* Sentence 4 explains how major case prints differ from standard fingerprints.

26. b. Sentence 3 introduces the general topic of community-oriented policing. The *concept . . . used effectively in Japan* in sentence 1 refers to the topic stated in sentence 3, so this sentence should follow the topic sentence. Sentence 4 introduces a type of community policing common in Japan, *Kobans.* Sentence 2 discusses how *Kobans* have made an impact in one particular Japanese city, Tokyo.

27. a. Sentence 1 introduces the topic of double jeopardy. Sentence 4 defines the term *double jeopardy* used in sentence 1. Sentence 2 gives another definition, signaled by *also.* Sentence 3 begins with the word *finally* and gives the last definition.

28. b. Sentence 3 establishes the general setting and situation, an officer patrolling a wealthy neighborhood. Sentence 4 states what the officer specifically notices while she is patrolling. Sentence 2 further details what the officer noticed in sentence 4. Sentence 1 sums up what the officer's observations lead her to believe, and what action she takes because of this belief.

29. c. Sentence 1 introduces the subject of the paragraph—former president of the United States Rutherford B. Hayes, and his lifelong advocacy for prison reform. Sentence 4 tells of how prior to his U.S. presidency, he served as the first president of the NPA. Sentence 2 would logically follow sentence 4, because it discusses how he had to relinquish his NPA presidency for the United States presidency. Sentence 3 is obviously the concluding sentence because it relates how after his U.S. presidential term, he served as the NPA president until his death.

30. d. The transitional word *Although* correctly establishes a contrast.

31. d. This answer establishes the causal relationship between the two sentences.

32. a. This is the only choice that uses the correct punctuation (a semicolon) necessary to combine the two sentences.

33. c. The transitional word *however* correctly establishes a contrast.

34. d. To *infer* is to come to a conclusion based on facts or premises. This word best fits the context of the sentence.

35. d. This is the only choice that contains the pronoun (*its*) that grammatically agrees with the noun *Mars Rover*. Choices **a** and **c** contain incorrect pronouns. Choice **b** mistakenly uses the contraction *it's* (*it is*).

36. c. Commas are used to set off a word or phrase that describes the subject but does not alter the meaning of the entire sentence.

37. b. There are two potential problems in this sentence: 1) the grammatical agreement between the nouns *Rodolfo* or *Randy* and the pronoun *his*; and 2) the formation of the verb *to bring*. Only in choice **b** are both of these correct. Because the sentence reads *Rodolfo* or *Randy*, the pronoun must be singular; only one of them brought the Frisbee. Choice **a** is wrong because the pronoun *their* is plural. Choice **c** is wrong because *there* is not a correct pronoun. Choices **d** is incorrect because *brang* is not the past tense of *bring*.

38. d. A semicolon can be used to separate two main clauses, which could each stand alone as complete sentences.

39. c. The word *principle* can only be used as a noun. *Principal* can be used as a noun or as an adjective. In this sentence, it is clearly an adjective, which rules out choices **a** and **b**. Choice **d** is wrong because the word *effect* is used incorrectly. The verb *affect* means to produce an *effect* (noun) on something.

40. c. *Carriage* is the correct spelling.

41. b. Before you multiply, count how many digits are to the right of each decimal point in the two numbers to be multiplied. They both have two digits to the right of their respective decimal point, which equals a total of four for the equation. Therefore, there must be four digits to the right of the decimal point in the answer.

42. d. Figure the amounts by setting up the following equations: First, S = $3 + $23 = $26. Now, B = ($1 × 5) + ($2 × 2) or $5 + $4 = $9; MR = $1 × 2 = $2; D = $4 × 1 = $4. Now, add: $9 + $2 + $4 = $15. Now subtract: $26 − $15 = $11.

43. a. For this problem, first perform the subtraction on the left side of the equation, and then do the addition. The correct answer is 5,507.

44. b. To find the total number of corrections officers, add up the total number in the row with the number of corrections officers (154 + 122 + 59 = 335).

45. c. To find the tasks per officer, divide the tasks by the corrections officers. The day shift has 2.5 tasks per person ($\frac{385}{154} = 2.5$), the night shift has 1.34 ($\frac{164}{122} = 1.34$) and the graveyard shift has 2.63 ($\frac{155}{59} = 2.63$). The graveyard shift has a higher number so more tasks are performed per officer.

46. c. Scott worked 4.75 hours on Tuesday (5.25 total hours − .5 lunch = 4.75) and he worked 6.75 hours on Wednesday (7.5 total hours − .75 lunch = 6.75) for a total of 11.5 hours (4.75 + 6.75 = 11.5). He charges $65/hour, so for labor alone he charged $747.50 (11.5 × 65 = 747.50) for this job. Add the initial fee of $35 and the materials ($47.35) to get the total (747.50 + 35 + 47.35 = 829.85).

47. d. 3^4 is three to the fourth power: $3 \times 3 \times 3 \times 3 = 81$.

48. c. The number of cans, n, must be multiplied by the number of servings in each can, which is 20. The algebraic expression that represents this calculation is $20 \times n$.

49. d. In the decimal 0.80, the 8 is in the tenths place (one place to the right of the decimal). Place the 8 over 10 to get $\frac{8}{10}$ and then reduce the fraction by dividing the top and bottom by 2 to get $\frac{4}{5}$.

50. b. Replace s with $2,200. The equation is then, $E = 0.22 \times 2,200 + 150$. The rules for order of operations state that multiplication is always done before addition. Therefore, complete the multiplication ($0.22 \times 2,200 = 484$) first, then add 150 to the result; $484 + 150 = \$634$.

51. d.

52. d.

53. c.

54. a.

55. c.

56. b.

57. a.

58. c.

59. b.

60. b.

61. b.

62. d.

63. b.

64. a.

65. c.

66. d.

67. c.

68. c.

69. b.

70. d.

71. c. If the pattern were complete there would be 24 hearts total because there should be six hearts across and four hearts down. There are only 20 hearts, so four are missing.

72. d. There are sixteen lowercase letters in the set:

DDD **d** DD **d d**

E E E E E E E **e**

F F **f** F **f** F **f f**

G **g g** G **g g** G **g**

H **h** H **h** H **h** H H

73. c. There are eleven letter o's in the sentence: *It too*k the rookie only a week to realize that there is never a dull day at the office for a corrections officer.

74. b. There are twelve 3s in the set:

3 7 4 9 3 8 2 7 4

4 8 3 2 9 8 4 6 7

0 9 7 4 3 0 9 7 3

3 3 2 9 8 6 3 4 7

6 3 6 3 6 3 6 3 8

75. a. There are nine circled tens in the set.

76. a. This is a First Amendment right of the United States constitution. Incarceration of an inmate does not override that inmate's United States constitutional rights.

77. b. All complaints by inmates must be logged and investigated.

78. a. The inmate may have unresolved issues regarding being in a wheelchair. The other choices violate the inmate's due process rights.

79. d. All complaints by inmates must be investigated.

80. b. It is the responsibility of the administration to provide protection and safety to all inmates.

81. c. Possession of contraband is a violation that threatens the safety and security of the institution.

82. d. It is a minor infraction unrelated to the planned visit. To deny visit will require a hearing.

83. a. The institution is responsible for the safety of the inmates.

84. a. It is the corrections officer's job to report incidents to the supervisory staff who are then supposed to take charge of the situation.

85. b. The inmate is not in a position to negotiate with the officer or to make demands. Confidentiality is important because snitches are despised and this information can place the inmate in grave physical danger.

86. b. Loss of keys can facilitate an escape.

87. c. An inmate's medical information is confidential.

88. a. Bringing contraband into the correctional facility is a violation.

89. d. Since no one has visited the inmate, it is the responsibility of the facility to provide underwear because this is possibly an indigent inmate.

90. c. Inmates can't be denied entrance to the law library.

91. c. According to the procedures for conducting a shakedown, an officer who finds a weapon should confiscate the contraband, investigate further, and report.

92. d. This is step 6 in the procedure for an officer who is standing guard at a gate.

93. d. The officer properly followed step 3 in the procedure for conducting a shakedown. Don't read information into the situation that isn't there: You don't know how far the day room is from the cells or how hard it would have been to control the inmate.

94. b. It's true Officer Millwood made sure everyone was outfitted (choice **a**) and checked for contraband (choice **c**), but he acted improperly because he didn't follow step 2 in the procedure for taking inmates to the clothing center. Choice **d** is incorrect because the procedure says only one officer is necessary.

95. b. Law and procedure say that in the event of an inmate's death the officer must file a report, or the officer will be guilty of a misdemeanor offense. The insurance company's needs (choice **d**) are not the officer's concern.

96. c. Both inmates have been in possession of a dangerous drug—one of them supplied it to the other, which is against the law. Both should therefore be charged with a felony.

97. b. Prison policy states that reports are to be completed in a timely manner.

98. d. Policy says that officers can't show favoritism—no matter how much it might seem warranted.

99. b. The officer is obligated to follow the procedure for taking inmates to the clothing center, and step 4 specifies that the officer should record what the inmate received. The officer may want to shake down other cells, but that would come later.

100. b. The prison rule regarding gates is clear that officers posted at around-the-clock gates aren't allowed to leave their post unless ordered to do so by an immediate supervisor. Officer Kittles received that order.

6 ▶ Reading Comprehension Review

CHAPTER SUMMARY

Good reading skills are vital for any potential corrections officer, so most corrections officer exams include reading comprehension questions. This chapter covers the most essential reading and reading comprehension strategies for success on your exam. You will learn to become an active reader, to understand the difference between main idea and supporting ideas, and to recognize information that is implied, but not stated in a passage.

eading comprehension passages and questions measure how well applicants understand what they read. Understanding written materials is part of almost any job, including law enforcement. Although you do not need any specialized knowledge to answer the reading questions on your exam, you do need to show that you can extract information from the passage. Some questions will focus on the explicit information offered in a passage: its main idea and supporting details. Other questions will ask you to interpret and evaluate the assumptions that are implicit in the passage: the text's underlying message, arguments, and logic.

Types of Questions

Some of the questions found in the reading comprehension section of your exam may focus on *what* information is presented in a passage; other questions may deal with *how* information is presented.

Literal Comprehension—The "What" Questions

Literal Comprehension questions measure your ability to understand the literal content of a passage. You might be asked to identify the main purpose of a passage, locate a specific fact or detail, or define how a word is used in a passage. Here are the three most common types of literal comprehension questions found on corrections officer exams:

1. **Main Idea.** For this question type, you need to be able to identify the main idea of the passage or a specific paragraph in the passage.
   Question Examples:
   - The passage is primarily concerned with
   - What is the author's main purpose in this passage?
   - Which of the following would be the best title for this passage?

2. **Supporting Idea or Detail.** This question type asks you to summarize a supporting idea in the passage. You will need to be able to locate specific details and information in the passage, such as a fact, figure, or name.
   Question Examples:
   - According to the passage, how many corrections officers retired in the past ten years?
   - The passage states that a *shakedown* is needed when
   - Which of the following is NOT mentioned as one of the reasons for recent reduction in crime?

3. **Vocabulary.** This question type asks you to determine the meaning of a word as it is used in the passage.
   Question Examples:
   - The word *protest* in the passage could best be replaced by
   - Which of the following is the best meaning of the word *experience* as it is used in the passage?

Critical and Inferential Comprehension— The "How" Questions

Whereas literal comprehension questions are straightforward, critical and inferential comprehension questions ask you to read between the lines of a text. These questions are about what is *implied* in the passage or statement. They ask you to identify the author's assumptions and attitudes and evaluate the weaknesses and strengths of the author's argument or logic. Critical and inferential comprehension questions include three types:

1. **Evaluation.** This question type asks you to evaluate the strengths and weaknesses of the argument presented in a passage. Evaluation questions will ask you to judge whether something is fact or opinion, or whether the evidence presented supports the message of the passage.
   Question Examples:
   - Which of the following is NOT mentioned in the passage as a weakness in the new law?
   - Which of the following sentences from the passage expresses a fact rather than an opinion?

2. **Inferences.** This type of question asks you to make an inference (draw a logical conclusion) based on the content of the passage. Inference questions will ask you to determine an author's underlying assumptions or attitude toward the subject of the passage.
   Question Examples:
   - This passage suggests that capital punishment is an effective deterrent because
   - The author would be LEAST likely to agree with which of the following statements?

3. **Generalizations.** This question type requires you to apply the ideas of a passage to new situations, recognize similar situations, and draw conclusions about the content of the passage.

Question Examples:
- Which of the following conclusions can you make based on the passage?
- Given the information in the passage, what appears to be an important quality for all corrections officers to possess?

Now that you have a better idea of what to expect on the reading comprehension portion of your exam, you can begin to review some reading comprehension skills and test-taking strategies. By honing these skills, you will be better equipped to understand reading passages and to do your very best on the exam.

Reading Skill Builders

Reading may seem like an inactive activity—after all, you are sitting, looking at words on a page. However, to improve your reading comprehension you need to read *actively,* meaning that you need to interact with the text. Incorporate these active-reading techniques into your study plan for your exam. Each time you read a magazine, newspaper, or book, sharpen your reading comprehension skills by using these strategies:

Skim ahead. Scan the text *before* you read. Look at how the text is organized: how it is broken into sections? In what order are the topics presented? Note key words and ideas that are highlighted in boldface type or in bulleted lists.

Jump back. Review the text after you read. By looking at summaries, headings, and highlighted information, you increase your ability to remember information and make connections between ideas.

Look up new words. Keep a dictionary on hand as you read. Look up unfamiliar words and list them with their definitions in a notebook or make flash cards. To help you remember new words, connect them to something in your life or reading. Make a point to use new words in your writing and conversation. By increasing your vocabulary, you build your reading comprehension.

Highlight key ideas. As you read, highlight or underline key terms, main ideas, or concepts that are new to you. Be selective—if you highlight too much of the text, nothing will stand out for you on the page. (If you don't own the book, use a notebook to jot down information.)

Take notes. Note-taking can help you remember material, even if you never look at your notes again. That's because it's a muscle activity, and using your muscles can actually aid your memory. Record your questions, observations, and opinions as you read. Write down the main idea of the passage, the author's point of view, and whether or not you agree with the author.

Make connections. When you connect two ideas, you improve your chances of remembering the material. For example, if you are reading about a current presidential race, you may note how it is similar or different to past elections. How have circumstances changed? You may also connect the topic to your own experience: How did you feel about past elections versus the current race?

Supporting Idea

How can you distinguish a main idea from a supporting idea? Unlike main ideas, supporting ideas present facts or **specific information.** They often answer the questions *what? when? why?* or *how?*

Reading passages on exams often follow a basic pattern of **general (main) idea → specific (supporting) idea.** In other words, a writer states her main idea (makes a general claim about her subject) and then provides evidence for it through specific details and facts. Do you always find main ideas in the first sentence of the passage? The answer is no. Although a first sentence may contain the main idea, an author may decide to build up to his or her main point. In that case, you may find the main idea in the last sentence of an introductory paragraph, or even in the last paragraph of the passage.

Practice answering main idea and supporting idea questions by working on the questions that follow this passage:

There is some evidence that crime rates are linked to social trends such as demographic and socio-economic changes. Crime statistics showed a decline in the post-World War II era of the 1940s and 1950s. Following the Vietnam War in the 1970s, however, reported crimes were on the rise again, only to be followed by lower numbers of such reports in the 1980s. One of the reasons for these fluctuations appears to be age. When the population is younger, as in the 1960s when the baby boomers came of age, there was a greater incidence of crime nationwide. A second cause for the rise and fall of crime rates appears to be economic. Rising crime rates appear to follow falling economies. A third cause cited for the cyclical nature of crime statistics appears to be the ebb and flow of public policy decisions, which sometimes protect personal freedoms at the expense of government control. A youthful, economically disadvantaged population that is not secured by the social controls of family and community or by government authority is likely to see an upswing in reported crimes.

1. Crime statistics seem to rise when populations are
   a. younger.
   b. older.
   c. veteran.
   d. richer.

Question type (circle one):
Main Idea / Supporting Idea

2. The main idea of the passage is that
   a. times of prosperity show lower crime statistics.
   b. when the economy slows, crime statistics rise.
   c. incidence of reported crime is related to several social and economic variables.
   d. secure families are less likely to be involved in crime.

Question type (circle one):
Main Idea / Supporting Idea

3. Which of the following would be the best title for this passage?
   a. *Wars and Crime Statistics*
   b. *Why Crime Statistics Rise and Fall*
   c. *Youth and Crime Statistics*
   d. *Poverty and Crime Statistics*

Question type (circle one):
Main Idea / Supporting Idea

4. Crime statistics show that crime is
   a. random.
   b. cyclical.
   c. demographic.
   d. social.

Question type (circle one):
Main Idea / Supporting Idea

Answers

1. a. Question type: supporting idea. This is a fairly clear example of how you can look quickly through a passage and locate a clearly stated detail. The word *young* appears in relation to the baby boomers; the idea is also suggested in the last sentence by the word *youthful*.

2. c. Question type: main idea. The other answer choices are supporting details—they're all in the passage, but they're not what the passage is mostly about. Choice **c** is the only one that combines several details into a statement that reflects the first sentence, which is also the topic sentence, of the paragraph.

3. b. Question type: main idea. Each of the other choices expresses a supporting idea, one of the reasons listed in the passage for fluctuation in crime rates. Choice **b** is the only one that expresses the sum of those details.

4. b. Question type: supporting idea. The passage mentions the *cyclical nature of crime statistics*. Other phrases that suggest this answer include *fluctuations*, *rise and fall*, and *ebb and flow*.

Strategies for Vocabulary Questions

If you encounter an unfamiliar word when you are reading, you may likely grab a dictionary and look it up. But, during your test, you won't have that luxury. However, you can use a number of strategies to figure out what an unknown word means.

Vocabulary questions measure your word power, but they also evaluate an essential reading comprehension skill, which is your ability to determine the meaning of a word from its **context.** The sentences that surround the word offer important clues about its meaning. Theoretically you should be able to substitute a nonsense word for the one being sought, and you would still make the right choice because you could determine meaning strictly from the sense of the sentence or its surrounding sentences. Try to determine the meaning of the nonsense word from the rest of the following sentence:

The chief noted with a smile that it gave him great terivinix to announce the award for Officer of the Year.

1. In this sentence, *terivinix* most likely means
  a. pain.
  b. sympathy.
  c. pleasure.
  d. anger.

Now, see if you can figure out the meaning of the word *incessant* from the context of these two sentences:

The incessant demands of the job are too much for me. The responsibilities are endless!

2. The word *incessant* most nearly means
  a. inaccessible.
  b. difficult.
  c. compatible.
  d. unceasing.

Answers

1. c. Clearly, the context of an award and the fact that the chief was smiling makes choice **c**, *pleasure*, the best choice. Awards don't usually bring *pain*, *sympathy*, or *anger*. When confronted with an unfamiliar word, try substituting a nonsense word and see if the context gives you the clue.

2. d. The second sentence, *The responsibilities are endless*, restates the phrase in the first sentence, *incessant demands*. This restatement suggests the meaning of *incessant:* continuing or following without interruption.

If the context of an unfamiliar word does not restate its meaning, try these two steps to figure out what the word means:

1. **Replace the vocabulary word** with the remaining answer choices, one at a time. Does the answer choice make sense when you read the sentence? If not, eliminate the answer choice. In the first practice question, *pain, sympathy,* and *anger* simply do not make sense in the sentence. Only choice **c**, *pleasure*, makes sense in the context.

2. **Is the word positive or negative?** Using the context of the passage, determine whether the unfamiliar word is a positive or negative term. If a word is used in a positive context, you can eliminate the answer choices that are negative. In the second practice question, you can guess that the word *incessant* is used negatively. The phrase, *too much for me*, suggests that the demands of the job are overwhelming and negative. Thus, you can eliminate answer choice **c** because it represents a positive term.

Fact vs. Opinion

Just because something is in print does not mean that it is fact. Most writing contains some *bias*—the personal judgment of a writer. Sometimes a writer's beliefs unknowingly affect how he or she writes about a topic. In other cases, a writer deliberately attempts to shape the reader's reaction and position. For example, a writer may present only one perspective about a subject or include only facts that support his or her point of view. These types of evaluation questions will ask you to judge the strengths or weaknesses of an author's argument. You will be required to distinguish between fact and opinion, and decide whether the supporting details, or evidence, effectively back up the author's main point.

To separate fact from opinion, consider these differences:

- A **fact** is a statement that can be verified by a reliable source.
- An **opinion** is a statement about the beliefs or feelings of a person or group.

Try to determine whether the information presented in each of these sentences is fact or opinion:

1. According to the most recent census, the U.S. population is growing older—in fact, adults over age 65 are the fastest growing segment of today's population.
2. Many believe that the population boom among elderly Americans will create a future healthcare crisis.

Answers

1. **Fact.** This is an example of a factual statement—it can be supported by the recent national census. When determining whether a statement is factual, consider whether a source gives researched, accurate information.
2. **Opinion.** This statement represents an opinion—it offers a belief about the future. Others may disagree with the prediction. Opinions reflect judgments that may or may not be true. Opinions include speculation or predictions of the future that cannot be proven at the present time.

Inference

Inference questions will ask you to make an inference, or draw a logical conclusion, about what you read. Sometimes a writer does not specifically state his main idea or offer a conclusion. The reader must infer the writer's meaning. To determine a writer's underlying assumptions or attitude, you need to look for clues in the context of the passage. One revealing clue to the writer's meaning is his word choice.

Word choice is the specific language the writer uses to describe people, places, and things. Word choice includes these forms:

- particular words or phrases a writer uses
- the way words are arranged in a sentence
- repetition of words or phrases
- inclusion of particular details

Style

Just as word choice can alert you to a writer's underlying message so can other aspects of a writer's style. **Style** is the distinctive way in which a writer uses language to inform or promote an idea. In addition to word choice, a writer's style consists of three basic components:

- sentence structure
- degree of detail or description
- degree of formality

When you read a magazine, newspaper, or book, consider how the writer uses sentences. Does the writer use short, simple sentences or long, complex sentences? Writers use different **sentence structures** to create different effects: they may make short declarative statements in order to persuade readers or long descriptions to create a flow that pleases the reader's ear.

Degree of detail refers to how specific an author is in describing something. For example, a writer may use a general term (*dog, beach, government*) or specific terms (*German Shepherd, Crane's Beach, House of Representatives*). In evaluating the strength of a writer's argument, consider whether terms are too general to provide adequate evidence.

Degree of formality refers to how formal or casual the writer's language is. Technical jargon or terminology is an example of formal language. Conversational phrases and slang are examples of casual language. Writers create a sense of objectivity when they use formal language, whereas the use of slang expresses familiarity.

Read the following passage and answer the practice questions. Consider the writer's choice of words, style, and point of view and how it affects the message presented in the text.

Although more and more people are exercising regularly, experts note that eating right is also a key to good health. Nutritionists recommend the "food pyramid" for a simple guide to eating the proper foods. At the base of the pyramid are grains and fiber. You should eat six to eleven servings of bread, cereal, rice, and pasta every day. Next up the pyramid are vegetables and fruit; five to nine daily servings from this group are recommended. The next pyramid level is the dairy group. Two or three servings a day of milk, yogurt, or cheese will help maintain good nutrition. Moving up the pyramid, the next level is the meat, poultry, fish, beans, eggs, and nuts group; everyone should eat only two to three servings from this group a day. At the very top of the pyramid are fats, oils and sweets; these foods should be eaten only infrequently.

One easy way to plan menus that follow the food-pyramid program is to shop only in the outer aisles of the grocery store. In most supermarkets, fresh fruit and vegetables, dairy, fresh meat, and frozen foods are in the outer aisles. Grains, such as pasta, rice, bread, and cereal, are located on the next aisles, the first inner rows. Finally, the farthest inside of the store is where you'll find chips and snacks, cookies, pastries, and soda pop. If you stay in the outer aisles of the grocery store, you won't be tempted to buy foods you shouldn't eat, and you'll find a wide variety of healthy foods. Another benefit of shopping this way is that grocery shopping takes far less time.

1. What best describes the tone of the passage?
   a. informative
   b. solemn
   c. trivial
   d. disapproving

2. The information in this passage is best described as
   a. opinion, because the passage is mainly about the way to grocery shop.
   b. opinion, because the food pyramid is simply a recommended guide to eating.
   c. fact, because the food pyramid was designed by nutrition experts.
   d. fact, because the author provides details to support his or her position.

3. Which of the following statements would most WEAKEN the author's argument?

   a. Complex carbohydrate foods, such as brown rice, beans, and whole-grain cereals supply the most nutrition for the least calories.

   b. Two servings of nonfat or low-fat dairy products provide your recommended daily requirement of calcium.

   c. Since many fresh fruits contain appreciable amounts of natural sugar, you should take care to limit your intake.

   d. Fruits, like vegetables, are excellent sources of fiber.

Answers

1. a. The passage is packed with information about foods on the pyramid, and the information is presented matter-of-factly, without any real emotion. So the best answer is choice **a**. Although the passage's subject is serious, the tone is certainly not *solemn* (choice **b**). Similarly, the author's methodical treatment of the subject rules out *triviality* (choice **c**). Finally. although the author may disapprove of poor diets, the tone of the passage is not *disapproving* (choice **d**).

2. b. The information presented in the passage is either the author's opinion (paragraph 2) or nutritionists' opinions (paragraph 1). This rules out choices **c** and **d**. Choice **a** can be ruled out because the main point of the passage is not shopping; that is the focus only of the second paragraph.

3. c. This statement weakens the argument because it contradicts the passage. The passage suggests that a person should eat lots of fruits and vegetables; in fact, it recommends eating five to nine servings from this group each day. Choice **c** suggests readers should limit the amount of fruit in their diet, therefore weakening the argument. Choice **a** would support the passage's recommendation to eat more servings of grains and fibers than any other food group. Likewise, choice **b** supports the passage's suggestion to have two to three servings of dairy products each day. Finally,

choice **d** is incorrect because the passage states that the base of the pyramid—the lowermost layers—are grains and fibers.

▶ How to Answer Fill-in-the-Blank Reading Questions

Some exams test your reading skills by having you fill in the missing words in a reading passage. If you're lucky, such questions come in standard multiple-choice format, and you'll be given choices of words to fill in the blank. Some tests, however, require you to fill in only the first letter of the missing word. To do well, you need both good reading skills and good test-taking skills. Below are some tips to help you sharpen your test-taking techniques, particularly for those tests that have you determine the first letter of the missing word.

Finding the Missing Word

You will be given reading passages with words omitted. Each missing word is indicated by a series of dashes. There is one dash for each letter in the missing word. You will have to determine the missing words and mark them correctly on your answer sheet. Here's how:

- Read through the paragraph quickly to get the general idea of it.
- Now go back to fill in the blanks by putting one letter on each line. Do the easy words first, then work on the harder ones. Choose only one word for each blank space. Make sure that word has exactly as many letters as there are dashes and makes sense in the sentence.
- Try to fill in every blank. Guess if you have to.
- Don't be alarmed if you're not sure of some of your answers. You can miss several words and still do well.

Look at the following sample sentence:

Fortunately, no one was hurt when the _ _ _ _ _ was derailed.

There are five dashes so the word you need must have five letters. The correct answer is *train* because it makes sense and has five letters. The word *engine* makes sense in the sentence, but it is incorrect because it is not a five-letter word. *Plane* is a five-letter word but is incorrect because planes cannot be derailed. Write the word *train* in the blank space.

Marking the Answer Sheet

Once you have completed the passage, you will have to mark your answers on the answer sheet. On the answer sheet, you will find numbered columns. Each column contains the letters A–Z, and the number at the top of the column corresponds to the number of a missing word in the passage. To mark your answer on the answer sheet, print the first letter of the word you wrote in the blank space in the passage in the box directly under the appropriate item number. Then, completely blacken the circle in that column containing the letter you wrote in the box.

Important:
The words you write in the blank spaces in the passage will not be scored. Neither will the letters you write at the top of the columns on the answer sheet. Only the darkened circles of the letters you choose will be scored. Make sure you mark your answers correctly.

As you mark your answer sheet, check to make sure that:

- the item number on the answer sheet is the same as the item number in the passage
- you have written the correct first letter in the box
- you have completely blackened the correct circle below the box

For example, if you chose *train* as the first missing word in a passage, you would find column 1, print T in the box, and blacken the circle with T in it.

Now, here's a practice fill-in-the-blank passage below. First write the answers in the blank spaces (one letter per line), then mark them on the answer sheet below. Work as quickly as you can without sacrificing

accuracy. Double check often to be sure you are marking your answers correctly. See the end of the chapter for answers.

Fortunately, no one was hurt when the 1)_ _ _ _ _ was derailed. The derailment occurred 2)_ _ _ _ _ _ _ lumber and other debris were piled on the tracks. Investigators believe a 3)_ _ _ _ _ _ of people were involved. They are looking into the possibility 4)_ _ _ _ a local gang caused the accident for 5)_ _ _. It would not be the first 6)_ _ _ _ that members of this 7)_ _ _ _ caused serious damage.

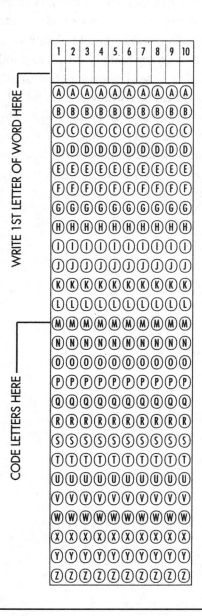

Additional Resources

Here are some other ways you can build the vocabulary and knowledge that will help you do well on reading comprehension questions.

- If you belong to a computer network such as America Online or Compuserve, search out articles related to law enforcement. Exchange views with others on the Internet. All of these exchanges will contribute to the knowledge needed to relate to the passage material on the tests.
- Use your library. Many public libraries have sections, sometimes called "Lifelong Learning Centers," that contain materials for adult learners. In these sections you can find books with exercises in reading and study skills. It's also a good idea to enlarge your base of information about the criminal justice field by reading books and articles on subjects related to criminology. Many libraries have computer systems that allow you to access information quickly and easily. Library personnel will show you how to use the computers and microfilm and microfiche machines.

- Begin now to build a broad knowledge of the law enforcement profession. Get in the habit of reading articles in newspapers and magazines on law enforcement issues. Keep a clipping file of those articles. This will help keep you informed of trends in the profession and aware of pertinent vocabulary related to policing issues.
- Consider reading or subscribing to professional journals.

If you need more help building your reading skills and taking reading comprehension tests, consider *Reading Comprehension Success, Second Edition,* published by LearningExpress.

Answers to Fill-in-the-Blank Reading Questions

1. train
2. because
3. number
4. that
5. fun
6. time
7. gang

7 ▶ Writing Review

CHAPTER SUMMARY

Did you know that law enforcement officers spend up to a third of their duty time writing reports? Because other professionals, such as lawyers and judges, base their actions and decisions on the data in these reports, solid writing skills are essential for all law enforcement candidates.

ost likely, the writing section of your corrections officer exam does not actually involve writing at all. Rather, you will be asked to answer multiple-choice questions that measure your knowledge of the basics of grammar, sentence construction, appropriate word choice, and your ability to locate errors in vocabulary and spelling. Therefore, a strong foundation in all these areas is key to scoring your best. Following is a comprehensive review to help you effectively deal with any writing question type you might encounter on your exam.

▶ Grammar Review

Structural Relationships

When you speak, you may leave your sentences unfinished or run your sentences together. But written expression makes a more permanent impression than speech. For example, the purpose of writing an incident report is to create a permanent record that clearly and accurately represents the facts. Sentence fragments, run-on sentences, misplaced modifiers, and dangling modifiers are structural writing problems that may obscure vital information in a report. The parts of sentences need to have a clear relationship to each other to make sense. This section reviews common errors in sentence structure.

Sentence Fragments

Sentences are the basic unit of written language. Most writing is done using complete sentences, so it's important to distinguish complete sentences from fragments. A sentence expresses a complete thought, while a fragment requires something more to express a complete thought. To be complete, a sentence needs more than punctuation at its end—it needs a subject and an active verb.

Look at the following pairs of word groups. The first in each pair is a sentence fragment; the second is a complete sentence.

Fragment: The dog walking down the street.
Complete Sentence: The dog was walking down the street.

Fragment: Exploding from the bat for a home run.
Complete Sentence: The ball exploded from the bat for a home run.

These examples show that a sentence must have a subject and a verb to complete its meaning. The first fragment has a subject (dog), but not a verb. *Walking* looks like a verb, but it is actually an adjective describing *dog*. The second fragment has neither a subject nor verb. *Exploding* looks like a verb, but it too is an adjective describing something not identified in the fragment.

Another common type of sentence fragment is a **subordinate clause** that stands alone. To review, *clauses* are groups of words that have a subject and a verb. An **independent clause** is one that stands alone and expresses a complete thought. Even though a

subordinate clause has a subject and a verb, it does not express a complete thought. It needs an independent clause to support it.

To identify a sentence fragment or subordinate clause on your exam, look for the following joining words, called **subordinating conjunctions.** When a clause has a subordinating conjunction, it needs an independent clause to complete an idea.

after	because	once	though	when
although	before	since	unless	where
as, as if	if	that	until	while

Examples:

The Canadian goose that built a nest in the pond outside our building.

As if the storm never happened, as if no damage was done.

In the first example, removing the connector *that* would make a complete sentence. In the second example, the subordinate clauses need an independent clause to make logical sense: *As if the storm never happened, as if no damage was done, Josie remained optimistic.*

Run-on Sentences

If you can tell when a group of words isn't a sentence, then you can tell when one or more sentences have been run together, sometimes with a comma in between. Some corrections officer exams will ask you to find run-on sentences. In speech, you may run your sentences together, but if you do so in writing, you will confuse your reader. There are four ways to correct a run-on sentence. Study how each fix listed below changes the following run-on sentence.

Example:

We stopped for lunch we were starving.

1. **Add a period.** This separates the run-on sentence and makes two simple sentences.

   We stopped for lunch. We were starving.

2. **Add a semicolon.**

   We stopped for lunch; we were starving.

3. **Use a coordinating conjunction** such as *and, but, or, for, nor, yet,* and *so* to connect the two clauses.

   We were starving, **so** we stopped for lunch.

4. **Use a subordinating conjunction** (see list of subordinating conjunctions on the previous page). By doing this, you turn one of the independent clauses into a subordinating clause.

   Because we were starving, we stopped for lunch.

Some of the questions on a corrections officer exam may test your ability to distinguish a complete sentence from a fragment or a run-on. Check for a subject and a verb, as well as for subordinating conjunctions. Check yourself with the following sample questions. The answers are at the end of this chapter.

1. Which of the following is a complete sentence?
   a. The treasure buried beneath the floorboards beside the furnace.
   b. After we spent considerable time examining all of the possibilities before making a decision.
   c. In addition to the methods the doctor used to diagnose the problem.
   d. The historical account of the incident bore the most resemblance to fact.

2. Which of the following is a complete sentence?
   a. This was fun to do.
   b. We looking.
   c. Before the door opened.
   d. If we ever see you again.

3. Which of the following is a run-on?
   a. Whenever I see the moon rise, I am awed by the deep orange color.
   b. The special services unit completed its work and made its report to the chief.
   c. Unless we hear from the directors of the board before the next meeting, we will not act on the new proposal.
   d. We slept soundly we never heard the alarm.

Misplaced Modifiers

Modifiers are phrases that describe nouns, pronouns, and verbs. In a sentence, they must be placed as closely as possible to the words they describe. If they are misplaced, you will end up with a sentence that means something other than what you intended. The results can be comical, but the joke may be on you!

Misplaced Modifier: My uncle told me about feeding cows in the kitchen. (Why are there cows in the kitchen?)
Correct: In the kitchen, my uncle told me about feeding cows.

Misplaced Modifier: A huge python followed the man that was slithering slowly through the grass. (Why was the man slithering through the grass?)
Correct: Slithering through the grass, a huge python followed the man.

OR

A huge python that was slithering slowly through the grass followed the man.

Most misplaced modifiers are **dangling modifiers.** Dangling modifiers are phrases, located at the beginning of a sentence and set off by a comma, that mistakenly modify the wrong noun or pronoun. To be correct, modifying phrases at the beginning of a sentence should describe the noun or pronoun (the subject of the sentence) that directly follows the comma.

Dangling Modifier: Broken and beyond repair, Grandma threw the serving dish away. (Why was Grandma broken?)

Correct: Broken and beyond repair, the serving dish was thrown away by Grandma.

OR

Grandma threw away the serving dish that was broken and beyond repair.

Use what you've just learned to choose which of the following choices is the correct version of the underlined portion of the sentence below. If you think the sentence is correct as it stands, choose option **a.** The answers are at the end of the chapter.

4. Subsidized by the federal government, <u>students can get help financing their post-secondary education through the Federal Work-Study Program</u>.
   a. students can get help financing their post-secondary education through the Federal Work-Study Program.
   b. since students finance their post-secondary education through the Federal Work-Study Program.
   c. to students who need help financing their post-secondary education.
   d. the Federal Work-Study Program helps students finance their post-secondary education.

Double Negatives

When you use two negatives such as *not* or *no* in a sentence, you may think that you are emphasizing your point. In fact, you are obscuring your meaning. As in math, two negatives result in a positive. When you write, "I don't have no money," you are actually saying that you do have money. Always avoid using double negatives—they are considered grammatically incorrect. *No* and *not* are obvious negatives, but on your test, be on the watch for any sentence that "doubles up" on any of the following words:

no one	neither	nobody	scarcely
nothing	nowhere	hardly	barely

Example:

Children don't hardly need computers in the classroom in order to learn basic skills like math and reading.

The negative verb *don't* and the adverb *hardly* cancel each other out. The double negative obscures the meaning of the sentence. To rewrite the sentence in a way that makes sense, you could remove either word.

Redundancy and Wordiness

Most writing required of corrections officers must be clear and to the point. Because of this, your exam may ask you to identify redundant or "wordy" language. To eliminate unnecessary repetitions or excessive wordiness, look for words that add no new information to a sentence.

Redundant: <u>Due to the fact that</u> the circumstances of the case were <u>sensitive in nature</u>, the proceedings were kept confidential.
Correct: <u>Because</u> the circumstances of the case were <u>sensitive</u>, the proceedings were kept confidential.

Redundant: Officer Charles <u>returned back</u> to the penitentiary <u>at 10:00 A.M. in the morning</u>.
Correct: Officer Charles <u>returned</u> to the penitentiary <u>at 10:00 A.M.</u>

Punctuation and Capitalization

Punctuation and capitalization are often tested on corrections officer exams, and are essential skills for all effective writers. This section will help you review the basics.

Commas

Commas create pauses, clarify meaning, and separate different parts of a sentence. For your exam, remember the six basic rules for using commas outlined below.

Use a comma:

■ To separate independent clauses joined by a coordinating conjunction, such as *and, but, nor, so, for,* or *or.* Use a comma before the conjunction.

My instinct was to solve the problem slowly and deliberately, *but* we only had a week before the deadline.

■ To set off nonessential clauses. A nonessential clause is one that can be removed from a sentence without changing its meaning.

My friend Ralph, *who is active in the local labor union,* is a fifth-grade teacher.

■ To set off words or phrases that interrupt the flow of thought in a sentence.

The certification program, *however,* works well for me.

Raimond Alvarez, *my adviser and mentor,* was present at the meeting.

■ To set off an introductory element, such as a word or phrase that comes at the beginning of a sentence.

Thrilled by the results, Phin presented the study to his colleagues.

■ To set apart a series of words in a list.

Micah, Jose, and Sam attended the conference.

■ To separate elements of dates and addresses. Commas are used to separate dates that include the day, month, and year. Dates that include just the month and year do not need commas. When the name of a city and state are included in an address, set off both with commas.

Margaret moved to *Portsmouth, New Hampshire,* for the job.

Maco came to Greensboro on *June 15, 2004,* right after she graduated from the program.

Maco came to Greensboro in *June 2004* after she graduated from the program.

Semicolons

Review how to use this mark correctly in the following guidelines and examples.

■ Use a semicolon to separate independent clauses that are not joined by a conjunction.

Officer Wilkens left the jail at 3 o'clock; Mrs. Wilkens was under the weather.

■ Use a semicolon to separate independent clauses that contain commas, even if the clauses are joined by a conjunction.

■ Use a semicolon to separate independent clauses connected with a conjunctive adverb, such as *however, therefore, then, thus,* or *moreover.*

The inmates were asked to wash, dry, and fold their clothes; however, inmate Rivera refused to comply.

Colons

Colons are used to introduce elements and to show an equivalent relationship (almost like an equals sign in math). Follow these guidelines to recognize the correct use of commas.

- Use a colon to introduce a list when the clause before the colon can stand as a complete sentence.

  These are the first-year teachers: Ellen, Ben, and Eliza.

  The first-year teachers are Ellen, Ben, and Eliza. (No colon here.)

- Use a colon to introduce a restatement or elaboration of the previous clause.

  James enjoys teaching *Measure for Measure* each spring: it is his favorite play.

- Use a colon to introduce a word, phrase, or clause that adds emphasis to the main body of the sentence.

  Carrie framed the check: it was the first paycheck she had ever earned.

- Use a comma to introduce a formal quotation.

  Writer Gurney Williams offered this advice to parents: "Teaching creativity to your child isn't like teaching good manners. No one can paint a masterpiece by bowing to another person's precepts about elbows on the table."

Apostrophes

Apostrophes are used to show possession. Consider these basic rules for using apostrophes.

- Add *'s* to form the singular possessive, even when the noun ends in *s*:

  Mr. Summers's essay convinced me.

- Add *'s* to plural words not ending in *s*.

  The *children's* ability to absorb the foreign language is astounding.

  The workshops focus on working *women's* needs.

- Add *s'* to plural words ending in *s*.

  The *students'* grades improved each semester.

- Add *'s* to indefinite pronouns that show ownership.

  Everyone's ability level should be considered.

- Never use apostrophes with possessive pronouns.

  This experiment must be *yours.*

- Use *'s* to form the plurals of letters, figures, and numbers, as well as expressions of time or money.

  Mind your *p's* and *q's.*

  The project was the result of a *year's* worth of work.

- Add *'s* to the last word of a compound noun, compound subject, or name of a business or institution.

  The *president-elect's* speech riveted the audience.

  Gabbie and Michael's wedding is in October.

  The *American Correctional Association's* meeting will take place next week.

- Use apostrophes to show that letters or words are omitted.

  Abby *doesn't* (does not) work today.

  Who's (who is) on first?

Capitalization

You may encounter questions that test your ability to capitalize correctly. Here is a quick review of the most common capitalization rules.

- Capitalize the first word of a sentence. If the first word is a number, write it as a word.
- Capitalize the pronoun *I*.
- Capitalize the first word of a quotation: I said, "What's the name of your dog?" Do not capitalize the first word of a partial quotation: He called me "the worst excuse for a student" he had ever seen.
- Capitalize proper nouns and proper adjectives.

Now try these practice questions. For each question, choose the option that is capitalized or punctuated correctly. Answers are at the end of the chapter.

5. a. This year we will celebrate christmas on Tuesday, December 25 in Manchester, Ohio.
  b. This year we will celebrate Christmas on Tuesday, December 25 in manchester, Ohio.
  c. This year we will celebrate Christmas on Tuesday, December 25 in Manchester, Ohio.
  d. This year we will celebrate christmas on Tuesday, December 25 in manchester, Ohio.

CAPITALIZATION

CATEGORY	EXAMPLE (PROPER NOUNS)
days of the week, months of the year	Friday, Saturday; January, February
holidays, special events	Christmas, Halloween; Two Rivers Festival, Dilly Days
names of individuals	John Henry, George Billeck
names of structures, buildings	Lincoln Memorial, Principal Building
names of trains, ships, aircraft	Queen Elizabeth, Chicago El
product names	Corn King hams, Dodge Intrepid
cities and states	Des Moines, Iowa; Juneau, Alaska
streets, highways, roads	Grand Avenue, Interstate 29, Deadwood Road
landmarks, public areas	Continental Divide, Grand Canyon, Glacier National Park
bodies of water	Atlantic Ocean, Mississippi River
ethnic groups, languages, nationalities	Asian-American, English, Arab
official titles	Mayor Daley, President Johnson
institutions, organizations, businesses	Dartmouth College, Lions Club, Chrysler Corporation
proper adjectives	English muffin, Polish sausage

6. a. When we interviewed each of the boys and the fathers, we determined that the men's stories did not match the boy's versions.

b. When we interviewed each of the boys and the fathers, we determined that the men's stories did not match the boys' versions.

c. When we interviewed each of the boys and the fathers, we determined that the mens' stories did not match the boys' versions.

d. When we interviewed each of the boys' and the fathers', we determined that the men's stories did not match the boys' versions.

7. a. Abraham Adams made an appointment with Mayor Burns to discuss the building plans.

b. Abraham Adams made an appointment with Mayor Burns to discuss the Building Plans.

c. Abraham Adams made an appointment with mayor Burns to discuss the building plans.

d. Abraham Adams made an appointment with mayor Burns to discuss the Building Plans.

8. a. After colliding with a vehicle at the intersection of Grand, and Forest Ms. Anderson saw a dark hooded figure crawl through the window, reach back and grab a small parcel, and run north on Forest.

b. After colliding with a vehicle at the intersection of Grand, and Forest, Ms. Anderson saw a dark hooded figure crawl through the window, reach back and grab a small parcel, and run north on Forest.

c. After colliding with a vehicle at the intersection of Grand and Forest Ms. Anderson saw a dark, hooded figure crawl through the window, reach back and grab a small parcel, and run north on Forest.

d. After colliding with a vehicle at the intersection of Grand and Forest, Ms. Anderson saw a dark, hooded figure crawl through the window, reach back and grab a small parcel, and run north on Forest.

9. a. Ms. Abigal Dornburg, M.D., was named head of the review board for Physicians Mutual.

b. Ms. Abigal Dornburg, M.D., was named Head of the Review Board for Physicians Mutual.

c. Ms. Abigal Dornburg, m.d. Was named head of the review board for Physicians mutual.

d. Ms. Abigal dornburg, M.D., was named head of the review board for Physicians Mutual.

10. a. Although it may seem strange, my partners purpose in interviewing Dr. E. S. Sanders Jr. was to eliminate him as a suspect in the crime.

b. Although it may seem strange my partner's purpose in interviewing Dr. E. S. Sanders, Jr. was to eliminate him, as a suspect in the crime.

c. Although it may seem strange, my partner's purpose in interviewing Dr. E. S. Sanders, Jr., was to eliminate him as a suspect in the crime.

d. Although it may seem strange, my partner's purpose in interviewing Dr. E. S. Sanders, Jr. was to eliminate him, as a suspect in the crime.

Grammatical Relationships

For your test you must be able to identify problems in the relationships between the parts of a sentence. You need to be on the lookout for the incorrect use of adjectives and adverbs, subject-verb agreement, pronoun agreement, and shifting verb tenses.

Adjectives and Adverbs

Adjectives and adverbs add spice to writing—they are words that describe, or *modify*, other words. However, adjectives and adverbs describe different parts of speech. Whereas adjectives describe nouns or pronouns, adverbs describe verbs, adjectives, or other adverbs. *Examples:*

We enjoyed the *delicious* <u>meal</u>.

The chef <u>prepared</u> it *perfectly*.

The first sentence uses the adjective *delicious* to modify the noun *meal.* In the second sentence, the adverb *perfectly* describes the verb *prepared*. Adverbs are easy to spot—most end in –*ly*. However, some of the trickiest adverbs does not end in the typical –*ly* form. The following are problem modifiers to look out for on your exam:

Good/Well—Writers often confuse the adverb *well* with its adjective counterpart, *good*.

Examples:

Ellie felt good about her test results.
(*Good* describes the proper noun *Ellie*.)

Ruben performed well on the test.
(*Well* modifies the verb *performed*.)

Fewer/Less—These two adjectives are a common pitfall for writers. To distinguish between them, look carefully at the noun described in the sentence. *Fewer* describes *plural* nouns, or things that can be counted. *Less* describes *singular* nouns that represent a quantity or a degree.

Examples:

The high school enrolls *fewer* students than it did a decade ago.

Emilia had *less* time for studying than Maggie.

Subject-Verb Agreement

They goes together, or *they go together*? You probably don't even have to think about which subject goes with which verb in this phrase—your ear easily distinguishes that the second version is correct. Subject-verb agreement is when a subject matches the verb *in number*. Singular nouns take singular verbs; plural nouns take plural verbs. If you are unsure whether a verb is singular or plural, apply this simple test. Fill in the blanks in the two sentences below with the matching form of the verb. The verb form that best completes the first sentence is singular. The verb form that best completes the second sentence is plural.

One person _____. [Singular]

Two people _____. [Plural]

Look at the following examples using the verbs *speak* and *do*. Try it yourself with any verb that confuses you.

One person *speaks*.   One person *does*.

Two people *speak*.   Two people *do*.

Special Singular Nouns—Some words that end is *s*, like *measles, news, checkers, economics, sports,* and *politics,* are often singular despite their plural form, because we think of them as one thing. Keep a watch out for collective nouns—nouns that refer to a number of people or things that form a single unit. These words, such as *audience, stuff, crowd, government, group,* and *orchestra,* need a singular verb.

Pronouns and Pronoun Agreement

Pronouns are words that take the place of a noun or another pronoun, called an **antecedent.** Just as subjects and verbs must agree in number, pronouns and their antecedents must match *in number*. If an antecedent is singular, the pronoun must be singular. If an antecedent is plural, the pronoun must be plural.

Pronouns also need to match their antecedent *in case.* Case refers to a word's grammatical relationship to other words in a sentence. A pronoun that takes the place of the subject of a sentence should be in the nominative case (*I, you, we, he, she, it, they*), whereas a pronoun that refers to the object in a sentence should be in the objective case (*me, us, you, him, her, it, them*).

Examples:

Matteo is funny, but *he* can also be very serious. (subject)

Bernadette hired Will, and she also fired *him*. (object)

In most cases, you will automatically recognize errors in pronoun agreement. The phrase "Me worked on the project with him" is clearly incorrect. However, some instances of pronoun agreement can be tricky. Review these common pronoun problems:

- **Indefinite pronouns** like *each, everyone, anybody, no one, one, either,* are singular.

Example:

> <u>Each</u> of the boys presented *his* science project.

- **Two or more nouns joined by *and*** use a plural pronoun.

Example:

> <u>Andy Warhol and Roy Lichtenstein</u> engaged popular culture in *their* art.

- **Two or more singular nouns joined by *or*** use a singular pronoun.

Example:

> <u>Francis or Andrew</u> will loan you *his* book.

- **He or she?** In speech, people often use the pronoun *they* to refer to a single person of unknown gender. However, this is incorrect—a singular antecedent requires a singular pronoun.

Example:

> <u>A person</u> has the right to do whatever <u>he or she</u> wants.

Choose the correct pronoun in the following sentences. Answers are at the end of the chapter.

11. Ravi or Yuri will bring (his, their) camera so (he, they) can take pictures of the party.

12. One of the inmate's files isn't in (its, their) drawer.

13. The caterer sent Bob and Ray the sandwiches (he, they) had ordered.

14. Lenny and (he, him) went to the courthouse with Bonnie and (I, me).

15. Neither my cousins nor my uncle knows what (he, they) will do tomorrow.

Easily Confused Word Pairs

The following lists some pronouns that are commonly confused with verb contractions or other words. Look out for these errors in the multiple-choice questions on your exam.

CONFUSING WORD	QUICK DEFINITION
its	belonging to it
it's	It is
your	belonging to you
you're	you are
their	belonging to them
they're	they are
there	describes where an action takes place
whose	belonging to whom
who's	who is *or* who has
who	refers to people
that	refers to things
which	introduces clauses that are not essential to the information in the sentence, unless they refer to people. (In that case, use *who*.)

The key to mastering the use of these easily confused words is to memorize each one and its meaning, and to think consciously when you see them in written language. Choose the correct form of these words in the following sentences. Answers are at the end of the chapter.

16. (Its, It's) (to, too, two) late (to, too, two) remedy the problem now.

17. This is the man (who, that) helped capture the escaped inmate.

18. (There, Their, They're) going (to, too, two) begin construction as soon as the plans are finished.

19. We left (there, their, they're) house after the storm subsided.

20. I think (your, you're) going (to, too, two) win at least (to, too, two) more times.

21. The corporation moved (its, it's) home office.

Verbs—Action Words

A verb is the action word of a sentence. The three basic verb tenses—present, past, and future—let you know when something happens, happened, or will happen. The important thing to remember about verb tense is to keep it consistent. If a passage begins in the present tense, keep it in the present tense unless there is a specific reason to change—to indicate that some action occurred in the past, for instance. If a passage begins in the past tense, it should remain in the past tense. Verb tense should never be mixed as it is in the following sentences.

Examples:

Incorrect: Terry opens the door and heard the crowd.
Correct: Terry opens the door and hears the crowd.

OR

Terry opened the door and heard the crowd.

Incorrect: When Kate visited Japan, she sees many Shinto temples.
Correct: When Kate visited Japan, she saw many Shinto temples.

However, sometimes it is necessary to use a different verb tense in order to clarify when an action occurred.

Examples:

The game warden sees the fish that you caught.

The verb *sees* is in the present tense, indicating that the action is occurring in the present. But, the verb *caught* is in the past tense, indicating that the fish were caught at some earlier time.

The house that was built over a century ago sits on top of the hill.

The verb phrase *was built* is in the past tense, indicating that the house was built in the past. However, the verb *sits* is in the present tense, indicating that the action is still occurring.

Try these practice questions. Choose the option that uses verb tense correctly. Answers are at the end of the chapter.

22. a. When I cry, I always get what I want.
   b. When I cry, I always got what I want.
   c. When I cried, I always got what I want.
   d. When I cried, I always get what I wanted.

23. a. It all started after I came home and am in my room studying for a big test.

b. It all started after I came home and was in my room studying for a big test.

c. It all starts after I come home and was in my room studying for a big test.

d. It all starts after I came home and am in my room studying for a big test.

24. a. The child became excited and dashes into the house and slams the door.

b. The child becomes excited and dashed into the house and slammed the door.

c. The child becomes excited and dashes into the house and slammed the door.

d. The child became excited and dashed into the house and slammed the door.

Vocabulary

Many corrections officer exams test vocabulary. There are three basic areas that you should be familiar with before you take your test:

- word parts: finding the meaning suggested by a part of a word, such as a root, prefix, or suffix
- synonyms and antonyms: words that mean the same or the opposite of given words
- context: determining the meaning of a word or phrase by noting how it is used in a sentence or paragraph

Word Parts—
Roots, Suffixes, and Prefixes

It is impossible to learn every vocabulary word that could possibly be tested on your corrections officer exam. But there are clues in many words that can help reveal a word's meaning even if you have never seen the word before. These "clues" are roots, prefixes, and suffixes, and they are the building blocks of many words in the English language. If you can learn the most common of these building blocks you can dramatically increase your odds of knowing a word's definition, or at least give yourself a fighting chance at figuring it out.

A **root** is the main part of a word that describes the word's basic origin.

Example:

The root of the words *beneficial, benefit,* and *benevolent* is *bene,* which means *good* or *well.* If something is *beneficial* or of *benefit* to you, it is good for you. A *benevolent* person is a good or kind person.

A **prefix** is a word part found at the beginning of a word, often before the root.

Example:

A common prefix is *anti-,* which means *against* or *opposite.* Two common words with the prefix *anti-* are *antibiotics* and *antifreeze. Antibiotics* are used to fight against sickness, and *antifreeze* is used in engines to protect against freezing.

A **suffix** is a word part found at the end of many words.

Example:

A common **suffix** is *–ology,* which means *the study of.* You can probably think of many words that have this suffix, such as *biology,* or *theology. Bio* is a common root that means *life. Theo* is common root that refers to god, or religion. If you did not know the meaning of biology or theology, but you recognized their roots and suffixes, you'd be able to figure out of their definitions. Biology is the *study of life.* Theology is the *study of god* or *religion.*

A List of Word Parts

Following are some of the word parts seen most often in vocabulary tests. Simply reading them and their examples for five to ten minutes a day will give you the quick recognition you need to make a good association with the meaning of an unfamiliar word.

COMMON PREFIXES AND THEIR MEANINGS

a (not, without) *ex*: amoral, apolitical	**ab** (away from, off) *ex*: abnormal, abhor	**bi** (two) *ex*: bifocals, bicentennial
contra (against, opposite) *ex*: contradict, contraceptive	**de** (take away from, down, do the opposite of) *ex*: deflate, derail	**dis** (not, opposite of, exclude) *ex*: disown, disarm
im, in, il (not, negative) *ex*: impossible, inappropriate, illegal	**inter** (between, among) *ex*: interstate, intervene	**mis** (wrong) *ex*: misspell, misplace
non (not, no) *ex*: nonsense, nonconformity	**ob, op** (toward, against, in the way of) *ex*: objection, oppose	**per** (through, very) *ex*: persecute, persuade
pre (before) *ex*: precede, predict	**pro** (forward, for) *ex*: protect, propel, provide	**port** (carry) *ex*: portable, portfolio
re (back, again) *ex*: remember, reply	**term** (end, boundary, limit) *ex*: terminology, termination	**trans** (across, beyond, change) *ex*: transformation, transfer
un (not, against, opposite) *ex*: unstoppable, untrustworthy, unhappy	**voc** (to call) *ex*: vocation, vocal	

COMMON ROOT WORDS AND THEIR MEANINGS

anim (mind, life, spirit, anger) *ex*: animal, animated, animosity	**cede, ceed, cess** (go, yield) *ex*: concede, success, exceed	**cred** (trust, believe) *ex*: credible, sacred, incredible
dic, dict (say, speak) *ex*: indication, dictionary, edict	**fid** (belief, faith) *ex*: confide, affidavit, fidelity	**flu, flux** (to flow, flowing) *ex*: fluid, fluctuate
form (shape) *ex*: conform, format, formality	**ject** (throw) *ex*: interject, object, intersect	**man** (by hand, make, do) *ex*: manage, craftsmanship, command
oper (work) *ex*: operation, cooperate	**path** (feel) *ex*: homeopathic, sympathy, psychopath	**pict** (paint, show, draw) *ex*: depiction, picture
pel/pulse (push) *ex*: impulse, compel	**rog** (ask) *ex*: interrogate	**rupt** (break) *ex*: interrupt, corrupt
sent, sens (feel, think) *ex*: resentment, sensitive	**sist** (to withstand, make up) *ex*: insist, resist, persist	**spir** (breath, soul) *ex*: inspire, perspire

COMMON SUFFIXES AND THEIR MEANINGS

ance, ence (quality or process) *ex*: dominance, dependence	**ant, ent** (something or someone that performs an action) *ex*: client, applicant	**ate** (office or function) *ex*: dedicate, candidate
dom (state of being) *ex*: boredom, wisdom	**er, or** (person or thing that does something) *ex*: officer, director	**ful** (amount or quality that fills) *ex*: handful, cheerful
ian, an (related to, one that is) *ex*: custodian, human	**ia** (names, diseases) *ex*: hysteria, anorexia	**ile** (capability, aptitude) *ex*: fragile, docile
ing (action, result of action) *ex*: singing, jumping, clinging	**ion** (condition or action) *ex*: abduction, selection, deduction	**ive** (condition) *ex*: motive, directive
ity (expressing state or condition) *ex*: sincerity, brevity	**ment** (action, product, result) *ex*: fragment, ornament, judgment	**ness** (state, condition, quality) *ex*: happiness, goodness, nervousness
or (property, condition) *ex*: candor, squalor, splendor	**otic** (relationship to action, process, or condition) *ex*: patriotic, psychotic, hypnotic	**ship** (status, condition) *ex*: partnership, friendship, courtship
ty (quality or state) *ex*: unity, civility, anonymity	**ure** (act, condition, process or function) *ex*: exposure, composure, assure	**y** (inclination, result of an activity) *ex*: dreamy, pesky, whiny

Choose the word or phrase below that best describes the meaning of the *underlined* portion of the word. Answers and explanations are at the end of the chapter.

25. <u>pro</u>active
  a. after
  b. forward
  c. toward
  d. behind

26. <u>re</u>cession
  a. against
  b. see
  c. under
  d. back

27. <u>con</u>temporary
  a. with
  b. over
  c. apart
  d. time

28. etymol<u>ogy</u>
  a. state of
  b. prior to
  c. study of
  d. quality of

29. vandal<u>ize</u>
  a. to make happen
  b. to stop
  c. to fill
  d. to continue

Synonym and Antonyms

A word is a synonym of another word if it has the same or nearly the same meaning as the other word. Antonyms are words with opposite meanings.

Questions that ask for synonyms and antonyms can be tricky because they require you to recognize the meaning of several words that may be unfamiliar—not only the words in the questions but also the answer choices. Usually the best strategy is to look at the structure of the word and to listen for its sound. See if a part of a word looks familiar. Think of other words you know that have similar key elements. How could those words be related?

Try your hand at identifying the word parts and related words in these sample **synonym** questions. Choose the word that means the same or about the same as the underlined word. Answers and explanations are found at the end of the chapter. Be sure to read the explanations thoroughly, they are just as important as the answers because they show you how to go about choosing a synonym if you don't know the word.

30. a set of <u>partial</u> prints
   a. identifiable
   b. incomplete
   c. visible
   d. enhanced

31. <u>substantial</u> evidence
   a. inconclusive
   b. considerable
   c. proven
   d. alleged

32. <u>corroborated</u> the statement
   a. confirmed
   b. negated
   c. denied
   d. challenged

33. <u>ambiguous</u> questions
   a. meaningless
   b. difficult
   c. simple
   d. vague

The main danger in answering questions with **antonyms** is forgetting that you are looking for opposites rather than synonyms. Most questions will include one or more synonyms as answer choices to distract you. The trick is to keep your mind on the fact that you are looking for the *opposite* of the word. If on your exam you're allowed to mark in the books or on the test papers, circle the word *antonym* or *opposite* in the directions to help you remember.

Otherwise, the same tactics that work for synonym questions work for antonyms as well: try to determine the meaning of part of the word or to remember a context where you've seen the word before.

Choose the word that means the *opposite* of the underlined word in the questions below. Answers and explanations are found at the end of the chapter.

34. <u>zealous</u> pursuit
   a. envious
   b. eager
   c. idle
   d. comical

35. <u>inadvertently</u> left
   a. mistakenly
   b. purposely
   c. cautiously
   d. carefully

36. <u>exorbitant</u> prices
   a. expensive
   b. unexpected
   c. reasonable
   d. outrageous

37. <u>compatible</u> workers
   a. comfortable
   b. conflicting
   c. harmonious
   d. experienced

38. <u>belligerent</u> attitude
   a. hostile
   b. reasonable
   c. instinctive
   d. ungracious

Context

Context is the surrounding text in which a word is used. Most people use context to help determine the meaning of an unknown word. A vocabulary question that gives you the vocabulary word within a sentence is usually easier to answer than one with little or no context. The surrounding text can help you as you look for synonyms (or antonyms) for the specified words in the sentences.

The best way to take meaning from context is to look for key words in sentences or paragraphs that convey the meaning of the text. If nothing else, the context will give you a means to eliminate wrong answer choices that clearly don't fit. The process of elimination will often leave you with the correct answer.

Try these practice questions. Choose the word that best describes the meaning of the underlined word in the sentence. Answers and explanations are found at the end of the chapter.

39. The members of the jury were <u>appalled</u> by the wild and uncontrolled behavior of the witness in the case.
   a. horrified
   b. amused
   c. surprised
   d. dismayed

40. Despite the fact that he appeared to have abundant financial resources, the defendant claimed to be <u>destitute</u>.
   a. wealthy
   b. ambitious
   c. solvent
   d. mpoverished

41. Though she was <u>distraught</u> over the disappearance of her child, the woman was calm enough to give the officer her description.
   a. punished
   b. distracted
   c. composed
   d. anguished

42. The unrepentant criminal expressed no <u>remorse</u> for his actions.
   a. sympathy
   b. regret
   c. reward
   d. complacency

Commonly Confused Words

The following list contains some commonly confused words that often appear on corrections officer exams. If you find some that you frequently confuse, study them and practice using them correctly in a sentence.

CONFUSING WORDS	QUICK DEFINITION
accept	recognize
except	excluding
affect (verb)	to influence
effect (noun)	result
effect (verb)	to bring about
all ready	totally prepared
already	by this time
allude	make indirect reference to

elude	evade
illusion	unreal appearance
all ways	every method
always	forever
among	in the middle of several
between	in an interval separating (two)
assure	to make certain (assure someone)
ensure	to make certain
insure	to make certain (financial value)
beside	next to
besides	in addition to
complement	match
compliment	praise
continual	constantly
continuous	uninterrupted
disinterested	no strong opinion either way
uninterested	don't care
elicit	to stir up
illicit	illegal
eminent	well known
imminent	pending
farther	beyond
further	additional
incredible	beyond belief, astonishing
incredulous	skeptical, disbelieving
loose	not tight
lose	unable to find
may be	something may possibly be
maybe	perhaps

overdo	do too much
overdue	late
persecute	to mistreat
prosecute	to take legal action
personal	individual
personnel	employees
precede	go before
proceed	continue
proceeds	profits
principal (adjective)	main
principal (noun)	person in charge
principle:	standard
stationary	still, not moving
stationery	writing material
than	in contrast to
then	next
to	on the way to
too	also
weather	climate
whether	if

Spelling

Generally, spelling is tested on corrections officers exams in a multiple-choice format. You will be given several possible spellings for a word and asked to identify the one that is correct. Thus, you must be able to see very fine differences between word spellings. The best way to prepare for a spelling test is to have a good grasp of the spelling fundamentals and be able to recognize when those rules don't apply. Remember that English is full of exceptions in spelling. You have to develop a good eye to spot the errors.

Even though there are so many variant spellings for words in English, corrections officer exams generally are looking to make sure that you know and can apply the basic rules. Here are some of those rules to review:

- *i* before *e*, except after *c*, or when *ei* sounds like *a*

    Examples: piece, receive, neighbor

- *gh* can replace *f* or be silent

    Examples: enough, night

- Double the consonant when you add an ending.

    Examples: forget / forgettable, shop / shopping

- Drop the *e* when you add *ing*.

    Example: hope / hoping

- The spelling of prefixes and suffixes generally doesn't change.

    Examples: *project, propel, pro*active

Following are some examples of how spelling could appear on a corrections officer exam. Choose the correctly spelled version of the underlined word in the following sentences. If the underlined word is spelled correctly, choose option **a**. Instead of checking to see if your answers are correct at the end of the chapter, use your dictionary for extra practice.

43. We went to an <u>exibition</u> of early Greek art.
  a. exibition
  b. exhibition
  c. excibition
  d. exebition

44. We will <u>probly</u> go to the movies tonight.
  a. probly
  b. probbaly
  c. probely
  d. probably

45. We took <u>allot</u> of pictures on our vacation.
  a. allot
  b. alot
  c. a lot
  d. alott

46. The high scorer had the greatest number of <u>accurate</u> answers.
  a. accurate
  b. acurate
  c. accuret
  d. acccurit

47. He was warned not to use <u>exessive</u> force.
  a. exessive
  b. excesive
  c. excessive
  d. excesive

Using Spelling Lists

Some test makers will give you a list to study before you take the test. If you have a list to work with, here are some suggestions:

- Divide the list into groups of three, five, or seven to study. Consider making flash cards of the words you don't know.
- Highlight or circle the tricky elements in each word.
- Cross out or discard any words that you already know for certain. Don't let them get in the way of the ones you need to study.
- Say the words as you read them. Spell them out in your mind so you can "hear" the spelling.

Here's a sample spelling list. These words are typical of the words that appear on corrections exams. If you aren't given a list by the agency that's testing you, study this one.

achievement	doubtful	ninety
allege	eligible	noticeable
anxiety	enough	occasionally
appreciate	enthusiasm	occurred
arraignment	equipped	offense
asthma	exception	official
autonomous	fascinate	pamphlet

auxiliary
ballistics
barricade
beauty
beige
brief
bureau
business
calm
cancel
capacity
cashier
circuit
colonel
comparatively
courteous
criticism
custody
cyclical
debt
definitely
descend

fatigue
forfeit
gauge
grieve
guilt
guarantee
harass
hazard
height
incident
indict
initial
innocent
irreverent
jeopardy
knowledge
leisure
license
lieutenant
maintenance
mathematics
mortgage

parallel
personnel
physician
politics
possess
privilege
psychology
recidivism
recommend
referral
salary
schedule
seize
separate
specific
statute
surveillance
suspicious
tentative
thorough
transferred
warrant

Here is a second set of vocabulary and spelling practice questions. Answers to all the questions except spelling questions are at the end of the chapter. For the spelling questions, use a dictionary before you use the answer key.

Choose the word that means the **same** or nearly the same as the underlined word.

48. convivial company
  a. lively
  b. dull
  c. tiresome
  d. dreary

49. meticulous record-keeping
  a. dishonest
  b. casual
  c. painstaking
  d. careless

50. superficial wounds
  a. life-threatening
  b. bloody
  c. severe
  d. shallow

51. impulsive actions
  a. cautious
  b. imprudent
  c. courageous
  d. cowardly

Choose the word that is most nearly **opposite** in meaning to the underlined word.

52. amateur athlete
  a. professional
  b. successful
  c. unrivaled
  d. former

53. lucid opinions
  a. clear
  b. strong
  c. hazy
  d. heartfelt

54. incisive reporting
  a. mild
  b. sharp
  c. dangerous
  d. insightful

55. <u>tactful</u> comments
   a. rude
   b. pleasant
   c. complimentary
   d. sociable

Using the context, choose the word that means the **same** or nearly the same as the underlined word.

56. Though he had little time, the student took <u>copious</u> notes in preparation for the test.
   a. limited
   b. plentiful
   c. illegible
   d. careless

57. Though flexible about homework, the teacher was <u>adamant</u> that papers be in on time.
   a. liberal
   b. casual
   c. strict
   d. pliable

58. The condition of the room after the party was <u>deplorable</u>.
   a. regrettable
   b. pristine
   c. festive
   d. tidy

In the following questions, decide whether the underlined word or one of the other choices best completes the sentence. If the underlined word in the sentence fits best, choose option **a.**

59. Her position as a(n) <u>primary</u> teacher took her all over the city.
   a. primary
   b. secondary
   c. itinerant
   d. permanent

60. Despite her promise to stay in touch, she remained <u>steadfast</u> and difficult to locate.
   a. steadfast
   b. stubborn
   c. dishonest
   d. elusive

Choose the word or phrase closest in meaning to the underlined part of the word.

61. <u>uni</u>verse
   a. one
   b. three
   c. under
   d. opposite

62. <u>re</u>entry
   a. back
   b. push
   c. against
   d. forward

63. <u>bene</u>fit
   a. bad
   b. suitable
   c. beauty
   d. good

64. educa<u>tion</u>
   a. something like
   b. state of
   c. to increase
   d. unlike

65. urban<u>ite</u>
   a. resident of
   b. relating to
   c. that which is
   d. possessing

Choose the correct spelling of the underlined word in the sentence. If the underlined word is spelled correctly, choose option **a.**

66. The information was <u>irelevent</u> to the action.
   a. irelevent
   b. irrevelent
   c. irrelevant
   d. irrevelent

67. He made no <u>comittment</u> to take the job.
   a. comittment
   b. commitment
   c. comitment
   d. comittmint

68. He made an income <u>adaquate</u> to meet his needs.
   a. adaquate
   b. adequate
   c. adiquate
   d. adequet

69. We went to eat at a fancy new <u>restarant</u>.
   a. restarant
   b. restaraunt
   c. restaurant
   d. resteraunt

70. The vote was <u>unannimous</u> to elect the chairman.
   a. unannimous
   b. unanimous
   c. unanimus
   d. unaminous

▶ Answers to Practice Questions

Grammar

1. d.

2. a.

3. d.

4. d. In the original sentence, the modifying phrase incorrectly describes the subject *students*. Choices **b** and **c** are subordinate clauses, and, therefore, incorrect. Only choice **d** answers the question "What is subsidized by the federal government?" in a way that makes sense.

5. c.

6. b.

7. a.

8. d.

9. a.

10. c.

11. his, he

12. its

13. they

14. he, me

15. he

16. It's, too, to

17. who

18. They're, to

19. their

20. you're, to, two

21. its

22. a.

23. b.

24. d.

Vocabulary

25. b. Think of *pro*peller. A propeller sends an airplane forward.

26. d. Think of *re*call: Manufacturers recall or bring back cars that are defective; people recall or bring back past events in memory.

27. a. Think of *con*gregation: a group of people gather with each other in a house of worship.

28. c. Think of bio*logy*, the study of life.

29. a. Think of scandal*ize*: to make something shocking happen.

30. b. *Partial* means *incomplete*. The key part of the word here is *part*. A partial print would only be *part* of the whole.

31. b. Something *substantial* has substance. Something of substance would be of considerable weight, size, or importance, so *substantial* evidence would considerable amount of evidence.

32. a. *Corroboration* is confirmation. The key part of the word here is the prefix *co-*, which means *with* or *together*. *Corroboration* means that one statement agrees *with* another.

33. d. *Ambiguous* questions are vague or uncertain. The key part of this word is *ambi-*, which means *two* or *both*. An ambiguous question can be taken two ways.

34. c. The key part or root of *zealous* is the word *zeal*. Maybe you've heard the word *zeal* before, and know *zeal* is *passion* or *enthusiasm*. A person who is *zealous* is full of passion or enthusiasm for something, so of the listed words, *idle* is most nearly its opposite. Don't be misled by the similar sounds of *zealous* and *jealous*. A synonym of *zealous—eager*—is there to distract you.

35. b. *Inadvertently* means *by mistake*, so *purposely* is the antonym. The key element in this word is the prefix *in-*, which usually means *not*, or *the opposite of*. As usual, one of the answer choices (choice **a**) is a synonym.

36. c. The key element here is *ex-*, which means *out of* or *away from*. Exorbitant literally means *out of orbit*. The opposite of an exorbitant or outrageous price would be a reasonable one.

37. b. The prefix, *com-*, means *with* or *together*. Words that usually begin with this prefix signify a joint relationship or agreeability. Something *conflicting* would be the opposite of that.

38. b. The key element in this word is the root *belli-*, which means *warlike*. The synonym choices, then, are *hostile* and *ungracious*; the antonym is *reasonable*.

39. a. While *surprised* and *dismayed* could both very well describe the reaction of the jurors, the sentence's key words *wild* and *uncontrolled* signify *horror* rather than the milder emotions described by the two other choices.

40. d. The key words here are *abundant financial resources*, but this is a clue by contrast. The introductory phrase *despite the fact* signals that you should look for the *opposite* of the idea of having abundant financial resources, which would be poor, or *destitute*.

41. d. The key word and phrase here are *though* and *disappearance of her child*, which signals that you are looking for an opposite of *calm* in describing how the mother spoke to the officer. The only word choice strong enough to match the situation is *anguished*.

42. b. Remorse means *regret for one's actions*. The part of the word here to beware of is the prefix *re-*. It doesn't signify anything in this word, though it often means *again* or *back*. Don't be confused by the two choices that also contain the prefix *re-*. The strategy here is to see which word sounds better in the sentence. The key words are *unrepentant* and *no*, indicating that you're looking for something that shows no repentance.

Spelling

43. b.
44. d.
45. c.
46. a.
47. c.

Vocabulary and Spelling

48. a.
49. c.
50. d.
51. b.
52. a.
53. c.
54. a.
55. a.
56. b.
57. c.
58. a.
59. c.
60. d.
61. a.
62. a.
63. d.
64. b.
65. a.
66. c.
67. b.
68. b.
69. c.
70. b.

Math Review

CHAPTER SUMMARY

This chapter gives you some important tips for dealing with math questions on a corrections officer exam and reviews some of the most commonly tested concepts. If you've forgotten most of your high school math or have math anxiety, this chapter is for you.

Not all corrections officer exams test your math knowledge, but many do. Knowledge of basic arithmetic, as well as the more complex kinds of reasoning necessary for algebra and geometry problems, are important qualifications for almost any profession. You have to be able to add up dollar figures, evaluate budgets, compute percentages, and other such tasks, both in your job and in your personal life. Even if your exam doesn't include math, you'll find that the material in this chapter will be useful on the job.

The math portion of the test covers the subjects you probably studied in grade school and high school. While every test is different, most emphasize arithmetic skills and word problems.

▶ Math Strategies

- Don't work in your head! Use your test book or scratch paper to take notes, draw pictures, and calculate. Although you might think that you can solve math questions more quickly in your head, that's a good way to make mistakes. Write out each step.

- Read a math question in chunks rather than straight through from beginning to end. As you read each chunk, stop to think about what it means and make notes or draw a picture to represent that chunk.
- When you get to the actual question, circle it. This will keep you more focused as you solve the problem.
- Glance at the answer choices for clues. If they're fractions, you probably should do your work in fractions; if they're decimals, you should probably work in decimals; etc.
- Make a plan of attack to help you solve the problem.
- If a question stumps you, try one of the backdoor approaches explained in the next section.
- When you get your answer, reread the circled question to make sure you've answered it. This helps avoid the careless mistake of answering the wrong question.
- Check your work after you get an answer. Test-takers get a false sense of security when they get an answer that matches one of the multiple-choice answers. Here are some good ways to check your work if you have time:

    Ask yourself if your answer is reasonable, if it makes sense.

    Plug your answer back into the problem to make sure the problem holds together.

    Do the question a second time, but use a different method.
- Approximate when appropriate. For example:

    $5.98 + $8.97 is a little less than $15. (Add: $6 + $9)

    $.9876 \times 5.0342$ is close to 5. (Multiply: 1×5)
- Skip hard questions and come back to them later. Mark them in your test book so you can find them quickly.

Backdoor Approaches for Answering Questions That Puzzle You

Remember those word problems you dreaded in high school? Many of them are actually easier to solve by backdoor approaches. The two techniques that follow are terrific ways to solve multiple-choice word problems that you don't know how to solve with a straightforward approach. The first technique, *nice numbers*, is useful when there are unknowns (like *x*) in the text of the word problem, making the problem too abstract for you. The second technique, *working backwards*, presents a quick way to substitute numeric answer choices back into the problem to see which one works.

Nice Numbers

1. When a question contains unknowns, like *x*, plug nice numbers in for the unknowns. A nice number is easy to calculate with and makes sense in the problem.
2. Read the question with the nice numbers in place. Then solve it.
3. If the answer choices are all numbers, the choice that matches your answer is the right one.
4. If the answer choices contain unknowns, substitute the same nice numbers into all the answer choices. The choice that matches your answer is the right one. If more than one answer matches, do the problem again with different nice numbers. You'll only have to check the answer choices that have already matched.

Example:

Officer Judi went shopping for uniforms with p dollars in her pocket. If the price of shirts was s shirts for d dollars, what was the maximum number of shirts Officer Judi could buy with the money in her pocket?

a. psd

b. $\frac{ps}{d}$

c. $\frac{pd}{s}$

d. $\frac{ds}{p}$

To solve this problem, let's try these nice numbers: $p =$ $100, $s = 2$; $d =$ $25. Now reread it with the numbers in place:

Officer Judi went shopping with $100 in her pocket. If the price of uniform shirts was 2 shirts for $25, what is the maximum number of shirts Judi could buy with the money in her pocket?

Since 2 shirts cost $25, that means that 4 shirts cost $50, and 8 shirts cost $100. So our answer is 8. Let's substitute the nice numbers into all 4 answers:

a. $100 \times 2 \times 25 = 5{,}000$

b. $100 \times \frac{2}{25} = 8$

c. $100 \times \frac{25}{2} = 1{,}250$

d. $25 \times \frac{2}{100} = \frac{1}{2}$

The answer is **b** because it is the only one that matches our answer of 8.

Working Backward

You can frequently solve a word problem by plugging the answer choices back into the text of the problem to see which one fits all the facts stated in the problem. The process is faster than you think because you'll probably only have to substitute one or two answers to find the right one.

This approach works only when:

- All of the answer choices are numbers.
- You're asked to find a simple number, not a sum, product, difference, or ratio.

Here's what to do:

1. Look at all the answer choices and begin with the one in the middle of the range. For example, if the answers are 14, 8, 2, 20, and 25, begin by plugging 14 into the problem.
2. If your choice doesn't work, eliminate it. Determine if you need a bigger or smaller answer.
3. Plug in one of the remaining choices.
4. If none of the answers work, you may have made a careless error. Begin again or look for your mistake.

Example:

Bob ate $\frac{1}{3}$ of the jellybeans. Cristobel then ate $\frac{3}{4}$ of the remaining jellybeans, which left 10 jellybeans. How many jellybeans were there to begin with?

a. 60

b. 80

c. 90

d. 120

Starting with the middle answer, let's assume there were 90 jellybeans to begin with:

Since Bob ate $\frac{1}{3}$ of them, that means he ate 30 ($\frac{1}{3} \times 90 = 30$), leaving 60 of them ($90 - 30 = 60$). Cristobel then ate $\frac{3}{4}$ of the 60 jellybeans, or 45 of them ($\frac{3}{4} \times 60 = 45$). That leaves 15 jellybeans ($60 - 45 = 15$).

The problem states that there were 10 jellybeans left, and we wound up with 15 of them. That indicates that we started with too big a number. Thus, 90 and 120 are all wrong! With only two choices left, let's use common sense to decide which one to try. The next lower answer is only a little smaller than 90 and may not be small enough. So, let's try 60:

Since Bob ate $\frac{1}{3}$ of them, that means he ate 20 ($\frac{1}{3} \times 60 = 20$), leaving 40 of them ($60 - 20 = 40$). Cristobel then ate $\frac{3}{4}$ of the 40 jellybeans, or 30 of them ($\frac{3}{4} \times 40 = 30$). That leaves 10 jellybeans ($40 - 30 = 10$).

Because this result of 10 jellybeans left agrees with the problem, the correct answer is **a**.

Word Problem Review

Many of the math problems on corrections officer exams are word problems. A word problem can include any kind of math, including simple arithmetic, fractions, decimals, percentages, even algebra and geometry.

The hardest part of any word problem is translating English into math. When you read a problem, you can frequently translate it word for word from English statements into mathematical statements. The following will be helpful in achieving this goal by providing common examples of English phrases and their mathematical equivalents.

Phrases meaning **addition:** *Increased by; sum of; more than; exceeds by.*

Examples:

A number increased by five: $x + 5$

The sum of two numbers: $x + y$

Ten more than a number: $x + 10$

Phrases meaning **subtraction:** *decreased by; difference of; less than; diminished by.*

Examples:

10 less than a number: $x - 10$

The difference of two numbers: $x - y$

Phrases meaning **multiplication:** *times; times the sum/difference; product of.*

Examples:

Three times a number: $3x$

Twenty percent of 50: $20\% \times 50$

Five times the sum of a number and three: $5(x + 3)$

Phrase meaning **division:** *per*

Examples:

15 drops per teaspoon: $\frac{15 \text{ drops}}{\text{teaspoon}}$

22 miles per gallon: $\frac{22 \text{ miles}}{\text{gallon}}$

Phrases meaning **equals:** *is; result is; are; has.*

Examples:

15 is 14 plus 1: $15 = 14 + 1$

10 more than 2 times a number is 15: $2x + 10 = 15$

There are 7 hats: $H = 7$

Ron has 5 books: $R = 5$

Practice what you've just learned about word problems with the following questions. Answers are at the end of the chapter.

1. John went shopping with $100 and returned home with only $18.42. How much money did he spend?
   a. $81.58
   b. $72.68
   c. $71.58
   d. $71.68

2. Marco invited ten friends to a party. Each friend brought 3 guests. How many people came to the party, excluding Marco?

   a. 3
   b. 10
   c. 30
   d. 40

3. The office clerk can type 80 words per minute. How many minutes will it take him to type a report containing 760 words?

   a. 8
   b. $8\frac{1}{2}$
   c. 9
   d. $9\frac{1}{2}$

4. Warden Diaz is writing a budget request to upgrade his personal computer system. He wants to purchase a CD burner, which will cost $100, two new software programs at $350 each, a new monitor for $249, and a bundle of blank CDs for $25. What is the total amount Warden Diaz should write on his budget request?

   a. $724
   b. $974
   c. $1,074
   d. $1,094

Addition Review

Addition is used when it is necessary to combine amounts. In addition, the numbers being added are called **addends**. The result is called a **sum**. The symbol for addition is called a **plus** sign. In the following example, 4 and 5 are addends and 9 is the sum:

$$4 + 5 = 9$$

It is easiest to add when the addends are stacked in a column with the place values aligned. Work from right to left, starting with the ones column.

Example:

   Add 40 + 129 + 24.

1. Align the addends in the ones column. Since it is necessary to work from right to left, begin to add starting with the ones column. Since the ones column totals 13, and 13 equals 1 ten and 3 ones, write the 3 in the ones column of the answer, and regroup or "carry" the 1 ten to the next column as a 1 over the tens column so it gets added with the other tens:

$$\begin{array}{r} \overset{1}{40} \\ 129 \\ +\ 24 \\ \hline 3 \end{array}$$

2. Add the tens column, including the regrouped 1.

$$\begin{array}{r} \overset{1}{10} \\ 129 \\ +\ 24 \\ \hline 93 \end{array}$$

3. Then add the hundreds column. Since there is only one value, write the 1 in the answer.

$$\begin{array}{r} \overset{1}{40} \\ 129 \\ +\ 24 \\ \hline 193 \end{array}$$

Try these addition problems. Answers are at the end of the chapter.

5. 567 + 389 + 267 =

   a. 1,123
   b. 1,223
   c. 1,232
   d. 1,323

6. Fairweather County employed 467 corrections officers last year, and recently hired 52 more. Cape Rose County employed 378 corrections officers last year, and recently hired 22 more. What is the total number of corrections officers currently employed by Fairweather and Cape Rose Counties?

a. 819
b. 820
c. 919
d. 920

Subtraction Review

Subtraction is used to find the difference between amounts. In subtraction, the number being subtracted is called the **subtrahend**. The number being subtracted FROM is called the **minuend**. The answer to a subtraction problem is called a **difference**. The symbol for subtraction is called a **minus** sign. In the following example, 15 is the minuend, 4 is the subtrahend, and 11 is the difference.

$$15 - 4 = 11$$

It is easiest to subtract when the minuend and subtrahend are in a column with the place values aligned. Again, just as in addition, work from right to left. It may be necessary to regroup.

Example:

If Cellblock North houses 52 inmates, and Cellblock East houses 36, how many more inmates does Cellblock North house?

1. Find the difference between the inmate numbers by subtracting. Start with the ones column. Since 2 is less than the number being subtracted (6), regroup or "borrow" a ten from the tens column. Add the regrouped amount to the ones column. Now subtract 12 − 6 in the ones column.

$$\begin{array}{r} \overset{4}{\cancel{5}}\overset{1}{2} \\ -\ 36 \\ \hline 6 \end{array}$$

2. Regrouping 1 ten from the tens column left 4 tens. Subtract 4 − 3 and write the result in the tens column of the answer. Cellblock North houses 16 more inmates than Cellblock East. Check by addition: 16 + 36 = 52.

$$\begin{array}{r} \overset{4}{\cancel{5}}\overset{1}{2} \\ -\ 36 \\ \hline 16 \end{array}$$

Practice with these subtraction problems. Answers are at the end of the chapter.

7.
$$\begin{array}{r} 1,332 \\ 601 \\ 102 \\ -\ 37 \\ \hline \end{array}$$
a. 491
b. 492
c. 592
d. 591

8. Rockville Penitentiary is slowly reducing its number of cells. Four years ago, there were a total of 310 cells. The following year it closed Cellblock 7, which contained 27 cells. The year after that is closed Cellblock 10, which had 25 cells, and Cellblock 3, which had 40 cells. How many open cells are there today?
a. 218
b. 318
c. 219
d. 419

Multiplication Review

In multiplication, the same amount is combined multiple times. When two or more numbers are being multiplied, they are called **factors**. The answer that results is called the **product**. In the following example, 5 and 6 are factors and 30 is their product.

$$5 \times 6 = 30$$

There are several ways to represent multiplication in the above mathematical statement.

- A dot between factors indicates multiplication:

$$5 \cdot 6 = 30$$

- Parentheses around any one or more factors indicate multiplication:

$$(5)6 = 30, \; 5(6) = 30, \text{ and } (5)(6) = 30$$

- Multiplication is also indicated when a number is placed next to a variable:

$$5a = 30$$

In this equation, 5 is being multiplied by a.

Instead of adding 30 three times, $30 + 30 + 30$, it is easier to multiply 30 by 3. If a problem asks for the product of two or more numbers, the numbers should be multiplied to arrive at the answer.

Example:

A courtroom contains 54 rows, each containing 34 seats. How many seats are there in total?

1. In order to solve this problem, you could add 34 to itself 54 times, but we can solve this problem easier with multiplication. Line up the place values vertically, writing the problem in columns. Multiply the number in the ones place of the top factor (4) by the number in the ones place of the bottom factor (4): $4 \times 4 = 16$. Since $16 = 1$ ten and 6 ones, write the 6 in the ones place in the first partial product. Regroup or carry the ten by writing a 1 above the tens place of the top factor.

$$\begin{array}{r} \overset{1}{34} \\ \times\, 54 \\ \hline 6 \end{array}$$

2. Multiply the number in the tens place in the top factor (3) by the number in the ones place of the bottom factor (4); $4 \times 3 = 12$. Then add the regrouped amount $12 + 1 = 13$. Write the 3 in the tens column and the one in the hundreds column of the partial product.

$$\begin{array}{r} \overset{1}{34} \\ \times\, 54 \\ \hline 136 \end{array}$$

3. The last calculations to be done require multiplying by the tens place of the bottom factor. Multiply 5 (tens from bottom factor) by 4 (ones from top factor); $5 \times 4 = 20$, but since the 5 really represents a number of tens, the actual value of the answer is 200 ($50 \times 4 = 200$). Therefore, write the two zeros under the ones and tens columns of the second partial product and regroup or carry the 2 hundreds by writing a 2 above the tens place of the top factor.

$$\begin{array}{r} \overset{2}{34} \\ \times\, 54 \\ \hline 136 \\ 00 \end{array}$$

4. Multiply 5 (tens from bottom factor) by 3 (tens from top factor); $5 \times 3 = 15$, but since the 5 and the 3 each represent a number of tens, the actual value of the answer is 1,500 ($50 \times 30 = 1,500$). Add the two additional hundreds carried over from the last multiplication: $15 + 2 = 17$ (hundreds). Write the 17 in front of the zeros in the second partial product.

$$\begin{array}{r} \overset{2}{3}4 \\ \times\,54 \\ \hline 136 \\ 1,700 \end{array}$$

5. Add the partial products to find the total product:

$$\begin{array}{r} \overset{2}{3}4 \\ \times\,54 \\ \hline 136 \\ +\,1,700 \\ \hline 1,836 \end{array}$$

Note: It is easier to perform multiplication if you write the factor with the greater number of digits in the top row. In this example, both factors have an equal number of digits, so it does not matter which is written on top.

Try these multiplication problems. Answers are at the end of the chapter.

9. $28 \times 87 \times 54 =$
   a. 13,554
   b. 13,544
   c. 132,554
   d. 131,544

10. A penitentiary contains 18 cellblocks, each containing 46 cells. How many cells are there in total?
    a. 528
    b. 828
    c. 628
    d. 738

11. 630
    $\times 67$
    a. 4,210
    b. 4,154
    c. 42,210
    d. 41,540

Division

In division, the same amount is subtracted multiple times. For example, instead of subtracting 5 from 25 as many times as possible, $25 - 5 - 5 - 5 - 5 - 5$, it is easier to simply divide, asking how many 5s there are in 25: $25 \div 5$. In division problems, the number being divided BY is called the **divisor**. The number being divided INTO is called the **dividend**. The answer to a division problem is called the **quotient**.

There are a few different ways to represent division with symbols. In each of the following equivalent expressions, 3 is the divisor and 8 is the dividend:

$$8 \div 3 \qquad {}^{8}\!/_{3} \qquad \frac{8}{3} \qquad 3\overline{)8}$$

Example:

Last week, 3 corrections officers worked a total of 54 hours of overtime. If they each worked the same amount of overtime, how many extra hours did each officer work?

1. Divide the total hours of overtime (54) by the number of corrections officers (3). Work from left to right. How many times does 3 divide 5? Write the answer, 1, directly above the 5 in the dividend, since both the 5 and the 1 represent a number of tens. Now multiply: since 1(ten) × 3(ones) = 3(tens), write the 3 under the 5, and subtract; 5(tens) − 3(tens) = 2(tens).

$$
\begin{array}{r}
1 \\
3\overline{)54} \\
-3 \\
\hline
2
\end{array}
$$

2. Continue dividing. Bring down the 4 from the ones place in the dividend. How many times does 3 divide 24? Write the answer, 8, directly above the 4 in the dividend. Since 3 × 8 = 24, write 24 below the other 24 and subtract 24 − 24 = 0.

$$
\begin{array}{r}
18 \\
3\overline{)54} \\
-3\downarrow \\
\hline
24 \\
-24 \\
\hline
0
\end{array}
$$

Remainders

If you get a number other than zero after your last subtraction, this number is your remainder.

Example:

9 divided by 4.

$$
\begin{array}{r}
2 \\
4\overline{)9} \\
-8 \\
\hline
1
\end{array}
$$

1 is the remainder

The answer is 2 r1. This answer can also be written as $2\frac{1}{4}$ since there was one part left over out of the four parts needed to make a whole.

Try these division problems. Answers are at the end of the chapter.

12. 6,900 ÷ 25 =
    a. 276
    b. 375
    c. 376
    d. 475

13. There are 988 inmates to be housed in 4 separate wings of a prison. If each wing houses the same amount of inmates, how many inmates can be housed each wing?
    a. 247
    b. 246
    c. 248
    d. 250

14. 8$\overline{)2,936}$ =
    a. 356
    b. 357
    c. 367
    d. 457

Fraction Review

Problems involving fractions may be straightforward calculation questions, or they may be word problems. Typically, they ask you to add, subtract, multiply, divide, or compare fractions.

Working with Fractions

A fraction is a portion of something.

Example:

Let's say that a pizza was cut into 8 equal slices and you ate 3 of them. The fraction $\frac{3}{8}$ tells you what part of the pizza you ate. The pizza below shows this: 3 of the 8 pieces (the ones you ate) are shaded.

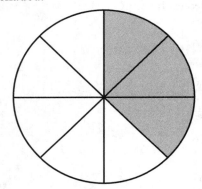

To work well with fractions, it is necessary to understand some basic concepts:

Three Kinds of Fractions

Proper fraction: The top number is less than the bottom number: $\frac{1}{2}$; $\frac{2}{3}$; $\frac{4}{9}$; $\frac{8}{13}$ The value of a proper fraction is less than 1.

Improper fraction: The top number is greater than or equal to the bottom number: $\frac{3}{2}$; $\frac{5}{3}$; $\frac{14}{9}$; $\frac{12}{12}$ The value of an improper fraction is 1 or more.

Mixed number: A fraction written to the right of a whole number: $3\frac{1}{2}$; $4\frac{2}{3}$; $12\frac{3}{4}$; $24\frac{3}{4}$ The value of a mixed number is more than 1: it is the sum of the whole number plus the fraction.

Factors

Factors are numbers that can be divided into a larger number without a remainder.

Example:

$12 \div 3 = 4$

The number 3 is, therefore, a factor of the number 12. Other factors of 12 are 1, 2, 4, 6, and 12. The common factors of two numbers are the factors that both numbers have in common.

Example:

The factors of 24 = 1, 2, 3, 4, 6, 8, 12, and 24.

The factors of 18 = 1, 2, 3, 6, 9, and 18.

From the above, you can see that the common factors of 24 and 18 are 1, 2, 3, and 6. From this list it can also be determined that the *greatest* common factor of 24 and 18 is 6. Determining the greatest common factor (GCF) is useful for simplifying fractions.

Example:

Simplify $\frac{16}{20}$.

The factors of 16 are 1, 2, 4, 8, and 16. The factors of 20 are 1, 2, 4, 5, and 20. The common factors of 16 and 20 are 1, 2, and 4. The greatest of these, the GCF, is 4. Therefore, to simplify the fraction, both the numerator and denominator should be divided by 4.

Simplifying Fractions

Rule:

$$\frac{ac}{bc} = \frac{a}{b}$$

- To simplify fractions, identify the greatest common factor (GCF) of the numerator and denominator and divide both the numerator and denominator by this number:

Example:

Simplify $\frac{63}{72}$.

The GCF of 63 and 72 is 9 so divide 63 and 72 each by 9 to simplify the fraction:

$$\frac{63 \div 9 = 7}{72 \div 9 = 8}$$

$$\frac{63}{72} = \frac{7}{8}$$

Whenever you do arithmetic with fractions, simplify your answer. On a multiple-choice test, don't panic if your answer isn't listed. Try to simplify it and then compare it to the choices.

Practice by simplifying these fractions to lowest terms:

15. $\frac{3}{12}$

16. $\frac{14}{35}$

17. $\frac{27}{72}$

Converting Mixed Numbers to and from Improper Fractions

Rule:

$$a\frac{b}{c} = \frac{ac + b}{c}$$

- A mixed number is number greater than 1 which is expressed as a whole number joined to a proper fraction. Examples of mixed numbers are $5\frac{3}{8}$, $2\frac{1}{3}$,

and $-4\frac{5}{6}$. To convert from a mixed number to an improper fraction (a fraction where the numerator is greater than the denominator), multiply the whole number and the denominator and add the numerator. This becomes the new numerator. The new denominator is the same as the original.

Note: if the mixed number is negative, temporarily ignore the negative sign while performing the conversion, and just make sure you replace the negative sign when you're done.

Example:

Convert $5\frac{3}{8}$ to an improper fraction.

Using the formula above, $5\frac{3}{8} = \frac{5 \times 8 + 3}{8} = \frac{43}{8}$.

Example:

Convert $4\frac{5}{6}$ to an improper fraction.

Perform the conversion: $4\frac{5}{6} = \frac{4 \times 6 + 5}{6} = \frac{29}{6}$.

The final answer: $\frac{29}{6}$.

Adding and Subtracting Fractions

Rules:

To add or subtract fractions with the same denominator:

$$\frac{a}{b} \pm \frac{c}{b} = \frac{a \pm c}{b}$$

To add or subtract fractions with different denominators:

$$\frac{a}{b} \pm \frac{c}{d} = \frac{ad \pm cb}{bd}$$

- To add or subtract fractions with like denominators, just add or subtract the numerators and keep the denominator.

Examples:

$$\frac{1}{7} + \frac{5}{7} = \frac{6}{7} \text{ and } \frac{5}{8} - \frac{2}{8} = \frac{3}{8}$$

- To add or subtract fractions with unlike denominators, first find the Least Common Denominator or LCD. The LCD is the smallest number divisible by each of the denominators.

For example, for the denominators 8 and 12, 24 would be the LCD because 24 is the smallest number that is divisible by both 8 and 12: $8 \times 3 = 24$, and $12 \times 2 = 24$.

Using the LCD, convert each fraction to its new form by multiplying both the numerator and denominator by the appropriate factor to get the LCD, and then follow the directions for adding/subtracting fractions with like denominators.

Example:

$$\frac{1}{3} + \frac{2}{5} = \frac{1(5)}{3(5)} + \frac{2(3)}{5(3)}$$

$$= \frac{5}{15} + \frac{6}{15}$$

$$= \frac{11}{15}$$

Try these addition and subtraction problems. The answers are at the end of the chapter.

18. $\frac{3}{4} + \frac{1}{6}$

19. $\frac{7}{8} + \frac{2}{3} + \frac{3}{4}$

20. $4\frac{1}{3} + 2\frac{3}{4} + \frac{1}{6}$

21. $\frac{4}{5} - \frac{2}{3}$

22. $\frac{7}{8} - \frac{1}{4} - \frac{1}{2}$

23. $4\frac{1}{3} - 2\frac{3}{4}$

Now let's put what you've learned about adding and subtracting fractions to work in some real-life problems.

24. Patrolman Gustav drove $3\frac{1}{2}$ miles to the police station. Then he drove $4\frac{3}{4}$ miles to his first assignment. When he left there, he drove 2 miles to his next assignment. Then he drove $3\frac{2}{3}$ miles back to the police station for a meeting. Finally, he drove $3\frac{1}{2}$ miles home. How many miles did he travel in total?

    a. $17\frac{5}{12}$

    b. $16\frac{5}{12}$

    c. $15\frac{7}{12}$

    d. $15\frac{5}{12}$

25. Before leaving the fire station, Firefighter Soriano noted that the mileage gauge on Engine 4 registered $4{,}357\frac{4}{10}$ miles. When he arrived at the scene of the fire, the mileage gauge then registered $4{,}400\frac{1}{10}$ miles. How many miles did he drive from the station to the fire scene?

    a. $42\frac{3}{10}$

    b. $42\frac{7}{10}$

    c. $43\frac{7}{10}$

    d. $47\frac{2}{10}$

Multiplying Fractions

Rule:

$$\frac{a}{b} \times \frac{c}{d} = \frac{a \times c}{b \times d}$$

Multiplying fractions is one of the easiest operations to perform. To multiply fractions, simply multiply the numerators and the denominators.

Example:

$$\frac{4}{5} \times \frac{6}{7} = \frac{24}{35}$$

If any numerator and denominator have common factors, these may be reduced to smaller numbers before multiplying, this is called **canceling**. To use canceling, divide the common multiples by a common factor. In the example below, 3 and 6 are both divided by 3 before multiplying.

Example:

$$\frac{\overset{1}{\cancel{2}}}{5} \times \frac{1}{\underset{2}{\cancel{6}}} = \frac{1}{10}$$

If you forget to cancel, you'll still get the right answer, but you'll have to simplify it.

Try these multiplication problems. The answers are at the end of the chapter.

26. $\frac{1}{5} \times \frac{2}{3}$

27. $\frac{2}{3} \times \frac{4}{7} \times \frac{3}{5}$

28. $\frac{3}{4} \times \frac{8}{9}$

To multiply a fraction by a whole number, first rewrite the whole number as a fraction with a bottom number of 1:

Example:

$$5 \times \frac{2}{3} = \frac{5}{1} \times \frac{2}{3} = \frac{10}{3}$$

(Optional: convert $\frac{10}{3}$ to a mixed number: $3\frac{1}{2}$)

To multiply with mixed numbers, it's easier to change them to improper fractions before multiplying.

Example:

$$4\frac{2}{3} \times 5\frac{1}{2}$$

1. Convert $4\frac{2}{3}$ to an improper fraction:

$$4\frac{2}{3} = \frac{4 \times 3 + 2}{3} = \frac{14}{3}.$$

2. Convert $5\frac{1}{2}$ to an improper fraction:

$$5\frac{1}{2} = \frac{5 \times 2 + 1}{2} = \frac{11}{2}.$$

3. Cancel and multiply the fractions:

$$\frac{\overset{7}{\cancel{14}}}{3} \times \frac{11}{\underset{1}{\cancel{2}}} = \frac{77}{3}.$$

4. Optional: convert the improper fraction to a mixed number:

$$\frac{77}{3} = 25\frac{2}{3}$$

Now try these multiplication problems with mixed numbers and whole numbers. The answers are at the end of the chapter.

29. $4\frac{1}{3} \times \frac{2}{5}$

30. $2\frac{1}{2} \times 6$

31. $3\frac{3}{4} \times 4\frac{2}{5}$

Here are a few more real-life problems to test your skills. Answers are at the end of the chapter.

32. After driving $\frac{2}{3}$ of the 15 miles to the courthouse, Officer Stone received a call from dispatch instructing him to return to the jailhouse. How many miles had he already driven when received the call?
   a. 5
   b. $7\frac{1}{2}$
   c. 10
   d. 12

33. If Corrections Officer Henry worked $\frac{3}{4}$ of a 40-hour week, how many hours did he work?
   a. $7\frac{1}{2}$
   b. 10
   c. 20
   d. 30

34. Dispatcher Chan makes $14.00 an hour. When she works more than 8 hours a day, she gets overtime pay of $1\frac{1}{2}$ times her regular hourly wage for the extra hours. How much did she earn for working 11 hours in one day?

   a. $77
   b. $154
   c. $175
   d. $210

Dividing Fractions

Rule:

$$\frac{a}{b} \div \frac{c}{d} = \frac{a}{b} \times \frac{d}{c} = \frac{a \times d}{b \times c}$$

To divide one fraction by a second fraction, invert the second fraction (that is, flip the top and bottom numbers) and then multiply.

Example:

$$\frac{1}{4} \div \frac{1}{2}$$

   1. Invert (flip) the second fraction: $\frac{1}{2} \to \frac{2}{1}$.
   2. Change the division sign ($\div$) to a multiplication sign ($\times$): $\frac{1}{4} \div \frac{2}{1} \to \frac{1}{4} \times \frac{2}{1}$.
   3. Now, work through the multiplication: $\frac{1}{4} \times \frac{2}{1} = \frac{1 \times 2}{4 \times 1} = \frac{2}{4}$.
   4. Can this be answer be simplified? Yes: $\frac{2}{4} = \frac{1}{2}$ (If you remembered to use canceling in the previous step, you would have automatically ended up with the simplified answer.)

To divide a fraction by a whole number, first change the whole number to a fraction by putting it over 1. Then follow the division steps above.

Example:

$$\frac{3}{5} \div 2 = \frac{3}{5} \div \frac{2}{1} = \frac{3}{5} \times \frac{1}{2} = \frac{3 \times 1}{5 \times 2} = \frac{3}{10}$$

When the division problem has a mixed number, convert it to an improper fraction and then divide as usual.

Example:

$$2\frac{3}{4} \div \frac{1}{6}$$

   1. Convert $2\frac{3}{4}$ to an improper fraction:

   $$2\frac{3}{4} = \frac{2 \times 4 + 3}{4} = \frac{11}{4}.$$

   2. Now, the division problem has become:

   $$\frac{11}{4} \div \frac{1}{6}.$$

   3. Flip $\frac{1}{6}$ to $\frac{6}{1}$, change $\div$ to $\times$, cancel, and multiply:

   $$\frac{11}{4} \div \frac{1}{6} \to \frac{11}{4} \times \frac{6}{1} \to \frac{11}{\overset{}{\underset{2}{4}}} \times \frac{\overset{3}{6}}{1} = \frac{11 \times 3}{2 \times 1} = \frac{33}{2}.$$

Here are a few division problems to try. Answers are at the end of the chapter.

35. $\frac{1}{3} \div \frac{2}{3}$

36. $2\frac{3}{4} \div \frac{1}{2}$

37. $\frac{3}{5} \div 3$

38. $3\frac{3}{4} \div 2\frac{1}{3}$

Let's wrap this up with some real-life problems. Answers are at the end of the chapter.

39. If the cook evenly split $6\frac{1}{2}$ pounds of beef for 4 inmates, how many pounds of beef does each inmate get?

   a. $\frac{8}{13}$
   b. $1\frac{5}{8}$
   c. $1\frac{1}{2}$
   d. $1\frac{5}{13}$

40. How many $2\frac{1}{2}$-pound chunks of cheese can be cut from a single 20-pound piece of cheese?
a. 2
b. 4
c. 6
d. 8

41. Ms. Goldbaum earned $36.75 for working $3\frac{1}{2}$ hours as an office clerk. What was her hourly wage?
a. $10.00
b. $10.50
c. $10.75
d. $12.00

Decimal Review

A decimal is a special kind of fraction. You use decimals every day when you deal with money—$10.35 is a decimal that represents 10 dollars and 35 cents. The decimal point separates the dollars from the cents. Because there are 100 cents in one dollar, 1¢ is $\frac{1}{100}$ of a dollar, or $.01.

Each decimal digit to the right of the decimal point has a name:

Example:

$.1 = 1 \text{ tenth} = \frac{1}{10}$

$.02 = 2 \text{ hundredths} = \frac{2}{100}$

$.003 = 3 \text{ thousandths} = \frac{3}{1,000}$

$.0004 = 4 \text{ ten-thousandths} = \frac{4}{10,000}$

When you add zeroes after the rightmost decimal place, you don't change the value of the decimal. For example, 6.17 is the same as all of these:

6.170

6.1700

6.17000000000000000

If there are digits on both sides of the decimal point (like 10.35), the number is called a *mixed decimal*. If there are digits only to the right of the decimal point (like .53), the number is called a *decimal*. A whole number (like 15) is understood to have a decimal point at its right (15.). Thus, 15 is the same as 15.0, 15.00, 15.000, and so on.

Changing Fractions to Decimals

To convert a fraction to a decimal, simply treat the fraction as a division problem. Divide the bottom number of the fraction into the top number of the fraction. Be sure to put a decimal point and a few zeroes on the right of the top number. When you divide, bring that decimal point up into your answer.

Example:

Change $\frac{3}{4}$ to a decimal.

1. Add a decimal point and 2 zeroes to the top number (3):3.00
2. Divide the bottom number (4) into 3.00:

$$\begin{array}{r} .75 \\ 4\overline{)3.00} \\ \underline{2\ 8} \\ 20 \\ \underline{20} \\ 0 \end{array}$$

Bring the decimal point up into the answer:
3. The quotient (result of the division) is the answer: .75

Some fractions may require you to add many decimal zeroes in order for the division to come out evenly. In fact, when you convert a fraction like $\frac{2}{3}$ to a decimal, you can keep adding decimal zeroes to the top number forever because the division will never come out evenly! As you divide 3 into 2, you'll keep getting 6's: $2 \div 3 = .6666666666$ etc.

This is called a *repeating decimal* and it can be written as $.66\overline{6}$ or as $.66\frac{2}{3}$. You can approximate it as .67, .667, .6667, and so on.

Changing Decimals to Fractions

To change a decimal to a fraction, write the digits of the decimal as the top number of a fraction and write the decimal's "name" (*tenths, hundredths, thousandths*) as the bottom number of the fraction. Then simplify the fraction, if possible.

Example:

Convert .125 to a fraction.

1. Write 125 as the top of the fraction: 125.
2. Three places to the right of the decimal means *thousandths*, so write 1,000 as the bottom number: $\frac{125}{1,000}$.
3. Simplify by dividing 125 into the top and bottom numbers: $\frac{125}{1,000} = \frac{125 \div 125}{1,000 \div 125} = \frac{1}{8}$.

Change the following decimals or mixed decimals to fractions. Answers are at the end of the chapter.

42. .005

43. 3.48

44. 123.456

Comparing Decimals

Because decimals are easier to compare when they have the same number of digits after the decimal point, tack zeroes onto the end of the shorter decimals. Then all you have to do is compare the numbers as if the decimal points weren't there:

Example:

Compare .08 and .1

1. Tack one zero at the end of .1: .10
2. To compare .10 to .08, just compare 10 to 8.
3. Since 10 is larger than 8, .1 is larger than .08.

Adding and Subtracting Decimals

Adding and subtracting decimals is very similar to adding and subtracting whole numbers. The most important thing to remember is to line up the decimal points. Zeros may be filled in as placeholders when all numbers do not have the same number of decimal places. If a number doesn't have a decimal point, then put one at the right end of the number.

Example:

1.23 + 57 + .038

1. Line up the numbers like this:

```
  1.230
 57.000
+  .038
```
2. Add: 58.268

Example:

1.23 + .038

1. Line up the numbers like this:
```
 1.230
- .038
```
2. Subtract: 1.192

Try these addition and subtraction problems. Answers are at the end of the chapter.

45. .905 + .02 + 3.075

46. .005 + 8 + .3

47. 3.48 − 2.573

48. 123.456 − 122

49. Officer Peterson drove 3.7 miles to the state park. He then walked 1.6 miles around the park to make sure everything was all right. He got back into the car, drove 2.75 miles to check on a broken traffic light and then drove 2 miles back to the police station. How many miles did he drive in total?
   a. 8.05
   b. 8.45
   c. 8.8
   d. 10

50. The average number of conjugal visits at State Penitentiary fell from 486.4 per week to 402.5 per week. By how many conjugal visits per week did the average fall?
   a. 73.9
   b. 83
   c. 83.1
   d. 83.9

Multiplying Decimals

To multiply decimals, ignore the decimal points and just multiply the numbers. Then count the total number of decimal digits (the digits to the right of the decimal point) in the numbers you're multiplying. Count off that number of digits in your answer beginning at the right side and put the decimal point to the left of those digits.

Example:

What is the product of 0.14 and 4.3?

1. Multiply as usual (do not line up the decimal points):

$$\begin{array}{r} 4.3 \\ \times\,.14 \\ \hline 172 \\ 430 \\ \hline 602 \end{array}$$

2. To figure out the answer, 4.3 has one decimal place and .14 has two decimal places. Add these in order to determine the total number of decimal places the answer must have to the right of the decimal point. In this problem there are a total of 3 (1 + 2) decimal places. When finished multiplying, start from the right side of the answer, and move to the left the number of decimal places previously calculated.

$$.602$$

In this example, 602 turns into .602 since there have to be three decimal places in the answer. If there are not enough digits in the answer, add zeros in front of the answer until there are enough.

Example:

$$.03 \times .006$$

1. Multiply 3 times 6: $3 \times 6 = 18$.
2. You need 5 decimal digits in your answer, so tack on 3 zeroes: 00018.
3. Put the decimal point at the front of the number (which is 5 digits in from the right): .00018

You can practice multiplying decimals with the following problems. Answers are at the end of the chapter.

51. $.05 \times .6$

52. $.053 \times 6.4$

53. $38.1 \times .0184$

54. Officer Joseph earns $14.50 per hour. Last week he worked 37.5 hours. How much money did he earn that week?
   a. $518.00
   b. $518.50
   c. $525.00
   d. $543.75

55. Peanuts cost $3.50 per pound. Approximately how much will 4.25 pounds of peanuts cost?
   a. $12.25
   b. $12.50
   c. $12.88
   d. $14.88

Dividing Decimals

To divide a decimal by a whole number, set up the division $(8\overline{).256})$ and immediately bring the decimal point straight up into the answer $(8\overline{)\,.256}$. Then divide as you would normally divide whole numbers:

Example:

```
      .032
   8)⌐256
       0
      25
      24
      16
      16
       0
```

   To divide any number by a decimal, there is an extra step to perform before you can divide. Move the decimal point to the very right of the number you're dividing by, counting the number of places you're moving it. Then move the decimal point the same number of places to the right in the number you're dividing into. In other words, first change the problem to one in which you're dividing by a whole number.

Example:

$$.06\overline{).218}$$

1. Because there are 2 decimal digits in .06, move the decimal point 2 places to the right in both numbers and move the decimal point straight up into the answer:

$$.06\overline{)1.21\,8}$$

2. Divide using the new numbers:

```
       20.3
   6)121.8
     12
     01
     00
      18
      18
       0
```

Under certain conditions, you have to tack on zeroes to the right of the last decimal digit in number you're dividing into:

- if there aren't enough digits for you to move the decimal point to the right OR
- if the answer doesn't come out evenly when you do the division OR
- if you're dividing a whole number by a decimal. Then you'll have to tack on the decimal point as well as some zeroes.

   Try your skills on the following division problems. Answers are at the end of the chapter.

56. $7\overline{)9.8}$

57. $.0004\overline{).0512}$

58. $.5\overline{)28.6}$

59. $.14\overline{)196}$

60. If Transport Officer Worthington drove his truck 92.4 miles in 2.1 hours, what was his average speed in miles per hour?
   a. 41
   b. 44
   c. 90.3
   d. 94.5

61. Inmate Sanders walked around the jail track a total of 18.6 miles in 4 days. On average, how many miles did she walk each day?
   a. 4.15
   b. 4.60
   c. 4.65
   d. 22.60

Percent Review

Percents are always "out of 100." Literally, the word *percent* means per 100 parts. The root *cent* means 100: a century is 100 years, there are 100 cents in a dollar, etc. For example, 17% is the same as $\frac{17}{100}$. Thus, 17% means 17 parts out of 100. Because fractions can also be expressed as decimals, 17% is also equivalent to .17, which is 17 hundredths.

Examples:

$$17\% = \frac{1}{3} = \frac{\%}{100} = 0.17$$

$$3\% = \frac{3}{100} = 0.03$$

$$124\% = \frac{124}{100} = 1.24$$

$$0.9\% = \frac{.9}{100} = \frac{9}{1,000} = 0.009$$

You come into contact with percents every day. Sales tax, interest, and discounts are just a few common examples.

If you're shaky on fractions, you may want to review the previous fraction section before reading further.

Changing a Decimal to a Percent and Vice Versa

To change a decimal to a percent, move the decimal point two places to the right and tack on a percent sign (%) at the end. If the decimal point moves to the very right of the number, you don't have to write the decimal point. If there aren't enough places to move the decimal point, add zeroes on the right before moving the decimal point.

To change a percent to a decimal, drop off the percent sign and move the decimal point two places to the left. If there aren't enough places to move the decimal point, add zeroes on the left before moving the decimal point.

Try changing the following decimals to percents. Answers are at the end of the chapter.

62. .45

63. .008

64. $.16\frac{2}{3}$

Now, change the following percents to decimals. Answers are at the end of the chapter.

65. 12%

66. $87\frac{1}{2}\%$

67. 250%

Changing a Fraction to a Percent and Vice Versa

To change a fraction to a percent, there are two techniques. Each is illustrated by changing the fraction $\frac{1}{4}$ to a percent:

Technique 1: Multiply the fraction by 100%.

Multiply $\frac{1}{4}$ by 100%: $\frac{1}{\overset{1}{4}} \times \frac{\overset{25}{100\%}}{1} = 25\%$.

Technique 2: Divide the fraction's bottom number into the top number; then move the decimal point two places to the right and tack on a percent sign (%).

Divide 4 into 1 and move the decimal point 2 places to the right:

$$\begin{array}{r} .25 \\ 4\overline{)1.00} \end{array} \qquad .25 = 25\%$$

To change a percent to a fraction, remove the percent sign and write the number over 100. Then reduce if possible.

Example:

Change 4% to a fraction.

1. Remove the % and write the fraction 4 over 100:
   $\frac{4}{100}$.
2. Simplify: $\frac{4 \div 4}{100 \div 4} = \frac{1}{25}$.

Here's a more complicated example:

Change $16\frac{2}{3}\%$ to a fraction.

1. Remove the % and write the fraction $16\frac{2}{3}$ over 100:
   $\frac{16\frac{2}{3}}{100}$
2. Since a fraction means "top number divided by bottom number," rewrite the fraction as a division problem: $\frac{100}{1} \rightarrow \frac{1}{100}$ $16\frac{2}{3} \div 100$
3. Change the mixed number ($16\frac{2}{3}$) to an improper fraction ($\frac{50}{3}$): $\frac{50}{3} \div \frac{100}{1}$
4. Flip the second fraction ($\frac{100}{1} \rightarrow \frac{1}{100}$) and multiply:
   $\frac{\overset{1}{50}}{3} \times \frac{1}{\underset{2}{100}} = \frac{1}{6}$

Try changing the following fractions to percents. Answers are at the end of the chapter.

68. $\frac{1}{8}$

69. $\frac{13}{25}$

70. $\frac{7}{12}$

Now change these percents to fractions.

71. 95%

72. $37\frac{1}{2}\%$

73. 125%

Percent Word Problems

Word problems involving percents come in three main varieties:

- Find a percent of a whole.

Example:

What is 30% of 40?

- Find what percent one number is of another number.

Example:

12 is what percent of 40?

- Find the whole when the percent of it is given.

Example:

12 is 30% of what number?

While each variety has its own approach, there is a single shortcut formula you can use to solve each of these:

$$\frac{is}{of} = \frac{\%}{100}$$

The **is** is the number that usually follows or is just before the word *is* in the question.

The *of* is the number that usually follows the word *of* in the question.

The **%** is the number that in front of the % or *percent* in the question.

Or you may think of the shortcut formula as:

$$\frac{part}{whole} = \frac{\%}{100}$$

To solve each of the three varieties, we're going to use the fact that the **cross-products** are equal. The cross-products are the products of the numbers diagonally across from each other. Remembering that product means multiply, here's how to create the cross-products for the percent shortcut:

$$\frac{part}{whole} = \frac{\%}{100}$$

$$part \times 100 = whole \times \%$$

Here's how to use the shortcut with cross-products:

- Find a percent of a whole.

  What is 30% of 40?

  30 is the % and 40 is the *of* number: $\frac{is}{40} = \frac{30}{100}$

  Cross-multiply and solve for *is*:
  $is \times 100 = 40 \times 30$

  $is \times 100 = 1,200$

  $12 \times 100 = 1,200$

  Thus, 12 is 30% of 40.

- Find what percent one number is of another number.

  12 is what percent of 40?

12 is the *is* number and 40 is the *of* number:
$\frac{12}{40} = \frac{\%}{100}$

Cross-multiply and solve for %:
$12 \times 100 = 40 \times \%$

$1,200 = 40 \times \%$

$1,200 = 40 \times 30$

Thus, 12 is 30% of 40.

- Find the whole when the percent of it is given.

  12 is 30% of what number?

  12 is the *is* number and 30 is the %: $\frac{12}{of} = \frac{30}{100}$

  Cross-multiply and solve for the of number:
  $12 \times 100 = of \times 30$

  $1,200 = of \times 30$

  $1,200 = 40 \times 30$

  Thus 12 is 30% of 40.

You can use the same technique to find the percent increase or decrease. The *is* number is the actual increase or decrease, and the *of* number is the original amount.

Example:

If a uniform supply store puts $20 hats on sale for $15, by what percent is the selling price decreased?

1. Calculate the decrease, the *is* number: $20 - $15 = $5.
2. The *of* number is the original amount, $20.
3. Set up the equation and solve for *of* by cross-multiplying: $\frac{5}{20} = \frac{\%}{100}$.

   $5 \times 100 = 20 \times \%$

   $500 = 20 \times \%$

   $500 = 20 \times 25$

4. Thus, the selling price is decreased by 25%.

If the merchant later raises the price of the hats from $15 back to $20, don't be fooled into thinking that the percent increase is also 25%! It's actually more, because the increase amount of $5 is now based on a lower original price of only $15:

$$\frac{5}{15} = \frac{\%}{100}$$

$$5 \times 100 = 15 \times \%$$

$$500 = 15 \times \%$$

$$500 = 15 \times 33\frac{1}{3}$$

Thus, the selling price is increased by 33%.

Find a percent of a whole. Answers are at the end of the chapter.

74. 1% of 25

75. 18.2% of 50

76. $37\frac{1}{2}$% of 100

77. 125% of 60

Find what percent one number is of another number.

78. 10 is what % of 20?

79. 4 is what % of 12?

80. 12 is what % of 4?

Find the whole when the percent of it is given.

81. 15% of what number is 15?

82. $37\frac{1}{2}$% of what number is 3?

83. 200% of what number is 20?

Now try your percent skills on some real-life problems.

84. Last Monday, 20% of the 140-member jail nursing staff was absent. How many nurses were absent that day?
a. 14
b. 20
c. 28
d. 112

85. 40% of State Penitentiary employees are women. If there are 80 women in State's service, how many men are employed there?
a. 32
b. 112
c. 120
d. 160

86. Out of 840 attempted escapes in the by inmates last year, 42 were successful. What percent of the escapes were successful?
a. .5%
b. 2%
c. 5%
d. 20%

87. Sam's Uniform Supply put all of its merchandise on sale for 20% off. If Jason saved $10 by purchasing one pair of shoes during the sale, what was the original price of the shoes before the sale?
a. $12
b. $20
c. $40
d. $50

▶ Answers to Practice Questions

Word Problems
1. a.
2. c.
3. d.
4. c.

Addition
5. b.
6. c.

Subtraction
7. c.
8. a.

Multiplication
9. d.
10. b.
11. c.

Division
12. a.
13. a.
14. c.

Fractions
15. $\frac{1}{4}$
16. $\frac{2}{5}$
17. $\frac{3}{8}$
18. $\frac{11}{12}$
19. $\frac{55}{24}$ or $2\frac{7}{24}$
20. $7\frac{1}{4}$
21. $\frac{2}{15}$
22. $\frac{1}{8}$
23. $\frac{19}{12}$ or $1\frac{7}{12}$
24. a.
25. b.

26. $\frac{2}{15}$
27. $\frac{8}{35}$
28. $\frac{2}{3}$
29. $\frac{26}{15}$ or $1\frac{11}{15}$
30. 15
31. $\frac{33}{2}$ or $16\frac{1}{2}$
32. c.
33. d.
34. c.
35. $\frac{1}{2}$
36. $5\frac{1}{2}$
37. $\frac{1}{5}$
38. $\frac{45}{28}$ or $1\frac{17}{28}$
39. b.
40. d.
41. b.

Decimals
42. $\frac{5}{1,000}$ or $\frac{1}{200}$
43. $3\frac{12}{25}$
44. $123\frac{456}{1,000}$ or $123\frac{57}{125}$
45. 4
46. 8.305
47. .907
48. 1.456
49. b.
50. d.
51. .03
52. .3392
53. .70104
54. d.
55. d.
56. 1.4
57. 128
58. 57.2

59. 1,400

60. b.

61. c.

Percents

62. 45%

63. .8%

64. 16.67% or $16\frac{2}{3}$%

65. .12

66. .875

67. 2.5

68. 12.5% or $12\frac{1}{2}$%

69. 52%

70. 58.33% or $58\frac{1}{3}$%

71. $\frac{19}{20}$

72. $\frac{3}{8}$

73. $\frac{5}{4}$ or $1\frac{1}{4}$

74. $\frac{1}{4}$ or .25

75. 9.1

76. $37\frac{1}{2}$ or 37.5

77. 75

78. 50%

79. $33\frac{1}{3}$%

80. 300%

81. 100

82. 8

83. 10

84. c.

85. c.

86. c.

87. d.

Memory,
Observation,
and Counting
Review

CHAPTER SUMMARY
This chapter contains hints and tips to help you answer questions that test your memory skills. Memory questions can be based on pictures or on written materials; you may get the materials ahead of time or on test day. However the memory questions are structured, this chapter will help you deal with them.

It's amazing what your mind will file away in that cabinet we call memory. You remember every snippet of dialogue uttered by Clint Eastwood in his first *Dirty Harry* movie from years ago, but you can't remember what you had for breakfast yesterday. Some people remember names well, but can't put them with the right faces. Others forget names quickly, but know exactly when, where, and why they met the person whose name they've forgotten. There are a few lucky individuals who possess what is commonly referred to as a "photographic memory," or total recall. And then there are those of us who need to look at a calendar every morning to remember what day of the week it is. Fortunately for most of us, having a good memory is actually something that can be developed—with the right incentive.

A high score on the corrections officer exam is plenty of incentive.

▶ Memory Skills

Most corrections officer exams may test your short-term memory or longer-term memory skills, or both. In tests of short-term memory, you're often required to look at a sketch of a street scene; drawings of men and women with differing facial features, weapons, and other property; or photographs. Usually, you will be given a set amount of time to look at the scene (five minutes is common), and then you will be asked to answer test questions about what you saw. Your goal is to memorize as much of that drawing or photograph as you can in the allotted time.

Some exams are more interested in longer-term memory skills. They may send you a study booklet a few weeks in advance of the test and ask you to memorize several items in the booklet. In that case, you will answer questions based on what you have been memorizing from the study booklet.

This chapter covers both kinds of memory questions, so you will be prepared for either one.

Short-Term Memory Questions

Questions Based on Written Passages
A common method of testing short-term memory is to have you read a lengthy, detailed block of text and then answer several multiple-choice questions based on that material. Here is an example:

Answer questions 1, 2, and 3 based on the following passage.

Officer Renteria is in the prison recreation yard when he notices that two inmates look as if they are about to start fighting. He walks over to the basketball court. Two white males are standing face-to-face arguing in the center of the court. One man is 6′ 5″ feet tall, wearing the orange prison uniform top and pants. He is holding a basketball under his right arm. The other man is 6 feet tall and is wearing the orange prison pants; he has no shirt on. Officer Renteria also notices that the other inmates have encircled the two men and are shouting at them to fight. He counts about 30 inmates standing on the basketball court, including the two men who are arguing. Officer Renteria puts out a call on his radio for backup and sees four officers trotting toward him from Gate 3. The officers surround the inmates and tell them to break it up. Officer Renteria and Officer Buffett escort the two men who are arguing back to their cells.

1. How tall was the tallest man involved in the argument?
   a. 5' 10"
   b. 6'
   c. 6' 2"
   d. 6' 5"

2. Which officer put out a call for backup?
   a. Officer Buffett
   b. Officer Renteria
   c. Officer Galway
   d. Officer Sears

3. Where did the officers take the two men who were arguing?
   a. to solitary confinement
   b. back to their cellblocks
   c. for a walk around the court to cool off
   d. back to their cells

What to Do
Short-term memory questions based on what you have read are fairly straightforward. Your best approach to these questions is to:

1. Read the instructions to find out what questions you will have to answer based on the passage you are about to read.
2. Read the questions before the passage so that your mind will be primed for the kind of information that should catch your eye as you read the passage.
3. After reading the passage, read the answers and try to eliminate the wrong ones first.
4. When you have the right answer, glance back at the passage to check your accuracy.

Using the example above, let's try these techniques. The instructions in the example tell you to answer questions 1 through 3 after reading the passage. That's simple enough. Let your eyes drop down to the first question: "How tall was the tallest man involved in the argument?" As you read the passage, your eyes will be on the lookout for that information. The next question asks, "Which officer put out a call for backup?" Once again, your brain is primed to wave red flags when you read the part of the passage that answers this question. The final question is, "Where did the officers take the two men who were arguing?" Since you are primed with the questions, you are ready to read the passage. You should find that the answers to the three questions are: **1. d**; **2. b**; and **3. d**.

What Not to Do

- Do not read through the passage looking for only the right answers. Read the entire story before you make your decisions. A lazy reader who skims this passage and stops reading as each question is apparently answered might get an unpleasant surprise when the "obvious" answer is wrong. For example, if you did not read the options carefully in the third question, you may have chosen option **c** because you see that the inmates were returned to their cellblocks. The last sentence in the passage tells you that the inmates who were arguing were returned to their cells, not cellblocks.

- Do not make this task harder than it is by trying to draw conclusions. Your memory skills are being tested here, not your reasoning abilities or your knowledge of the law.

Questions Based On Pictures

Looking at a picture for a set length of time—usually five minutes—and then answering a series of questions about details in the scene is a very common way for corrections officer exams to test your short-term memory. It is a simple test of your ability to recall specific details. You aren't being asked to solve crimes, use judgment skills, or draw conclusions about what you see.

The picture will often be a scene of a busy city street with plenty of details for you to pick up on: store names, buses, taxis, people, clothing, action scenes (a mugging or maybe someone changing a flat tire on a car), and street signs. You will be asked to study this drawing or photograph for a specific amount of time, then you will turn to a set of questions in the test booklet. Let's assume that the picture you studied for five minutes showed a man holding a knife in his left hand while stealing a woman's purse. You might see a test question like this:

4. What is the man who is stealing the woman's purse holding in his left hand?
   a. a gun
   b. a stick
   c. a bottle
   d. a knife

The questions are simple and the answers are simple. If you don't remember what the perpetrator had in his hand or didn't even notice the scene in the picture, then you will have to give this question your best guess.

What to Do

Use a methodical approach to studying what you see. When you read sentences on a page, you read from left to right. This skill is as unconscious as breathing for most English-language readers. Approach memorizing a picture the same way you read, taking in the information from left to right. Instead of staring at the street scene with the whole picture in focus, make yourself start at the left and work your way across the page until you get to the right.

What Not to Do

- Do not go into brain-lock when you first see the busy street scene. Take a deep breath and decide to be methodical.

- Do not try to start memorizing with a shotgun approach, letting your eyes roam all over the page without really taking in the details.

Questions Based on a Video

Some exams will show you a video and then have you answer questions about what you have observed. This method is not widely used because it's difficult to administer to large numbers of people, but it is possible that you may encounter it. Check with your state or jurisdiction to make sure if this is an aspect of your particular test. If it is, a good way to prepare is to rent a movie and ask a friend to pick out a scene and prepare questions for you. After you watch the scene, have the friend ask you about the specific things that you observed.

Long-Term Memory Questions

For questions that test long-term memory, you will be sent a study booklet a few weeks in advance of the test. The booklet contains detailed instructions on what you will be expected to know for the test. The expectation is that you will have plenty of time to memorize the information and that you will be able to answer questions based on what you have memorized.

For example, you may see several pictures of items confiscated during a search of a prisoner's cell—maybe a wristwatch, a brown belt, or a pen. On test day, you may see a question like this:

5. In the study booklet provided to you, there are several drawings of items confiscated in a search of an inmate's cell. One of the items was a belt. What color was the belt?
   a. navy
   b. tan
   c. black
   d. brown

The questions are simple. You just have to be able to recall details.

What to Do

If you get material to study in advance, study it in advance. Don't start to study the day before the test. Spend a little time on your study booklet every day from the day you get it until the day before the test. Make up your own questions from the study booklet, there are only so many questions that could possibly be asked of you on the test. You may find at test time that you are asked questions similar to the ones you have asked yourself.

What Not to Do

- Do not read the questions too quickly. If you're having trouble remembering the details, going with what initially feels like the correct answer is usually a good idea—but you must make sure you are answering the right question. Rushing yourself can produce errors that were easily avoidable if you exercised patience.

Memorization Tips

Memorization is much easier if you approach the task with the expectation that you will remember what you see. Call it positive thinking, self-hypnosis, or concentration—it doesn't really matter as long as you get results. When you run through the practice questions in this book, prepare your mind before you begin. Repeat to yourself over and over that you will remember what you see as you study the images. Your performance level will naturally rise to meet your expectations.

Yes, it's easy for your brain to seize up when you see a drawing filled with many details, a test section full of questions, and a test proctor standing above you with a stopwatch in one hand barking, "You have five minutes to study this drawing. You may begin." But if you have programmed yourself to stay calm, stay alert, and execute your plan, you will remember the details when you need them.

Plan? Yes, you need a plan. If you have a method for memorizing, say, a busy urban street scene—like the left-to-right scheme previously outlined—then you will be more likely to relax and allow yourself to retain what you have seen long enough to answer the test questions. Keep in mind that you aren't trying to memorize the scene to learn it for life, you are doing it to retain the information long enough to answer the test questions. What will it matter if you remember the scene three months from now? Your goal is to retain the information long enough to get through this test.

Observation Tips

It's almost impossible to talk about memorization without bringing up observation. Some people are naturally observant. Others drift off into daydreams and have no awareness of the world around them. Whatever category you think you are in, it's never too late to sharpen, or acquire, strong observation skills. How? By practicing, of course.

Newspaper photos make great practice tools. News photos are normally action-oriented and usually have more than one person in the scenes. Sit down in a quiet place, clear your mind, remind yourself for several minutes that you will retain all the details you need when you study the picture, and then turn to a picture and study it for about five minutes. At the end of the time you allot yourself, turn the picture over, get a piece of paper and a pencil, then write down all the details you can think of in the picture. Make yourself do this as often as possible before the test.

You can sharpen your observation skills on the way to work or school, too. Instead of sitting in your car waiting for the light to change with a blank stare on your face, look around you and say out loud what you see. "I'm at the corner of Seventeenth and Peabody. I see a man in a black, full-length raincoat standing on the northeast corner looking in the display window of Frank's Motorcycle Shop. There's a black Ford station wagon parked at a meter near the motorcycle shop. The license plate is . . ." (If you ride to work on a bus or train, say these things silently to yourself!) Not only are you practicing a basic skill you will need to become an excellent corrections officer, you are training your mind to succeed at whatever memory questions the test maker throws your way.

Memory and Observation Practice

Refer to the street scene on pages 66–67. Below are several questions asking about details of the scene. Use this scene to practice your memory skills. Take five minutes (no more!) to study the picture and then answer the questions that follow, without looking back at the picture.

Then check your answers by looking back at the scene. If you get all the questions right, you know you're well prepared for memory questions. If you miss a few, you know you need to spend more time practicing, using the tips outlined above. Remember, you can improve your memory with practice.

6. What number is on the bag being carried by the woman on the sidewalk?
   a. 31
   b. 23
   c. 13
   d. 18

7. The woman walking the dogs is holding how many leashes?
   a. 3
   b. 2
   c. 4
   d. 1

8. The intersection in this scene is labeled
   a. W 2nd Av and 7 Av
   b. W 2nd St and 7 Av
   c. W 7th St and 2nd Av
   d. W 7th Av and 7th St

9. What is the name of the bank?
   a. Gotham Bank
   b. Gotham Savings
   c. Gotham Loan
   d. Gotham Savings and Loan

10. What name is printed on the front of the taxi driving down the street?
  a. Arthur's Taxis
  b. Adam's Taxis
  c. Akim's Taxis
  d. Al's Taxis

11. What is the man leaning over the subway entrance doing?
  a. snatching a woman's purse
  b. dropping a water balloon
  c. selling flowers
  d. zipping his jacket

12. What phone number is written on the Rent-A-Van moving truck?
  a. 553-2277
  b. 555-2272
  c. 555-2212
  d. 553-2177

Counting Practice

Many corrections officer exams test your counting skills. There are many possible ways your exam may do this.

A question may give you a set of different letters and ask you to count only one specific letter or letter case from the set:

13. If many lower case letters are there in this set?

```
B B B b B B b b
Z Z Z Z Z Z Z z
F F f F f F f f
X x x X x x X x
N h N h N h N N
```

  a. 13
  b. 14
  c. 15
  d. 16

Or you may encounter questions that employ shapes and patterns in sets:

14. How many diamonds are needed to complete this pattern?

♦ ♦ ♦ ♦ ♦
♦ ♦   ♦
♦
♦ ♦ ♦   ♦
♦   ♦ ♦ ♦

  a. 6
  b. 7
  c. 8
  d. 9

15. How many hearts are in the following set?

♥ ♥ ♣ ♥ ♣ ♣
♣ ♣ ♣ ♣ ♣ ♥
♥ ♣ ♥ ♥ ♣ ♣
♥ ♣ ♥ ♥ ♣ ♥

  a. 9
  b. 10
  c. 11
  d. 12

Answers: **13. d.; 14. c.; 15. c.**

Other types of counting questions may give you a short paragraph or sentence, and ask you to count the number of times something such as a word, letter, or punctuation mark occurs. You may be given a picture similar to the memory and observation questions and be asked to count something that occurs in the picture. Without a time limit, counting questions are extremely simple. But take five questions similar to the previous examples, and add a time limit of thirty seconds, and the whole situation changes doesn't it? Test jitters add to that time limit and what was once a simple question has now become a difficult brainteaser.

What to Do

There is only one thing you can do, and that's relax. Take a deep breath, don't fight the clock, and make sure you know the task at hand. Remember, counting questions are simple, don't make them into something they are not. Work through each question as quickly as you can without confusing yourself, and know that when you get into trouble, jitters grow. Counting questions are the easiest questions to practice—look all around you. On the bus, quickly count how many people have brown hair, in the library how many black books on a shelf, etc. Sharpening your counting skills is not only important for your exam it's important for your career as a corrections officer as well.

What Not to Do

Don't make the questions complicated by rushing through them. Don't look at the clock, it will only add to your anxiety and make you prone to mistakes. Know what you have to do, and do it. Calmness and preparation are the marks of a good test-taker, and it's no surprise they are the marks of a good corrections officer, as well.

10 ▶ Situational Reasoning and Applying Written Material Review

CHAPTER SUMMARY

This chapter will teach you how to best handle exam questions that test your judgment and ability to use common sense. The keys to doing well on these questions are being sure to read everything carefully, and learning to think like a corrections officer.

In the civilian world when employers search for worker, the emphasis is most often on training and education. They want workers who are trained and ready to function after a brief adjustment time. This is not usually the case in corrections. Agencies who hire corrections officers always like to see college degrees and law enforcement training, but what they prize most of all are enthusiastic applicants who come armed with the tools of common sense and good judgment. Every corrections officer must be trained—the hiring agency wants to know whether or not you will be able to safely and effectively apply what you learn. They'll do this with the quickest, most cost-effective method—the multiple-choice exam.

Judgment questions are designed to see if you can make a sound decision—pick the right multiple-choice answer—based on information given to you. To arrive at the right conclusion, you will need to apply common sense, good judgment, and good reading skills. (A little good luck never hurts either!)

Judgment questions generally fall into two categories: situational judgment and application of rules and procedures. This chapter looks at each category, takes apart an example of each type of judgment question, and then identifies the best approach to answering the question. There are also tips on what is most likely to trip up an unprepared test-taker.

► Situational Judgment Questions

Situational judgment questions ask you to climb inside the mind of a corrections officer and make decisions from this viewpoint. It isn't necessary for you to know the laws of any state or the policies and procedures of any prison system. The test itself will give you all the information you need to answer the question.

Some exams put you right into the hot seat with language such as "You are a corrections officer in charge of . . ." while other exams use a more subtle approach: "Officer Jerod is conducting a shakedown of inmate Smythe's cell and finds a homemade knife." Although the approach is different, both test makers are asking you to look at their questions from the same viewpoint—a corrections officer's.

The structure of the questions is pretty simple. You'll be given a situation, and then you'll be asked to choose how you would handle the situation if you were the corrections officer on duty. The best part about a multiple-choice test is that you don't have to come up with your own plan—you get to choose the best answer from the four options listed below the question. Test-day jitters, of course, may make all of the options appear to be the right one, but keep in mind that there is only one best answer.

Here's an example:

Officer Ellenbee has searched inmate Franks and has found a knife in his pants pocket. He has not completed his search of the inmate. What should he do with the knife?

a. Ask the inmate to hold it in his hand until the search is completed.
b. Put the knife in his own pocket to keep it safely out of reach of the inmate.
c. Put the knife back in the inmate's pocket and instruct him to leave it alone until he has completed the search.
d. Put the knife on the floor until he has completed the search.

In this situation, all of the options could conceivably happen, and probably have, but only one answer is the best answer. Only one answer truly appeals to your common sense and ability to apply good judgment. Which one is it?

The best way to approach this type of question is to start by eliminating the options that right off you know aren't going to work. Option **a** is not as appealing as some of the other options because the idea of an inmate holding a weapon in his hand while the officer searches him should cause that officer considerable unease, if not downright fear for his life. Feel free to apply common sense liberally here. Option **c** is not much better. It wouldn't take a whole lot of effort for the inmate to reach into his pocket to get at the weapon. Option **d** is safer than the other two, but once again, it wouldn't take much effort for the inmate to reach down and pick up the knife. Option **b** is the winner in this contest. The inmate would have his hands full trying to get at the knife in the officer's pocket.

The temptation with situational judgment questions is to project your thoughts and feelings into the scenario. You may catch yourself chewing on your pencil thinking, "Well, this guy is an idiot. I'd never handle this situation using any of these choices." Probably not. Unfortunately, you will never see the following option:

e. The above choices stink. I would _____.

Another temptation is to read more into the situation than is there. You may think, "Maybe this inmate is a decent guy. Maybe he's in prison for a nonviolent crime and wouldn't be likely to use that knife on anyone. The officer might know that this guy wouldn't hurt him . . ." And so on. Use only the information you see on the page, not the information that *could* be there, to make your decision.

Just remember: You'll be asked to exercise your good judgment and common sense to each question you read. And it certainly helps to know what it means to "think like a corrections officer."

Through Their Eyes

Think like a corrections officer—that's easy to say. But how do you do it? The ideal way to learn is to find an officer who works in a facility that allows visitors. This facility doesn't necessarily have to be a state prison. Local or county jails have been known to be fairly sympathetic to requests to tour the facility. It's always easiest if you get to know someone who is already working in the corrections field. If you don't, though, never be afraid to keep trying until you find an agency willing to let you see with your own eyes what officers handle in real, day-to-day settings. Do what you can to look at the world through their eyes.

Safety First

If you got tired of hearing your mother say, "Safety first!" when you were growing up, get ready for an exhausting experience. In every action a corrections officer takes, the safety and well-being of everyone involved is Priority Number One.

When you look at a test question, remember that officers have the importance of safety drilled into them from day one. Is it safer to let the inmate stand in front of an officer or behind an officer? Is it safer to call for backup when a big fight breaks out, or should the officer just wade in and hope that when the fighters see the uniform the fight will end?

The safety issue may not surface in every question, but when it does, be aware that safety is one of a corrections officer's highest priorities.

Use of Force

The smallest amount possible is the right amount of force. You don't need to go through six months of training to recognize that it's a monumental waste of effort to swat a fly with a ten-pound sledgehammer when a one-ounce plastic flyswatter will achieve the same result. Common sense comes heavily into play in this area. Expect to see test questions that ask you what the proper amount of force is for an officer to use when physical control is necessary, and what kind of force is appropriate out of the choices you are given. When

answering judgment questions, keep in mind that the test makers know that the best officers will use the least force possible in *all* situations.

It's Up to You

Many situations that arise in a correctional facility may not be covered in a procedural manual or list of regulations. Things happen quickly and you have no time to consult the policy manual or ask a coworker what to do. It's all up to you how you handle the situation. For example, you might see a question like this:

> You are on duty during the lunch hour. You are seating inmates at tables, always alert for any potential problems. As you direct one of the inmates to a chair, that inmate whispers to you that she has information about drug smuggling within the prison and asks that you find her later to talk about this when no one else can hear. What should you do?
> a. Take the inmate out of the cafeteria immediately and make her talk.
> b. Ignore the inmate. She probably just wants the attention.
> c. Continue the seating as if you didn't hear her, and then contact her later in private as she asked.
> d. Confront her right there and make her say what is on her mind in front of the other inmates.

Once again, the process of elimination will come in handy to answer this question. Look at option **a** first: Is there any particular urgency to the situation? No one is apparently in any immediate danger, so it would not make much sense to call attention to this possible informant by singling her out. Option **b** is not a good choice because you certainly want to be able to stop illegal drugs from coming into the prison population. If the inmate has good information, you don't want to lose it. Because you don't want to single the inmate out and make the other inmates suspicious of her, option

c looks like the best choice so far. Option **d** would put the inmate in danger by identifying her to other inmates as a possible snitch.

Application of Laws, Policy, and Procedures

Another kind of test question asks you to read rules, laws, policies, or procedures and then apply those guidelines to a hypothetical situation. You may still be able to use your good judgment and common sense in these questions, but even more important is your ability to read carefully and accurately.

These kinds of questions ask you to do something corrections officers do every day: take their knowledge of the laws of their state or of their agency's procedures and use that knowledge to decide how to act in a given situation. The questions don't expect you to know the laws or procedures; they are right there as part of the test question. And that's why your reading skills are extra important.

Application of procedures questions will supply you with information about corrections procedures and then ask you to apply those procedures to a hypothetical situation. You might have to decide which step in a set of procedures is the next step to be taken in the situation, or you might have to decide whether a hypothetical officer followed the procedures properly in a given situation. In either case, you are being tested on your ability to follow directions, and that ability directly relates to your reading comprehension skills.

The question is usually preceded by a brief passage telling you about the procedure; for example:

When an officer decides that an inmate requires disciplinary action following a minor infraction of prison rules, the officer should follow these procedures:

1. Write a report identifying whom the inmate is, what rule the inmate broke, and the details surrounding the incident.
2. The officer should place his or her signature at the bottom of the report.

3. Recommend appropriate disciplinary action.
4. Place a copy of the report in the inmate's file.
5. Turn the report in to the supervisor in charge of the inmate's cellblock.

Officer Luke is in charge of the prison library. Inmate Foster has been allowed to use the library for several days in a row to prepare for his defense in an upcoming trial. Inmate Foster has been loud and disruptive in the library for two days in a row and has had to be returned early to his cell. Officer Luke decides to write up inmate Foster so that disciplinary action can be taken. What is the next step he should take after he places a copy of the report in the inmate's file?
a. Sign the report.
b. Give a copy of the report directly to the inmate.
c. Turn the report in to the supervisor in charge of the inmate's cellblock.
d. Make sure the report gives the details of inmate Foster's behavior in the library.

What the test maker wants you to do is study the list of procedures so that when you are reading questions like the one above, you will be able to return to the proper list of procedures, scan the steps, and answer the question properly. These questions can be tricky if you read too fast or read only a part of the answers. Take your time and make sure the answer can be linked to a step in the procedure.

In the example above, the question asks the reader to pick out the next step Officer Luke should take after he places a copy of the report in the inmate's file. Find the procedures that pertain to reporting an inmate for disciplinary action and look at the steps. Find the step that pertains to the question. In this case, your eyes should light on step 4: *Place a copy of the report in the inmate's file.* Since the question asks you what the officer's NEXT step is (after step 4) then you should be looking at step 5 to see if it matches choice **a**, **b**, **c**, or **d**.

Turn back to the list of choices below the question and start reading. It's not choice **a** because that happens to be the second step in the procedure, and not what we are looking for. Choice **b** isn't listed as an option anywhere in the procedures so we can cross it right off the list. Choice **c** is, however, and it looks to be step 5 of the procedure, word-for-word. Still, check the other options just to make sure. Choice **d** matches up with the first step in the procedure and isn't what the question asks for either. Therefore, choice **c** is the right answer.

Remember, you can only choose *one* answer. Often, two answers will look good, but only one will be the BEST answer. That is why it is important to read the questions and answers thoroughly.

Improving Your Judgment Skills

You have more options than you may realize when it comes to sharpening your judgment skills—not only for the exam, but also for your career as a corrections officer. There are some surprisingly simple exercises you can do in your everyday life that will get you ready.

What If . . .

There's a game most officers play in their minds called "What if." You play too, but you may not be aware of it. "What if I won the lottery tomorrow? If I did, I'd empty my desk drawers on top of the boss's desk and move to an island somewhere." Sound familiar?

Some professional baseball players watch slow-motion videos of a batter with perfect form in the hope that by memorizing and studying his moves, they will be able to improve their own performance. And research shows that this works: In times of stress, people are more likely to carry out a task if they've practiced it—mentally or physically.

"What if" uses the same logic. If you have thought about a situation and you have arrived at a conclusion about what you would do under the given circumstances, then you have given your brain a plan for the situation if it ever actually occurs. Maybe you have heard someone say, "I didn't have any idea what to do.

I just froze." That brain didn't have a plan to follow. Playing "What if" could have given it a plan.

Train yourself to play "What if." Suppose you are standing in a long line at the grocery store. You have got time on your hands. Imagine that instead of a grocery store, you are standing in a prison and the man in front of you in line is really an inmate waiting in line at the cafeteria. Suddenly, you notice that he has a bulge in his back pocket. It looks like a knife. What do you do?

This situation could turn out to be one of the situational judgment questions you will find on your exam. Practice. At the very least it may add a little excitement to your grocery shopping.

Self-Confidence Checks

Practice your self-confidence. Odd advice? Not really. Self-confidence is what makes most officers able to make decisions with a minimum of confusion and self-doubt. Although you aren't a corrections officer yet, you need the same self-confidence of corrections officer to make the right decisions as a test-taker. If you aren't confident about your judgment skills and your ability to decide what to do in a situation, then you are likely to torture yourself with every judgment question.

Believe it or not, it is possible to practice self-confidence. Many people practice the opposite of self-confidence by thinking and saying negative things like "I don't know if I can do that" or "What if I can't do that?"

Do you talk like that? If so, now is your chance to turn it around. Tell yourself and others, "The corrections officer test is coming up and I intend to ace it." And "I know I will make a great corrections officer. I know that when I read the test questions I can rely on my own good judgment to help me. My common sense will point me in the right direction."

This isn't bragging. It's how you prepare for success. You will start thinking of what you need to do to ace the test. You are practicing self-confidence right now by reading this book. You are getting the tools you need to do the job. Your self-confidence has no option but to shoot straight up—and your score along with it.

Read, Read, Read

Reading is crucial on judgment questions. This isn't the kind of reading you do when you are skimming a novel or skipping through articles in a newspaper. It's the kind where you not only have to pay attention to what the writer is telling you, but also make decisions based on the information you have received.

11 ▶ Corrections Officer Exam II

CHAPTER SUMMARY

This is the second of the three practice exams in this book based on exams used by departments of correction around the country to assess candidates applying for positions as corrections officers. After working through the instructional material in the previous chapters, take this test to see how much your score has improved since you took the first exam.

The test that follows is based on the exams used throughout the country to select corrections officers. Though written examinations for corrections officers vary depending on the state, county, or municipal corrections agency, most exams test just a few basic skills, like the ones covered in this exam.

This test is similar to the one you took in Chapter 5. There are a total of one hundred questions in the following areas: reading, writing, math, memory and observation, counting, situational reasoning, and applying written material.

For this exam, simulate the actual test-taking experience as much as possible. Find a quiet place to work where you won't be interrupted. Tear out the answer sheet on the next page and find some number 2 pencils to fill in the circles with. Find a timer or a stopwatch to time yourself during the memory, observation, and counting sections of the exam.

After the exam, use the answer key that follows it to see how you did and to find out why the correct answers are correct.

1.	ⓐ	ⓑ	ⓒ	ⓓ	35.	ⓐ	ⓑ	ⓒ	ⓓ	69.	ⓐ	ⓑ	ⓒ	ⓓ
2.	ⓐ	ⓑ	ⓒ	ⓓ	36.	ⓐ	ⓑ	ⓒ	ⓓ	70.	ⓐ	ⓑ	ⓒ	ⓓ
3.	ⓐ	ⓑ	ⓒ	ⓓ	37.	ⓐ	ⓑ	ⓒ	ⓓ	71.	ⓐ	ⓑ	ⓒ	ⓓ
4.	ⓐ	ⓑ	ⓒ	ⓓ	38.	ⓐ	ⓑ	ⓒ	ⓓ	72.	ⓐ	ⓑ	ⓒ	ⓓ
5.	ⓐ	ⓑ	ⓒ	ⓓ	39.	ⓐ	ⓑ	ⓒ	ⓓ	73.	ⓐ	ⓑ	ⓒ	ⓓ
6.	ⓐ	ⓑ	ⓒ	ⓓ	40.	ⓐ	ⓑ	ⓒ	ⓓ	74.	ⓐ	ⓑ	ⓒ	ⓓ
7.	ⓐ	ⓑ	ⓒ	ⓓ	41.	ⓐ	ⓑ	ⓒ	ⓓ	75.	ⓐ	ⓑ	ⓒ	ⓓ
8.	ⓐ	ⓑ	ⓒ	ⓓ	42.	ⓐ	ⓑ	ⓒ	ⓓ	76.	ⓐ	ⓑ	ⓒ	ⓓ
9.	ⓐ	ⓑ	ⓒ	ⓓ	43.	ⓐ	ⓑ	ⓒ	ⓓ	77.	ⓐ	ⓑ	ⓒ	ⓓ
10.	ⓐ	ⓑ	ⓒ	ⓓ	44.	ⓐ	ⓑ	ⓒ	ⓓ	78.	ⓐ	ⓑ	ⓒ	ⓓ
11.	ⓐ	ⓑ	ⓒ	ⓓ	45.	ⓐ	ⓑ	ⓒ	ⓓ	79.	ⓐ	ⓑ	ⓒ	ⓓ
12.	ⓐ	ⓑ	ⓒ	ⓓ	46.	ⓐ	ⓑ	ⓒ	ⓓ	80.	ⓐ	ⓑ	ⓒ	ⓓ
13.	ⓐ	ⓑ	ⓒ	ⓓ	47.	ⓐ	ⓑ	ⓒ	ⓓ	81.	ⓐ	ⓑ	ⓒ	ⓓ
14.	ⓐ	ⓑ	ⓒ	ⓓ	48.	ⓐ	ⓑ	ⓒ	ⓓ	82.	ⓐ	ⓑ	ⓒ	ⓓ
15.	ⓐ	ⓑ	ⓒ	ⓓ	49.	ⓐ	ⓑ	ⓒ	ⓓ	83.	ⓐ	ⓑ	ⓒ	ⓓ
16.	ⓐ	ⓑ	ⓒ	ⓓ	50.	ⓐ	ⓑ	ⓒ	ⓓ	84.	ⓐ	ⓑ	ⓒ	ⓓ
17.	ⓐ	ⓑ	ⓒ	ⓓ	51.	ⓐ	ⓑ	ⓒ	ⓓ	85.	ⓐ	ⓑ	ⓒ	ⓓ
18.	ⓐ	ⓑ	ⓒ	ⓓ	52.	ⓐ	ⓑ	ⓒ	ⓓ	86.	ⓐ	ⓑ	ⓒ	ⓓ
19.	ⓐ	ⓑ	ⓒ	ⓓ	53.	ⓐ	ⓑ	ⓒ	ⓓ	87.	ⓐ	ⓑ	ⓒ	ⓓ
20.	ⓐ	ⓑ	ⓒ	ⓓ	54.	ⓐ	ⓑ	ⓒ	ⓓ	88.	ⓐ	ⓑ	ⓒ	ⓓ
21.	ⓐ	ⓑ	ⓒ	ⓓ	55.	ⓐ	ⓑ	ⓒ	ⓓ	89.	ⓐ	ⓑ	ⓒ	ⓓ
22.	ⓐ	ⓑ	ⓒ	ⓓ	56.	ⓐ	ⓑ	ⓒ	ⓓ	90.	ⓐ	ⓑ	ⓒ	ⓓ
23.	ⓐ	ⓑ	ⓒ	ⓓ	57.	ⓐ	ⓑ	ⓒ	ⓓ	91.	ⓐ	ⓑ	ⓒ	ⓓ
24.	ⓐ	ⓑ	ⓒ	ⓓ	58.	ⓐ	ⓑ	ⓒ	ⓓ	92.	ⓐ	ⓑ	ⓒ	ⓓ
25.	ⓐ	ⓑ	ⓒ	ⓓ	59.	ⓐ	ⓑ	ⓒ	ⓓ	93.	ⓐ	ⓑ	ⓒ	ⓓ
26.	ⓐ	ⓑ	ⓒ	ⓓ	60.	ⓐ	ⓑ	ⓒ	ⓓ	94.	ⓐ	ⓑ	ⓒ	ⓓ
27.	ⓐ	ⓑ	ⓒ	ⓓ	61.	ⓐ	ⓑ	ⓒ	ⓓ	95.	ⓐ	ⓑ	ⓒ	ⓓ
28.	ⓐ	ⓑ	ⓒ	ⓓ	62.	ⓐ	ⓑ	ⓒ	ⓓ	96.	ⓐ	ⓑ	ⓒ	ⓓ
29.	ⓐ	ⓑ	ⓒ	ⓓ	63.	ⓐ	ⓑ	ⓒ	ⓓ	97.	ⓐ	ⓑ	ⓒ	ⓓ
30.	ⓐ	ⓑ	ⓒ	ⓓ	64.	ⓐ	ⓑ	ⓒ	ⓓ	98.	ⓐ	ⓑ	ⓒ	ⓓ
31.	ⓐ	ⓑ	ⓒ	ⓓ	65.	ⓐ	ⓑ	ⓒ	ⓓ	99.	ⓐ	ⓑ	ⓒ	ⓓ
32.	ⓐ	ⓑ	ⓒ	ⓓ	66.	ⓐ	ⓑ	ⓒ	ⓓ	100.	ⓐ	ⓑ	ⓒ	ⓓ
33.	ⓐ	ⓑ	ⓒ	ⓓ	67.	ⓐ	ⓑ	ⓒ	ⓓ					
34.	ⓐ	ⓑ	ⓒ	ⓓ	68.	ⓐ	ⓑ	ⓒ	ⓓ					

PART ONE: READING COMPREHENSION

Following are several reading passages. Answer the questions that come after each, based solely on the information in the passages.

Most criminals do not suffer from antisocial personality disorder; however, nearly all persons with this disorder have been in trouble with the law. Sometimes labeled "sociopaths," they are a grim problem for society. Their crimes range from con games to murder, and they are set apart by what appears to be a complete lack of conscience. Often attractive and charming, and always inordinately self-confident, they nevertheless demonstrate a disturbing emotional shallowness, as if they had been born without a faculty as vital as sight or hearing. These individuals are not legally insane, nor do they suffer from the distortions of thought associated with mental illness; however, some experts believe they are mentally ill. If so, it is an illness that is exceptionally resistant to treatment, particularly since these individuals have a marked inability to learn from the past. It is this latter trait that makes them a special problem for law enforcement officials. Their ability to mimic true emotion enables them to convince prison officials, judges, and psychiatrists that they feel remorse. When released from incarceration, however, they go back to their old tricks, to their con games, their impulsive destructiveness, and their sometimes lethal deceptions.

1. Based on the passage, which of the following is likely NOT a characteristic of the person with antisocial personality disorder?
   a. delusions of persecution
   b. feelings of superiority
   c. inability to suffer deeply
   d. inability to feel joy

2. Which of the following careers would probably best suit the person with antisocial personality?
   a. soldier with ambition to make officer
   b. warden of a large penitentiary
   c. loan officer in a bank
   d. salesperson dealing in nonexistent real estate

3. Based on the passage, which of the following words best sums up the inner emotional life of the person with antisocial personality?
   a. angry
   b. empty
   c. anxious
   d. repressed

4. According to the passage, which of the following characteristics is most helpful to the person with antisocial personality in terms of getting out of trouble with the law?
   a. inability to learn from the past
   b. ability to mimic the emotions of others
   c. attractiveness and charm
   d. indifference to the suffering of others

Police officers are held to a higher standard of conduct than most citizens. Should an officer behave in a disruptive manner, make an offensive joke, or behave in an otherwise uncivil manner, even while off duty, community leaders, public officials, and the media react not only with disapprobation and censure, but even with surprise. A police officer is expected to be an idealist even though he or she confronts human nature at its most disillusioning every day.

This is as it should be. As police officers are the keepers of civil order, they must exemplify civil behavior. Civil order depends less upon legal coercion than upon mutual respect and common ideals. Committed to the ideals of justice and truth, police officers must practice fairness and accuracy, even in their speech. Sworn to uphold individual rights, they must treat every individual with respect. A high standard of civil conduct is not merely a matter of community relations, but speaks to the essence of a police officer's role. By the same token, the public should treat police officers with the respect due those who must adhere to a higher standard of tolerance, understanding, moderation, and civility, even while working under extraordinarily trying conditions.

5. Which of the following best expresses the main idea of the passage?
- **a.** High standards should apply to businessmen as well as to police officers.
- **b.** Police officers are held to unrealistic standards of behavior.
- **c.** Police officers must remain idealistic, despite the disillusioning nature of their work.
- **d.** A police officer should uphold common ideals, both as expressed in law and as required to keep the peace.

6. The passage suggests that police officers should refrain from racial slurs for all of the following reasons EXCEPT
- **a.** As generalizations, such slurs are unfair and inaccurate.
- **b.** Such slurs are disrespectful to individuals.
- **c.** Such slurs harm the relationship between the community and the police.
- **d.** Such slurs are hurtful to the morale of a multiracial police force.

7. Which of the following is the best title for the passage?
- **a.** The Definition of Civil Order
- **b.** Why the Police Deserve Respect
- **c.** Civil Conduct for Police Officers
- **d.** Why Police Officers Should Be Tolerant

8. Why does civil conduct *speak to the very essence of a police officer's role?*
- **a.** because a police officer is a public servant
- **b.** because a police officer who behaves in an uncivil manner meets with public censure
- **c.** because civil conduct is necessary in order to keep the civil peace
- **d.** because a police officer upholds the law

9. Which of the following is NOT mentioned in the passage as a quality a police officer must exemplify?
- **a.** politeness
- **b.** courage
- **c.** justice
- **d.** moderation

In the past two decades, law enforcement officers have welcomed the advent of new technologies, which have aided them greatly in their work. These include long-range eavesdropping devices and computer scanners that allow police to identify possible suspects by merely typing a license number into a computer in the patrol car. The scanner allows instant access to motor vehicle and criminal records, and gives officers the opportunity to snare wrongdoers, even when they are not involved in criminal activity at the time. Police departments have praised the use of computers, which they say help them get criminals off the streets and out of the way of honest citizens. Not all of those citizens agree with this attitude, however, some believe that arrests made solely on the basis of scanner identification constitute an invasion of privacy. They regard the accessing of records as illegal search and seizure. In New Jersey, Florida, and Arizona, citizens who believe that their constitutional rights have been violated have filed lawsuits. They believe that much computer-generated information is inaccurate and vulnerable to hackers who invade computer databases. Some believe that such information from scanners could be used to charge innocent citizens with crimes, or to target particular neighborhoods for harassment.

10. Which of the following best expresses the main idea of the passage?
a. New technologies are available to police officers.
b. Police officers are skeptical of new policing technologies.
c. New technologies raise questions of privacy.
d. New technologies may be discriminatory.

11. Computer scanners allow police to
a. identify suspects.
b. access computer databases.
c. locate wrongdoers.
d. all of the above

12. In this passage, the word *snare* most nearly means
a. to question.
b. to interrupt.
c. to capture.
d. to free.

Law enforcement officers often do not like taking time from their regular duties to testify in court, but testimony is an important part of an officer's job. To be good witnesses, officers should keep complete notes detailing any potentially criminal or actionable incidents. When on the witness stand, officers may refer to those notes to refresh their memory about particular events. It is also very important for officers to listen carefully to the questions asked by the lawyers and to provide only the information requested. Officers should never volunteer opinions or any extra information that is beyond the scope of a question.

13. According to the passage, an officer who is testifying in court
a. will be questioned by the judge.
b. may refer to his or her notes while on the witness stand.
c. must do so without pay.
d. appreciates taking a break from routine assignments.

14. This passage is probably taken from a
a. memo entitled "Proper Arrest Procedure."
b. newspaper article about crime prevention.
c. recruitment pamphlet for law enforcement officers.
d. officers' training manual.

15. According to the passage, testifying in court is
a. an important part of a law enforcement officer's job.
b. difficult, because lawyers try to trick witnesses.
c. less stressful for law enforcement officers than for other witnesses.
d. a waste of time, because judges usually let criminals off.

Police officers should be aware of the cultural beliefs and habits of the subcultures they are likely to serve in an urban environment. In one case, an African-American man was arrested for the murder of a woman who had been strangled with a pair of stockings missing their tops because he had similar stocking tops in his drawer. The white police officers were not aware that stocking tops were used in a hair styling process common in African-American communities at that time. Neither was the all-white jury. This shows why it is important not only that officers be culturally aware, but also that both police forces and juries reflect the diversity of their communities.

16. According to the passage, police officers need to be aware of the subcultures they serve because
   a. they are likely to be prejudiced.
   b. there could be hostility between the police and cultural minorities.
   c. their ignorance could lead to injustice.
   d. improved community relations will lead to more effective law enforcement.

17. The passage suggests that juries should reflect the diversity of the communities they serve in order to
   a. ensure that juries will be able to place the suspect in the context of the community.
   b. make juries more sympathetic to members of cultural minorities.
   c. reduce the possibility of bias in their verdicts.
   d. improve relations between the community and the criminal justice system.

The rules for obtaining evidence, set down in state and federal law, usually come to our attention when they work to the advantage of defendants in court, but these laws were not created with the courtroom in mind. They were formulated with the practical intent of shaping police procedure before the arrest, in order to ensure justice, thoroughness, and the preservation of civil liberties. A good police officer must be as well schooled in the rules for properly obtaining evidence as a defense lawyer is, or risk losing a conviction. When a case is thrown out of court or a defendant is released because of these evidentiary "technicalities," we are often angered and mystified, but we are not always aware of how these rules of evidence shape police procedure in positive ways every day.

18. According to the passage, rules of evidence are designed to ensure all of the following EXCEPT
   a. meticulousness in gathering evidence.
   b. proof of guilt.
   c. protection of individual rights.
   d. fairness of treatment.

19. According to the passage, why should a police officer know the rules of evidence?
   a. The rules protect the rights of the accused.
   b. The public does not appreciate the rules' importance.
   c. An officer must follow the rules to obtain a conviction.
   d. Following the rules protects officers from accusations of misconduct.

20. In saying that the intent of rules of evidence is *practical*, the author most likely means that
   a. the focus of the rules is on police procedures in the field rather than on legal maneuvers in court.
   b. the practical nature of the rules enables lawyers to use them in court to protect defendants.
   c. the framers of these rules designed them to maintain idealistic standards of fairness.
   d. the rules are often misused in court because of their limited scope.

PART TWO: PREPARING WRITTEN MATERIAL

Questions 21–29 consist of four numbered sentences. Choose the sentence order that would result in the best paragraph.

21. 1) Murder in the first degree is usually defined as the willful and premeditated killing of another. 2) A third definition of murder in the first degree is the killing of a police officer or corrections officer. 3) Finally, in some states, killing of a person while attempting to escape from lawful custody may be defined as first-degree murder. 4) It may also apply to situations where a person is killed during the commission of a felony.
   a. 4, 3, 1, 2
   b. 2, 1, 3, 4
   c. 3, 2, 4, 1
   d. 1, 4, 2, 3

22. 1) The jurors were, in fact, expected to investigate the facts of the case themselves. 2) When court was in session during the colonial times in America, the entire community gathered at the local courthouse to watch the proceedings. 3) Unlike today, colonial juries were encouraged to ask questions of the parties in the courtroom. 4) If jurors conducted an investigation today, the case would be thrown out.
   a. 2, 3, 1, 4
   b. 3, 4, 1, 2
   c. 3, 4, 2, 1
   d. 3, 2, 4, 1

23. 1) It was originally used as a military fort because of its strategic location. 2) The first civilian prisoners were transferred to the island after the 1906 earthquake in San Francisco; from that point on until it was officially closed in 1963, Alcatraz was regarded as one of the most impregnable civilian prisons in the world. 3) Alcatraz's first inmates were Civil War military prisoners who arrived in 1861. 4) Alcatraz, also known as "The Rock," is located at the mouth of San Francisco Bay.
   a. 1, 4, 2, 3
   b. 2, 1, 4, 3
   c. 4, 1, 3, 2
   d. 4, 2, 4, 1

24. 1) It would not be fair if the suspect was, for example, much taller than all the other people in the line-up. 2) Police are allowed to require a suspect to participate in a line-up in front of a witness for identification. 3) Nor should the witness be allowed to see the suspect away from the other participants, perhaps in handcuffs or other restraints. 4) However, the police cannot construct the line-up in a way that suggests to the witness which person he or she should identify.
   a. 3, 2, 1, 4
   b. 1, 3, 4, 2
   c. 2, 4, 1, 3
   d. 4, 1, 2, 3

25. 1) Among these exceptions is the exigent circumstances exception. 2) There are only a few exceptions to the requirement that a police officer must obtain a search warrant before searching for evidence of a crime. 3) However, whether a search is conducted with a warrant or without, an officer must always be able to show that there was probable cause to believe a search was necessary. 4) In order for a warrantless exigent search to be valid, a police officer must show both that there was no time to obtain a warrant and that it was reasonable to believe evidence would be destroyed or that people were in danger.

    a. 2, 1, 4, 3
    b. 4, 2, 3, 1
    c. 2, 3, 4, 1
    d. 2, 3, 1, 4

26. 1) You'll quickly learn that a prison is like a small community, and each corrections officer has a particular responsibility within that community. 2) If you decide to become a corrections officer, every day on the job will bring a different challenge. 3) Most important of all, you'll soon realize that the risks involved in the occupation are far outweighed by the rewards. 4) But no matter what your particular role, all corrections officers must be effective at handling crises, resolving conflicts, and be willing to serve as mentors and teachers.

    a. 1, 4, 2, 3
    b. 2, 1, 4, 3
    c. 1, 2, 4, 3
    d. 4, 2, 1, 3

27. 1) Finally, about 16,000 jobs for corrections officers were in federal correctional institutions, and about 16,000 jobs were in privately owned and managed prisons. 2) Roughly three out of every five jobs were in state correctional institutions. 3) According to the U.S. Department of Labor, corrections officers held about 476,000 jobs in 2002. 4) Most of the remaining jobs were in city and county jails, or other institutions run by local governments.

    a. 2, 3, 1, 4
    b. 3, 4, 1, 2
    c. 2, 4, 3, 1
    d. 3, 2, 4, 1

28. 1) Officer Harris is three blocks away from the warehouse and tells the dispatcher she will respond to the call. 2) In the call, the dispatcher states that the alarm has already sounded three times in the past four hours. 3) She then parks down the block from the warehouse and radios the dispatcher that she has arrived. 4) The dispatcher puts out a call of a burglar alarm at a warehouse at 410 Fourth Avenue.

    a. 4, 3, 1, 4
    b. 4, 2, 1, 3
    c. 2, 4, 1, 3
    d. 3, 4, 2, 1

29. 1) For example, a man in Texas was convicted of stealing the guns belonging to Clayton Moore, TV's Lone Ranger. 2) Another example of this kind of sentence is when convicted drunk drivers are ordered to place a bumper sticker on their car that publicizes their crime. 3) In addition to a fine and probation, the gun thief was ordered to complete 600 hours of community service cleaning the Houston Police Department's horse stables. 4) In recent years, courts have begun handing down criminal sentences that include an element of humiliation.
   a. 1, 4, 2, 3
   b. 2, 1, 4, 3
   c. 4, 1, 3, 2
   d. 3, 2, 4, 1

For questions 30–33, choose the sentence that best describes the underlined sentence into one.

30. I ate a very large plate of spaghetti.
   I still have room for dessert.
   a. Because I ate a very large plate of spaghetti, I still have room for dessert.
   b. I ate a very large plate of spaghetti, because I still have room for dessert.
   c. However I ate a very large plate of spaghetti; I still have room for dessert.
   d. I ate a very large plate of spaghetti, but I still have room for dessert.

31. Joseph is an intelligent man.
   Joseph cannot read or write.
   a. Joseph cannot read or write, while he is an intelligent man.
   b. Joseph cannot read or write and is an intelligent man.
   c. Although Joseph cannot read or write, he is an intelligent man.
   d. Being an intelligent man, Joseph cannot read or write.

32. Everybody in John's family is tall.
   His brother is almost seven feet.
   a. Everybody in John's family is tall; for example, his brother is almost seven feet.
   b. Everybody in John's family is tall; rather, his brother is almost seven feet.
   c. Everybody in John's family is tall; in contrast, his brother is almost seven feet.
   d. Everybody in John's family is tall; on the contrary, his brother is almost seven feet.

33. This area of the country is called "tornado alley."
   Many tornadoes roar through here every spring.
   a. Many tornadoes roar through here every spring, while this area of the country is called "tornado alley."
   b. Many tornadoes roar through here every spring, but this area of the country is called "tornado alley."
   c. Many tornadoes roar through here every spring; therefore, this area of the country is called "tornado alley."
   d. This area of the country is called "tornado alley"; meanwhile, many tornadoes roar through here every spring.

In questions 34–40, a portion of the sentence is underlined. Under each section there are four ways of phrasing the underlined option. Choice **a** repeats the original underlined portion; the other three provide alternative choices. Select the choice that best expresses the meaning of the original sentence. If the original sentence is better than any of the alternatives, chose option **a**.

34. The case-breaking tip came from an anynonimous source.
   a. anynonimous
   b. anonimous
   c. anounymous
   d. anonymous

35. The lacrosse team scored <u>less goals today than they did</u> last Monday.
  a. less goals today than they did
  b. lesser goals today than they did
  c. few goals today than they did
  d. fewer goals today than they did

36. Nobody on the team <u>skates more graceful than me.</u>
  a. skates more graceful than me.
  b. skates more gracefully than I do.
  c. skates gracefuller than I do.
  d. skates more graceful than I do.

37. Many criminologists <u>maintain, that severe</u> sentences do deter crime.
  a. maintain, that severe
  b. maintain that, severe
  c. maintain that severe
  d. maintain—that severe

38. <u>The Mississippi River, it originates in Minnesota,</u> empties into the Gulf of Mexico.
  a. The Mississippi River, it originates in Minnesota,
  b. The Mississippi River, that originates in Minnesota,
  c. The Mississippi River, who originates in Minnesota,
  d. The Mississippi River, which originates in Minnesota,

39. <u>There wasn't never a comedian that was funnier.</u>
  a. There wasn't never a comedian that was funnier.
  a. There never was a funnier comedian.
  a. Never was there a comedian more funnier.
  a. There was never a comedian more funnier.

40. The corrections officer presented a(n) <u>ultimatum</u> to inmate Willis regarding the contraband found in his cell—next time, he would be placed in solitary.
  a. ultimatum
  b. petition
  c. question
  d. inquiry

PART THREE: MATH

Questions 41–50 are followed by four answer choices. Select the choice that best answers the question.

41. Police confiscated 6,000 kg of marijuana in a drug bust. The marijuana was packaged in 5-kg bags. How many bags of marijuana did the police confiscate?
a. 1,200 bags
b. 600 bags
c. 300 bags
d. 20 bags

42. $\frac{3}{4}$ is equal to
a. 0.50.
b. 0.25.
c. 0.75.
d. 0.30.

43. You are trying to keep your employees from working overtime, which is anything over 40 hours in a week. If there is an employee who already has worked 9 hours on Monday, 6.5 hours on Tuesday, 8 hours on Thursday, and 10.5 hours on Friday, how many hours can you schedule that employee to work on Saturday?
a. 5 hours
b. 5.5 hours
c. 6 hours
d. 4.5 hours

44.   292
         $\times$ 50
a. 14,600
b. 14,500
c. 10,500
d. 1,450

45. The prison kitchen just received a shipment of 1,260 cans of soup that need to be stored. If each shelf holds 9 cans, how many shelves will be needed to store all of the soup?
a. 90 shelves
b. 140 shelves
c. 160 shelves
d. 320 shelves

46. $76\frac{1}{2}$
         $+\quad 11\frac{5}{6}$
         _____

a. $87\frac{1}{2}$
b. $88\frac{2}{3}$
c. $88\frac{1}{3}$
d. $89\frac{1}{6}$

47. There are 65 applicants for 4 job openings. Approximately how many people are applying per job?
a. 15
b. 16
c. 17
d. 18

Refer to the following table for questions 48–49

	PORTION OF ASSIGNMENT
Doug	0.25
Jane	0.10
A.J.	0.05
Marie	0.60

48. What fraction of the project was Marie responsible for?

a. $\frac{1}{4}$

b. $\frac{3}{5}$

c. $\frac{2}{5}$

d. $\frac{1}{5}$

49. If Jane dropped out of the group and A.J. took over her part of the project, what fraction was A.J. then responsible for?

a. $\frac{1}{4}$

b. $\frac{1}{5}$

c. $\frac{1}{10}$

d. $\frac{3}{20}$

50. $3^2 \times 3^4 =$

a. 3^6

b. 3^8

c. 6^6

d. 6^8

PART FOUR: MEMORY, OBSERVATION, AND COUNTING

Following are a a drawing of a street scene, and a short reading passage. Study these for ten minutes. At the end of ten minutes, turn the page and answer the 20 questions without referring back to the study material. You have five minutes to answer the questions. If you refer back to the study material after ten minutes are up, you will be disqualified. When the five minutes are up, you may continue with the rest of the test.

On Friday, October 1, 2004, Corrections Officer Todd Rodriguez reported to his new assignment in the visitor's room in the main building of Rockland Prison. Senior Corrections Officer Mike Ling was training him on the day shift. Officer Rodriguez had graduated from the academy just two months prior. Besides Officer Ling, Officer Rodriguez would also be working with Officer Rodney White and Officer Jim Tuttle. They were veterans with three and four years of day shift experience, respectively.

At 8:00 A.M. sharp, Officer Rodriguez reported to duty. Officer Ling took Officer Rodriguez into the visitor's room and told him to familiarize himself with the layout of the room. He was introduced to Officers White and Tuttle. Ling told the young officer that the room holds a maximum of 16 inmates at a time. One inmate and one visitor are to sit at one of the 16 metal tables. Each table has two metal chairs, one on each side of each table. All furnishings are bolted to the floor in the room. The concrete floor is painted white, except for a red line leading from the inner hallway that the inmates use to get to the visitor's room. The red line is painted 14 inches from the right-hand side of the wall and goes completely around the room to end up back at the doorway. Officer Ling instructed Officer Rodriguez that all inmates are expected to walk along the red line to enter and exit the room. If they refuse to walk the line, their visiting privileges are immediately revoked. The walls are white and the ceiling is gray. There are no windows.

Officer Ling told Officer Rodriguez that he is responsible for doing a pat-down search of each inmate before allowing the inmate into the room. The visitors are all thoroughly searched before they are allowed to enter the room. After Officer Rodriguez pats the inmates down, he is to allow the visitors into the room. Each visitor is allowed a maximum of 30 minutes with the inmate. If the inmate has two visitors, one visitor must remain in the waiting room next door until it is his or her turn. But no matter how many visitors come for an inmate, the inmate is allowed only one session of 30 minutes. At the end of this time period, the officer is to make sure the visitors stay seated while the inmates are escorted to the doorway leading back into the corridor. Officer Rodriguez is to do another pat-down search of each inmate before the inmate passes through the doorway and into the hall. After each inmate is searched and turned over to the escorting officer, Officer Rodriguez is to let the visitors know that they may exit the room.

51. What color is the line painted on the floor of the visitor's room?
  a. beige
  b. yellow
  c. red
  d. green

52. What is Officer Rodriguez's training officer's last name?
  a. Lang
  b. White
  c. Tuttle
  d. Ling

53. What is the maximum number of inmates allowed into the visitor's room at one time?
  a. 15
  b. 16
  c. 14
  d. 12

54. What time did Officer Rodriguez report for duty on his first day at his new assignment?
  a. 8:00 A.M.
  b. 7:30 A.M.
  c. 7:00 A.M.
  d. 6:45 A.M.

55. What should Officer Rodriguez instruct visitors to do while inmates are exiting the visitor's room?
   a. exit by another door
   b. remain seated until the inmates have left
   c. stand by their chairs and wait to be searched
   d. stand on the line on the floor until the inmates have left

56. How far from the wall is the line painted that the inmates are required to walk along?
   a. 10 inches
   b. 12 inches
   c. 14 inches
   d. 16 inches

57. What day of the week did Officer Rodriguez report to his new duty assignment?
   a. Monday
   b. Friday
   c. Thursday
   d. Wednesday

58. What kind of search is Officer Rodriguez required to conduct on each inmate?
   a. strip
   b. spread
   c. pat-down
   d. full-body

59. How long is a visitor permitted to see an inmate?
   a. 15 minutes
   b. 20 minutes
   c. 25 minutes
   d. 30 minutes

60. What color is the ceiling in the visitor's room?
   a. gray
   b. red
   c. white
   d. blue

61. The scene is taking place on which street corner?
   a. Grand Dr. at 8 St.
   b. Green Blvd. at 6 Ave.
   c. Grant Sq. at 7 Ave.
   d. Georges Blvd. at 5 St.

62. The street number of the drug store is
   a. 311.
   b. 312.
   c. 411.
   d. 412.

63. The man with the gun is standing next to
   a. the hot dog stand.
   b. Johnny's Bar.
   c. the woman carrying the shopping bag.
   d. the trash can.

64. What is the name printed on the newsstand?
   a. Al's News
   b. Ace News
   c. Abe's News
   d. A + G News

65. What is exiting from the bus?
   a. a group of senior citizens
   b. a group of middle-aged tourists
   c. a group of school children
   d. a group of teenagers

66. The name printed on the truck in the street is
   a. Adam's Market.
   b. Alfonse's Fine Merchandising.
   c. Alvin's Fresh Produce.
   d. Al's Fruit Market.

67. What name is printed on the hot dog stand?
   a. Tony
   b. Frank
   c. Henry
   d. Toby

68. What is written above the bus's open door?

a. Al's Tour Bus

b. Ajax Tours

c. All Around Tours

d. A-1 Bus Tours

69. What is the phone number for the dentist office?

a. 555-3030

b. 555-2020

c. 555-2200

d. 555-3300

70. The elderly man about to be mugged is carrying

a. a shopping bag.

b. an umbrella.

c. a suit coat.

d. an overcoat.

You have 1 minute to answer questions 71–75. When the minute is up, you may continue with the rest of the test.

71. How many letter r's are there in the following sentence?

The warden, Margaret Appleton, started out as a corrections officer in this prison and was promoted all the way up through the ranks to reach the pinnacle of her career.

a. 13

b. 14

c. 15

d. 16

72. How many diamonds are needed to complete this pattern?

a. 6

b. 7

c. 8

d. 9

73. How many upper case vowels are there in this set?

```
M q u c A A B F
N E n A N r r G
O o o V S s I E
P P e A p U p p
```

a. 8

b. 9

c. 10

d. 11

74. How many circled white 2s (②) are in the following set?

②③②①③②③
②③❶②②❶❸
❸③❷①❶②❸
①❷①②②②❶

a. 7

b. 8

c. 9

d. 10

75. How many 7s are in the following set?

```
4 8 3 2 9 8 4 6 7
4 2 6 3 8 3 6 3 8
3 3 2 9 8 6 3 4 7
3 7 4 9 3 8 2 7 4
0 9 7 4 3 0 9 7 3
```

a. 5
b. 6
c. 7
d. 8

PART FIVE: APPLYING WRITTEN MATERIALS

Following is a set of rules and procedures for corrections officers. Please read them and choose the best answer to the following questions, based on good judgment and common sense.

The Rules and Regulations of the Corrections Officer Manual states:

Inmates that are housed in a separate secure facility for their and the general population's safety are handled in a manner that is indigenous to that population. The inmates that are housed here are listed under the following categories: pedophiles, former members of law enforcement, those afflicted with contagious diseases, and those under protective custody.

Officers must not communicate with inmates in a manner that would suggest nepotism, favoritism, or prejudice. All officers must be screened and instructed to reveal any pre-association with inmates, conflict of interest, or prior family history.

In the event of an officer becoming aware that he has prior knowledge of an inmate, the officer should complete the following steps:

1. The officer should not communicate with the inmate. Remove himself or herself from the environment where the inmate is housed.
2. The officer should immediately request a change in officer assignment for the area.
3. The officer should proceed to his supervisor's office and notify him or her, of the potential conflict of interest, familial association or prior association with the inmate.
4. A written record of the contact of the past history as well as the current contact should be noted.
5. An assignment which would provide future non-contact with the inmate should be initiated: transfer to another wing, level, or the special assignment of an officer to handle all details for that specific inmate.
6. In the event that the inmate initiates contact with the officer, the administration should be notified immediately to prevent potential problems.
7. Maintenance of the correctional facility is the responsibility of the administration.

Life Threatening Illness

Inmates with life threatening or contagious diseases should be treated with confidentiality. The type of illness should not be disclosed since it interferes with the inmates' Rights and Privileges. Officers should be warned about protecting themselves from becoming infected. All officers, male or female, are barred from having sexual contact with ALL inmates.

The commanding officer is responsible for maintaining all confidential records and assigning officers to various tasks. Written directions must be posted so that all officers are aware of the necessary steps to take to prevent illness or injury and maintain their health.

All documents pertaining to an inmate's medical needs must be secured in a locked and secure environment.

A list of the ACCESS ONLY individuals should be posted.

If an officer becomes aware of an inmate's illness, great attempts must be made to maintain confidentiality.

In the event that an officer knowingly divulges an inmate's medical status, he or she will be brought up on disciplinary charges.

In the event that an inmate with a contagious illness knowingly tries to harm an officer, he or she will be prosecuted by the full extent of the law.

Telephone Access

Officers are barred from conducting personal telephone calls for inmates. Officers are barred from providing inmates with access to cellular telephones to make personal calls.

All telephone calls must be made from the designated telephones assigned by the Department of Corrections. Inmates are not allowed to request personal favors from officers.

All requests should be reported to a superior officer. The name of the inmate, the contact person, and the number requested should be reported and recorded. The information should be forwarded to the Information officer.

76. During a routine bed check, Officer Motant realizes that the inmate in Cellblock 15 is a former fraternity brother from college. What should Officer Motant do?
    a. He should introduce himself and recount their past histories.
    b. He should remove himself from the area and notify his supervisor.
    c. He should mandate that the inmate keep quiet about past associations.
    d. He should identify himself, contact his supervisor, and write a detailed report of his association.

77. During a casual conversation with inmate Orangy, Officer Creek was informed that inmate Orangy was HIV+. What should Officer Creek do?
    a. Tell the inmate that he is glad that he was notified of the HIV status.
    b. Tell the inmate that he should remain quiet about his medical status.
    c. Contact all officers that are assigned to the unit and inform them of the inmate's revelations.
    d. Keep the information confidential.

78. During roll call, inmates Chui and Wong noticed that Officer Williams possessed a cellular telephone in his belt pocket. They requested that he contact a family member at 123-456-7890 to send them money for the commissary. Officer Williams should:
    a. state to the inmates that officers are barred from making personal calls.
    b. take their request and forward it to his superior officer.
    c. make the phone call and proceed to record the request.
    d. a and b

79. Officers have become aware that two inmates are involved in sexual activities. One of the inmates is HIV positive. Upon realizing this, the officer should
    a. alert the other staff members about the possible danger.
    b. inform his/her immediate supervisor of this knowledge.
    c. maintain strict confidentiality and keep it to himself/herself.
    d. discreetly confront the two inmates and inform them of the possible danger.

80. While on vacation, Officer Hughley received a call on his personal cellular telephone from inmate White's father requesting an update on his son's status. What statement should Officer Hughley choose to inform the father?
  a. I am not privileged to provide that data.
  b. I am on vacation.
  c. Where and how did you get my number? I will be notifying my supervisor of this incident immediately.
  d. a and c

81. Officer Hotley hears an inmate talking intimately after lockdown. He realizes that two inmates are discussing potential sexual intimacy. One of them has been diagnosed with tuberculosis. Officer Hotley should
  a. write a report outlining the incident.
  b. inform his supervisors, who will have a medical team discuss proper health procedures with the inmates separately.
  c. reprimand them for conversing after the designated lock down period.
  d. refuse future privileges for each inmate after he has been brought before a specific committee convened to handle incidents among inmates.

82. Officer Nariz has decided to review inmate personnel files. He is not one of the members with ACCESS. What action should be taken by administration?
  a. He should be brought up on charges for invading the privacy of the inmates.
  b. No action should be taken against him since he is assigned to the inmates' level.
  c. He should be issued a warning and advised not to divulge any information learned from his activity.
  d. He should be fined and the infraction recorded in his personnel file.

83. During the course of his rounds, Officer Postage noticed an unwrapped package detailing pedophile activities in inmate Harkey's cell. In this situation, what order of operations should be conducted?
  1. Confiscate the materials.
  2. Prepare a detailed incident report.
  3. Notify the supervisor on duty.
  a. 1, 2, 3
  b. 3, 1, 2
  c. 3, 2, 1
  d. 1, 3, 2

84. Inmate Jadgarric has been observed sharing personal fluids with inmate Jones. Administration should be commanded to do the following:
  a. Have AIDS/HIV related seminars to advise the inmate population of the need to be safe when engaging in high risk behavior.
  b. Take no action since inmates should know better than to conduct activity that would be deemed high risk.
  c. Advise all of the other inmates to refrain from communicating with inmate Jadgarric.
  d. none of the above

85. Officer Sockbond conducts casual conversations with an inmate who was indicted for Insider Information. From the information that is garnered, he proceeds to invest in the stock market. Due to a down turn in the market, he loses his investment. Officer Sockbond should
  a. disclose his investments in his I-9.
  b. confront the inmate and demand that he give him further advice.
  c. take the loss and move on, but not directly ask for advice.
  d. casually mention it to the inmate but not directly ask for advice.

86. Inmate Lector was sexually intimate with Officer Santiago ten years ago. Fifteen years later inmate Lector is assigned to Officer Santiago's unit. During inmate Lector's confinement the relationship was rekindled. Officer Johnson recently discovered the relationship. Officer Johnson should
   a. tell Officer Santiago to terminate the relationship.
   b. mind her own business and stay out of it.
   c. notify her superior officer.
   d. tell the inmate to terminate the relationship.

87. Officers Brac, Crucksank, Sawyer, and Hoyt were discussing recent inmates that were admitted. Two of the officers failed to divulge a familial connection between two inmates with different last names. The inmates requested a meeting with the superior officer to discuss cruel and unusual punishment at the hands of the officers in the unit. All the officers except Hoyt and Sawyer were named in the petition. A number of officers requested a review to ascertain why these officers were exempt. An investigation by the Inspector General's office revealed the following information: Sawyer and Hoyt are married to second cousins of three of the inmates assigned to their unit. Describe, in order of operation, what Officers Hoyt and Sawyer should have done. This is an open question with a number of acceptable responses. Pick the best answer.
   a. Officers Hoyt and Sawyer may not have been aware of the familial connection.
   b. The inmates may have been using prior knowledge of their familial connection to gain negotiations supremacy.
   c. Officers Hoyt and Sawyer may have kept quiet because they may not have wanted to be reassigned and did not believe that the extended familial connection was of any consequence.
   d. Both officers should have notified the supervisor immediately.

88. During Officer Levy's tour, he realizes that there are three showers and 30 inmates assigned to his housing area. One of the showers is inoperable. the officer should
   a. have the inmates plunge the shower that is not working.
   b. notify the maintenance staff to do immediate repairs.
   c. allow inmates to go to another housing unit's shower.
   d. do nothing since two showers are functioning.

89. A prison gang, who call themselves "The Black Angels," have been responsible for a recent string of violence. Officer Manning observes a group of suspected gang members conferring during dinner. They are heard discussing the details of a planned attack on a rival inmate. Officer Manning should
   a. perform a search of their cells while they are absent.
   b. immediately inform the supervisor and then request a lockdown of the cellblock in order to perform an immediate search of their cells, and conduct a body cavity search.
   c. separate the prisoners and place them in different cellblocks.
   d. put in a request for the transfer of the suspected gang leader and place him in isolation.

90. Officer Samson observed an inmate writing on the wall which constitutes defacing institutional property. In this situation the officer should
   a. Write the inmate a disciplinary ticket.
   b. Verbally counsel the inmate about his/her actions.
   c. a and b
   d. none of the above

PART SIX: APPLYING WRITTEN MATERIALS

Following is another set of rules and procedures for corrections officers. Based on these, answer the questions that follow them. You may refer back to the rules and procedures as often as needed.

Corrections officers are often required to use force to subdue inmates in certain situations or when physical altercations occur. It is each officer's duty to use the least amount of force possible in these situations, starting with voice control and progressing to departmentally approved holds and/or weapons.

Often inmates must be transported from prison facilities to courthouses for trials or other legal proceedings. Certain high-risk inmates must be transported in full restraints. To transport an inmate to the courthouse:

1. The officer should first check the vehicle in which the inmate will be transported, to make sure no weapons or contraband have been left by previous occupants.
2. The transport officer should thoroughly search the inmate.
3. After ensuring that the inmate has no weapons or contraband, the officer should place the inmate in leg irons and handcuffs with the inmate's hands behind his or her back with palms facing outward.
4. The officer should seat the inmate in the vehicle and secure him or her with a seat belt, if seat belts are available.
5. The officer will transport the inmate directly to the appropriate location without stopping.
6. Upon arrival, the transport officer will remove the inmate from the vehicle and then check the vehicle for contraband or weapons left by the inmate.

7. The transport officer will turn the inmate over to a receiving officer at the courthouse.

If an inmate should escape during transport, the transport officer should:
1. Immediately contact dispatch to request assistance.
2. Report the location and means of the escape.
3. Report the direction and method of travel of the escapee.
4. Provide the name and a physical description of the inmate.
5. Use all reasonable and necessary means to recapture the prisoner.
6. Be prepared to submit a detailed report outlining the circumstances of the escape.

Corrections officers are encouraged to develop open communication with the inmates in their care. Officers should never make promises to inmates that they cannot keep, nor should they fail to follow through with what they promise the inmate they will do.

91. Transport Officer Ming is preparing to drive inmate Polk to the courthouse for a hearing on her part in last month's escape attempt. Officer Ming thoroughly searches the van for weapons or contraband, searches the inmate, and then places her in leg irons and handcuffs. What should she do next?
   a. Drive directly to the courthouse.
   b. Call the courthouse to let them know she is on the way.
   c. Sign the logbook to show that she is the transporting officer.
   d. Seat inmate Polk in the vehicle and secure the seat belt around her.

92. While transporting inmate Hayes to the prison, Officer Presotto's transport vehicle is involved in an accident with another vehicle and is forced off the road. Officer Presotto is temporarily dazed by the accident, but when he regains his bearings he realizes that inmate Hayes has managed to escape; he spots him on the other side of the highway. Officer Presotto immediately takes off in foot pursuit of inmate Hayes. Officer Presotto acted

   a. properly; Officer Presotto was forced to make a snap judgment.

   a. properly; the accident was not his fault.

   a. improperly; Officer Presotto should have radioed dispatch before engaging in pursuit.

   a. improperly; he should have first fired a warning shot in the air to slow inmate Hayes down.

93. Officers Romney and Pagel break up a fight between two inmates in Cellblock D. The fighters calm down and voluntarily walk with the officers when the officers order them to accompany them to segregation cells. On the way to the cell, Officer Romney strikes one of the inmates in the back of the head when the inmate asks where they are going. Officer Romney acted

   a. improperly; his use of force against an unresisting inmate is unwarranted and illegal.

   b. improperly; he should have hit the inmate on the leg, not the head, as this would be less injurious.

   c. properly; the inmate might possibly stir up trouble again by talking.

   d. properly; the inmate should be punished for fighting.

94. A female motorist with a flat tire tried to flag Officer Goldberg over while he was transporting inmate Vincent to the courthouse. Although he had time to spare in reaching his destination, Officer Goldberg continued on his way to the courthouse without stopping. The officer acted

   a. improperly; as a public servant he was obligated to stop and render assistance.

   b. improperly; he easily had the time to stop.

   c. properly; transporting officers must take inmates directly to the appropriate location without stopping.

   d. properly; the officer would not be able to see what the inmate was doing if he pulled off the road to help the motorist.

95. Officer Gonzalez is about to place inmate Rhodes into the transport vehicle to take him to the courthouse. Rhodes has already been searched and properly shackled. As Officer Gonzalez is about to secure Rhodes in the seatbelt, Rhodes says he claustrophobic and would prefer to not be seat belted. What should Officer Gonzalez do?

   a. Allow inmate Rhodes to travel without a seatbelt, as long as he promises not to tell any other officer that he was allowed to do so.

   b. Secure Rhodes in the seatbelt, but unlock his handcuffs so he is more at ease.

   c. Handcuff Rhodes to the vehicle and then search out a supervisor to ask what to do.

   d. Secure Rhodes in the seatbelt, and tell him there are no exceptions to the rules.

96. Two inmates are talking in the doorway to the recreation yard. Inmate Washburn pushes inmate Wong, who hits his head on the concrete and is knocked unconscious. Officer Dodrill runs up with his nightstick at the ready to break up the fight. Inmate Washburn drops to his knees, throws his hands over his head, and says "I'll stop fighting. I give up, I give up." What should Officer Dodrill do?

a. He should strike the inmate once to make certain he is truly subdued.

b. He should tackle him and hold him down until help arrives.

c. He should restrain inmate Wong just in case he is faking his unconsciousness.

d. He should handcuff inmate Washburn.

97. Officer Quintana promises inmate Janikowski that before he leaves for the day he will let the next officer on duty know that he has given inmate Janikowski permission to make two trips to the library. Quintana leaves the facility thirty minutes later without relaying the promise to the officer who relieves him. Officer Quintana acted

a. properly; Inmate Janikowski can ask the next officer for permission to make two trips.

b. properly; officers are under no obligation to do favors for inmates.

c. improperly; officers should follow through with all promises they make to inmates.

d. improperly; it is not up to officers to make decisions about where inmates are allowed to go in a prison facility.

98. Officer Fitz is preparing to transport an inmate from the prison to the courthouse. When he arrives, the inmate has already been placed in leg irons. Officer Melvin tells Officer Fitz that he has already searched the inmate. Officer Fitz searches the inmate again. Officer Fitz acted

a. properly; the correct procedure for transporting officers is to thoroughly search the inmate.

b. properly; Officer Fitz has no way of knowing whether Officer Melvin really conducted the search.

c. improperly; Officer Fitz has insulted Officer Melvin's professionalism.

d. improperly; Officer Fitz is violating the inmate's civil rights by searching him again.

99. Officer Yardley arrives at the courthouse with an inmate and the inmate's lawyer greets him at the receiving entrance. The lawyer says that he will handle everything from there, and Yardley can return to the prison. What should Officer Yardley do?

a. Ask the lawyer for proper identification, and if everything checks out, hand the inmate over.

b. Find the proper receiving officer at the courthouse and hand the inmate over to only that officer.

c. Telephone the prison warden to find out if he is allowed to hand the inmate over to the inmate's lawyer.

d. Take the inmate directly to the judge presiding over the inmate's case.

100. Corrections Officer Pan has a hunch that inmate Gordon is going to assault inmate Wade at lunch. During lunch, inmate Gordon gets up from his table with his empty tray and walks in the direction of the garbage can, close to where inmate Wade is sitting. Officer Pan runs across the cafeteria and tackles inmate Gordon before he reaches the area where Wade is sitting. Officer Pan acted

a. properly; he successfully prevented a possible assault upon inmate Gordon.

b. properly; Pan set an example for the inmates that he won't tolerate violence amongst inmates.

c. improperly; Officer Pan should have first warned inmate Gordon of his hunch.

d. improperly; a simple hunch is not reason enough to subdue an inmate.

ANSWERS

Use the answers below not only to see how you did but also to understand why the correct answers are correct. For Memory and Observation questions, refer to the memory material to see why the answers are right.

1. a. The discussion of the traits of a person with anti-social personality disorder in the middle of the passage specifies that such a person does not have distortions of thought, such as delusions of persecution. The passage speaks of the antisocial person as being *inordinately self-confident* (choice **b**) and of the person's *emotional shallowness* (choices **c** and **d**).

2. d. The third sentence of the passage speaks of *con games*. None of the other professions would suit an impulsive, shallow person who has been in trouble with the law.

3. b. The passage mentions *emotional shallowness*. The other choices hint at the ability to feel meaningful emotion.

4. b. The passage says that a person with antisocial personality disorder can mimic real emotion, thereby conning prison officials, judges, and psychiatrists. The other choices are mentioned in the passage, but not in connection with getting out of trouble with the law.

5. d. The passage deals not only with the sphere of law, but more centrally with the sphere of values and civil conduct. Nowhere does the passage say that police officers should be *idealistic* (choice **c**).

6. d. Fairness and accuracy, respect for individuals, and the importance of maintaining community relations are all mentioned in the second paragraph. Maintaining morale on a multiracial force is also important, but it is not mentioned in the passage.

7. c. The importance of a police officer's civil conduct is mentioned several times throughout the passage. Therefore, choice **c**, *Civil Conduct for Police Officers*, is the best choice for the title.

8. c. The second sentence of the second paragraph states that because police officers are the *keepers of civil order, they must exemplify civil behavior.*

9. b. Moderation is explicitly referred to near the end of the second paragraph. Justice and politeness are synonymous with fairness and civil conduct. It's true that most police officers are certainly courageous, but courage is never mentioned in the passage.

10. c. This purpose of this passage is to describe the usefulness of some the new technologies (such as scanner identification) available to law enforcement officials, but also discuss the fact that some citizens *believe that arrests made solely on the basis of scanner identification constitute an invasion of privacy.*

11. d. The third and fourth sentences of passage state that computer scanners *allow police to identify possible suspects*, gain *instant access to motor vehicle and criminal records*, and give *officers the opportunity to snare wrongdoers.*

12. c. The word *snare* as it used in this passage most nearly means *to capture*. If you did not know the definition of *snare*, you could deduce its meaning in context from the very next sentence: *Police departments have praised the use of computers, which they say help them get criminals off the streets . . .*

13. b. The second and third sentences of the passage state that *officers should keep complete notes detailing any potentially criminal or actionable incidents* and the officers *may refer to those notes to refresh their memory about particular events.*

14. d. The passage provides information for law enforcement officers; so choice **d** is therefore the most logical choice. Choice **a** refers to a memo directed to police officers, but the subject matter is incorrect. The subject matter of choice **b** is also incorrect. The wording and tone of the passage do not seem to be attempting recruitment, as in choice **c**.

15. a. The first very first sentence of the passage states that testimony *is an important part of an officer's job . . .*

16. c. The suspect mentioned in the passage was arrested because the police were ignorant of a cultural practice in the African American community. The passage doesn't discuss racial prejudice.

17. a. Because neither the jury nor the police officers in the case mentioned in the passage were African American, they were unaware of the African-American community's hair-styling practice.

18. b. Proof of guilt is the whole point of gathering evidence, but this is never referred to in the passage.

19. c. This third sentence states that if an officer does not know or follow the rules, he or she *may risk losing a conviction.* Don't be fooled by choice **a**: The rules of evidence do protect the accused, but that is not the reason given for why an officer must know them.

20. a. The *practical intent* the author refers to in the second sentence is the purpose of shaping police procedure before arrest.

21. d. Sentence 1 introduces the topic, murder in the first degree. The phrase *it may also* in sentence 4 indicates a second definition of the topic; sentence 2 is a third definition; sentence 3, beginning as it does with the word *finally*, gives the last definition.

22. a. Sentence 2 introduces the general topic, courtroom proceedings during the colonial times. Sentence 3 explains how modern juries differ from colonial juries. Sentence 1 details the difference stated in sentence 3. Sentence 4 explains what

would happen if what was discussed in sentence 1 occurred today.

23. c. Sentence 4 introduces the topic, Alcatraz Island. Sentence 1 tells of the original use of the island; Sentence 3 expands upon those details. Sentence 2 discusses Alcatraz's transition to a civilian prison, and the mention of the prison's official closing in 1963 should indicate to you that this is the final sentence.

24. c. Sentence 2 is the topic sentence and notes what police are allowed to do. Sentence 4, introduced by *however*, indicates a limitation on police action. Sentences 1 and 3 give examples of the limitation, and since sentence 3 begins with *nor*, it must come after sentence 1.

25. a. Sentence 2 is the topic sentence. Sentence 1 gives an example of the topic; sentence 4 defines the example, and sentence 3 begins with *however*, indicating it is expanding on the example.

26. b. Sentence 2 establishes the topic, what a prospective corrections officer can expect on the job. Sentence 1 expands upon the topic sentence. Sentence 4 draws further upon the idea of the different roles of corrections officers indicated in sentence 1, and therefore should follow it. Sentence 3, introduced by *Most important of all*, wraps the four sentences up.

27. d. Sentence 3 introduces the topic, the number of jobs corrections officers held in 2002. Sentence 2 details where the majority of the corrections jobs were found; sentence 4 tells of where *Most of the remaining jobs were* found. Sentence 1 is introduced by *Finally*, which signals that it should be the concluding sentence.

28. b. Sentence 4 introduces the dispatcher and the burglar alarm call at the warehouse; sentence 2 goes into more detail about the burglar alarm. Sentence 1 introduces Officer Harris; sentence 3 details what she does after responding to the dispatcher's call.

29. c. Sentence 4 is the general topic sentence, relating how recently courts have been handing down sentences that include elements of public humiliation. Sentence 1, with the phrase *for example,* gives a specific case of this public humiliation; sentence 3 gives the details of the example. Sentence 2 provides another more general example.

30. d. The transitional word *but* correctly establishes a contrast.

31. c. The transitional word *although* correctly establishes a contrast.

32. a. The transitional phrase *for example* correctly establishes an example.

33. c. This answer establishes the causal relationship between the two sentences.

34. d. *Anonymous* is the correct spelling.

35. d. When a comparison is made, the word *fewer* is used with nouns that can be counted; the word *less* is used with quantities that cannot be counted.

36. b. This is the only choice that uses the adverb correctly and establishes the appropriate comparison. Choices **a**, **c**, and **d** are incorrect because an adverb (*gracefully*) is required to modify the verb *skates.*

37. c. No punctuation is necessary; in fact, any use of punctuation would unnecessarily separate the verb *maintain* from its object.

38. d. This is the only sentence that uses the correct pronoun, *which.* Use *which* when introducing clauses that are not essential to the information in the sentence, unless they refer to people, then use *who.* The second clause in choice **c** is referring to a river, not a person, so the use of *who* is incorrect.

39. b. This is only sentence that does not contain a double negative or a double comparison.

40. a. An *ultimatum* is a final, non-negotiable proposition, condition, or demand. This definition best fits the context of the sentence.

41. a. Divide the total amount of marijuana (6,000 kg) by the amount in each bag (5 kg), to get the number of bags (1,200).

42. c. To convert a fraction to a decimal, divide the numerator, 3, by the denominator, 4:

$$4)\overline{3.00}\quad 0.75$$

43. c. Take the total time allowed (40 hours) and subtract the time already used (9 + 6.5 + 8 + 10.5 = 34) to find the left over time (40 − 34 = 6).

44. a. All the other choices are common errors in computation, particularly not carrying digits to the next place.

45. b. Since each shelf can hold 9 cans, divide 1,260 by 9; 1,260 ÷ 9 = 140.

46. c. If you convert $\frac{1}{2}$ to sixths, you get $\frac{3}{6}$. Add $\frac{3}{6}$ and $\frac{5}{6}$ to get $1\frac{2}{6}$, or $1\frac{1}{3}$, and then add 1 to the whole numbers.

47. b. To find out how many people are applying for each job, divide the total number of applicants by the total number of positions available ($\frac{65}{4}$ = 16.25). The answer is closer to 16 than 17 people.

48. b. Look at the table to find out what portion Marie was responsible for (0.60). Convert this to a fraction and reduce; $\frac{6}{10} \div \frac{2}{2} = \frac{3}{5}$.

49. d. Look at the table to find out Jane's portion (0.10). Add this to A.J.'s portion (0.05); 0.10 + 0.05 = 0.15. Convert this to a fraction and then reduce; $\frac{15}{100} \div \frac{5}{5} = \frac{3}{20}$.

50. a. When multiplying the same number with different exponents, keep the number and add the exponents. Therefore: $3^2 \times 3^4$ is 3^6.

51. c.
52. d.
53. b.
54. a.
55. b.
56. c.
57. b.
58. c.
59. d.
60. a.
61. c.
62. a.

63. a.

64. b.

65. c.

66. d.

67. a.

68. d.

69. b.

70. d.

71. c. There are 15 letter r's in the sentence: *The warden, Margaret Appleton, started out as a corrections officer in this prison and was promoted all the way up through the ranks to reach the pinnacle of her career.*

72. c. If the pattern were complete there would be 25 diamonds total because there should be five diamonds across and five diamonds down. There are only 17 diamonds, so eight are missing.

73. b. There are nine upper case vowels in the set:

M q u c **A A** B F

N **E** n **A** N r r G

O o o V S s **I E**

P P e **A** p **U** p p

74. a. There are seven circled white *2*s in the set.

75. b. There are six *7*s in the set:

4 8 3 2 9 8 4 6 7

4 2 6 3 8 3 6 3 8

3 3 2 9 8 6 3 4 7

3 7 4 9 3 8 2 7 4

0 9 7 4 3 0 9 7 3

76. b. The officer is following all protocol for written directives as mandated by the Department of Corrections.

77. d. Due to patients', inmates', and medical confidentiality, information must not be divulged to others that are not in direct relationship to the illness. Medical personnel should be notified to maintain secure measures.

78. d. Officers are barred from conducting personal telephone calls for inmates. All requests should be reported to thr superior officer.

79. c. An Officer must maintain confidentiality regarding medical information; but sexual activity is not condoned.

80. d. Officer Hughley should immediately notify his supervisor. Officer Hughley should be concerned about how his cell phone number got out.

81. a. A report should be written immediately. Sexual activity is not consensual. Sexual activity is not condoned.

82. a. Officer Nariz should be reprimanded since he is not an authorized ACCESS user.

83. b. This answer corresponds to the set of rules and procedures

84. d. Sexual activity is not condoned.

85. c. Staff should not be using inmates to solicit information.

86. c. This is a violation of the rules.

87. d. There is a conflict of interest.

88. b. Inmates are required to have running showers.

89. b. Searches can detect contraband and they deter the movement of contraband within the institution. Attacks threaten the safety and security of the institution, its staff, and inmates.

90. c. These actions are appropriate to the situation.

91. d. This is step 4 in the procedure for transporting inmates. Choices **b** and **c** are not listed in the procedure, and choice **a** is a later step in the procedure.

92. c. Officer Presotto should have radioed dispatch before he attempted to recapture inmate Hayes. This is covered in steps 1–4 of the procedures for a prisoner who escapes during transport.

93. a. Officer Romney's use of force in this situation is totally unnecessary and is a violation of the inmate's civil rights.

94. c. Step 5 in the procedure for transporting inmates specifies that the officer is to proceed directly to the destination.

95. d. Again, step 4 of the procedures for transporting a prisoner states that if seatbelts are available in the transport vehicle, they must be used. However, the prisoner should not be allowed to have his or her handcuffs taken off during a transport (choice **b**).

96. d. Policy and law instruct the officer to use the least amount of force. No force is necessary in this instance because the inmate is surrendering.

97. c. The policy on open communication with inmates states that officers should not make promises they can't keep. The officer acted improperly by not following through with his promise to let the inmate make two trips to the library.

98. a. The officer has followed the proper procedure for transporting inmates, which says that the transport officer should search the inmate.

99. b. Step 7 in the procedure for transporting inmates specifies that the officer is to only turn the inmate over to the proper receiving officer at the courthouse.

100. d. Corrections officers are often required to use force to subdue inmates in certain situations or when physical altercations occur, but when Officer Pan subdued inmate Gordon, Gordon was simply walking toward the garbage. Perhaps Officer Pan prevented an altercation, but a hunch that something may happen is not reason enough to apply the use of force on a prisoner.

12 ▶ Corrections Officer Exam III

CHAPTER SUMMARY

This is the final corrections officer exam in this book. Now that you've had plenty of study and preparation, this exam will show you how much you've improved.

L ike the previous two exams in this book, this final corrections officer exam assesses the most commonly tested skills on corrections officer exams in various jurisdictions throughout the United States. Part One, Reading Comprehension, consists of questions on passages that you will have in front of you as you answer. Part Two, Preparing Written Material, includes questions on how to express given information in writing. Part Three, Math, is simple arithmetic problems. For Part Four, Memory and Counting, you will read a passage and answer questions about this passage without looking back. Also, you will answer five simple counting questions in one minute. For Part Five, Situational Reasoning, you will choose the best answer to the questions, using your good judgment and common sense. Part Six, Applying Written Material, will ask you to apply the corrections rules and procedures it gives you to specific situations.

You should allow two hours for this exam. Set yourself up in an area that's as much like a real testing room as possible, with no distractions. Use number 2 pencils to fill in the answer sheet on the next page. When you finish, check your answers against the Answers section that follows the exam.

1.	a	b	c	d	31.	a	b	c	d	61.	a	b	c	d
2.	a	b	c	d	32.	a	b	c	d	62.	a	b	c	d
3.	a	b	c	d	33.	a	b	c	d	63.	a	b	c	d
4.	a	b	c	d	34.	a	b	c	d	64.	a	b	c	d
5.	a	b	c	d	35.	a	b	c	d	65.	a	b	c	d
6.	a	b	c	d	36.	a	b	c	d	66.	a	b	c	d
7.	a	b	c	d	37.	a	b	c	d	67.	a	b	c	d
8.	a	b	c	d	38.	a	b	c	d	68.	a	b	c	d
9.	a	b	c	d	39.	a	b	c	d	69.	a	b	c	d
10.	a	b	c	d	40.	a	b	c	d	70.	a	b	c	d
11.	a	b	c	d	41.	a	b	c	d	71.	a	b	c	d
12.	a	b	c	d	42.	a	b	c	d	72.	a	b	c	d
13.	a	b	c	d	43.	a	b	c	d	73.	a	b	c	d
14.	a	b	c	d	44.	a	b	c	d	74.	a	b	c	d
15.	a	b	c	d	45.	a	b	c	d	75.	a	b	c	d
16.	a	b	c	d	46.	a	b	c	d	76.	a	b	c	d
17.	a	b	c	d	47.	a	b	c	d	77.	a	b	c	d
18.	a	b	c	d	48.	a	b	c	d	78.	a	b	c	d
19.	a	b	c	d	49.	a	b	c	d	79.	a	b	c	d
20.	a	b	c	d	50.	a	b	c	d	80.	a	b	c	d
21.	a	b	c	d	51.	a	b	c	d	81.	a	b	c	d
22.	a	b	c	d	52.	a	b	c	d	82.	a	b	c	d
23.	a	b	c	d	53.	a	b	c	d	83.	a	b	c	d
24.	a	b	c	d	54.	a	b	c	d	84.	a	b	c	d
25.	a	b	c	d	55.	a	b	c	d	85.	a	b	c	d
26.	a	b	c	d	56.	a	b	c	d	86.	a	b	c	d
27.	a	b	c	d	57.	a	b	c	d	87.	a	b	c	d
28.	a	b	c	d	58.	a	b	c	d	88.	a	b	c	d
29.	a	b	c	d	59.	a	b	c	d	89.	a	b	c	d
30.	a	b	c	d	60.	a	b	c	d	90.	a	b	c	d

PART ONE: READING COMPREHENSION

Following are several reading passages. Answer the questions that come after each, based solely on the information in the passages.

Evidence concerning the character of a witness must be limited to questions of truthfulness. The credibility of a witness can be attacked by any party, and by evidence of a prior conviction for a felony, so long as the relevance of the conviction to the question of truthfulness is deemed by the court to outweigh the prejudicial damage caused to the witness. If, for example, the witness is guilty of some crime which the jury might find repugnant but which is not relevant to the witness's credibility, this would be deemed unacceptably prejudicial. The elements of credibility that can be impeached are perception, memory, clarity, and sincerity. Police officers should not base an arrest on the testimony of an untruthful or otherwise unreliable witness—for example, a witness who is mentally unstable, senile, or intoxicated. Officers should recognize that a case based on the testimony of a witness with prior felony convictions is vulnerable to dismissal.

1. What is the primary purpose of the passage?
   a. to review the criteria for impeaching the credibility of a witness
   b. to argue for the importance of determining the credibility of a witness before arresting a suspect
   c. to raise questions concerning the reliability of witnesses with prior convictions
   d. to teach police officers proper witness interrogation techniques

2. Which of the following would NOT be admissible to impeach the credibility of a witness?
   a. proof of a felony conviction
   b. a psychiatric evaluation
   c. a neighbor's claim that the witness is a liar
   d. a claim that the witness is prone to spousal abuse

3. According to the passage, why shouldn't the police base their case on the testimony of an untruthful witness?
   a. The accused might be innocent.
   b. The case might be dismissed.
   c. The police will be embarrassed in court.
   d. The police will be vulnerable to a lawsuit.

4. Which of the following witnesses would be least likely to be vulnerable to having their credibility impeached, according to the criteria set forth in the passage?
   a. a nearsighted person who wasn't wearing glasses
   b. an alcoholic
   c. a petty thief
   d. a person with a psychiatric history

The criminal justice system needs to change. The system could be more just if it allowed victims the opportunity to confront the person who has harmed them. Also, mediation between victims and their offenders would give the offenders a chance to apologize for the harm they have done.

5. This paragraph best supports the statement that victims of a crime should
   a. learn to forgive their offenders.
   b. have the right to confront their offenders.
   c. learn the art of mediation.
   d. insist that their offenders be punished.

6. The views of the author of this passage could be characterized as which of the following?
  a. conservative
  b. revolutionary
  c. uninformed
  d. reformist

At 12:45 A.M. on October 15, while parked at 1910 Sherman, Police Officers Fung and Janikowski were asked to respond to a disturbance at 1809 Washington. When they arrived at the one-story dwelling, the complainant, Dan Leary, who resides next door at 1807 Washington, told them that he had been kept awake for two hours by the sound of yelling and breaking glass. He said the occupant of 1809 Washington, a Mr. Everett Macy, lived alone, was crazy, and had always been crazy. As they approached the house, they heard yelling coming from inside. When the officers knocked on the door, Mr. Macy answered promptly and said, "It's about time you got here." Inside, broken furniture was strewn about. Mr. Macy stated he had been protecting himself from persons who lived inside the woodwork of his home. He went willingly with the officers to Duke County Hospital at 1010 Main, where he was admitted to the psychiatric unit for observation. No arrests were made.

7. Which of the following is most likely a fact?
  a. Dan Leary had been kept awake by noise.
  b. Mr. Macy had been making noise for two hours.
  c. Mr. Macy had always been crazy.
  d. The police heard Mr. Macy shouting inside his house.

8. The call to the police was most likely made from which of the following addresses?
  a. 1910 Sherman
  b. 1809 Washington
  c. 1807 Washington
  d. 1010 Main

9. Based on the passage, what was the most likely reason the police were called?
  a. A neighbor was bothered by the noise coming from Mr. Macy's home.
  b. A neighbor was worried for Mr. Macy's safety.
  c. A neighbor was worried for the safety of Mr. Macy's family.
  d. A neighbor was curious about Mr. Macy's personal life.

10. What was Mr. Macy's demeanor when the police arrived at his door?
  a. He seemed surprised.
  b. He seemed to have been expecting them.
  c. He seemed frightened and distrustful.
  d. He seemed angered by their presence.

Adolescents are at high risk for violent crime. Although they make up only 14% of the population age 12 and over, 30% of all violent crimes—1.9 million—were committed against them. Because crimes against adolescents are likely to be committed by offenders of the same age (as well as same sex and race), preventing violence among and against adolescents is a twofold challenge. Adolescents are at risk for becoming both victims and perpetrators of violence. New violence-prevention programs in urban middle schools help reduce the crime rate by teaching both victims and perpetrators of such violence the skills of conflict resolution and how to apply reason to disputes, as well as by changing attitudes towards achieving respect through violence and towards the need to retaliate. These programs provide a safe place for students to discuss their conflicts and therefore prove appealing to students at risk.

11. What is the main idea of the passage?
   a. Adolescents are more likely to commit crimes than older people and must therefore be taught nonviolence in order to protect society.
   b. Middle school students appreciate the conflict resolution skills they acquire in violence-prevention programs.
   c. Middle school violence-prevention programs are designed to help to lower the rate of crimes against adolescents.
   d. Violence against adolescents is increasing.

12. Which of the following is NOT mentioned in the passage as a skill taught by middle school violence-prevention programs?
   a. keeping one's temper
   b. settling disputes without violence
   c. avoiding the need for vengeance
   d. being reasonable in emotional situations

13. According to the passage, which of the following statements about adolescents is true?
   a. Adolescents are disproportionately likely to be victims of violent crime.
   b. Adolescents are more likely to commit violent crimes than other segments of the population.
   c. Adolescents are the victims of 14% of the nation's violent crimes.
   d. Adolescents are reluctant to attend violence-prevention programs.

14. According to the passage, why is preventing violence against adolescents a *twofold challenge*?
   a. because adolescents are twice as likely to be victims of violent crime as members of other age groups
   b. because adolescents must be prevented from both perpetrating and being victimized by violent crime
   c. because adolescents must change both their violent behavior and their attitudes towards violence
   d. because adolescents are vulnerable yet reluctant to listen to adult advice

In the last decade, community policing has been frequently touted as the best way to reform urban law enforcement. The idea of putting more officers on foot patrol in high crime areas, where relations with police have been frequently strained, was initiated in Houston in 1983 under the leadership of then-Commissioner Lee Brown. He believed that officers should be accessible to the community at the street level. If officers were assigned to the same area over a period of time, those officers would eventually build a network of trust with neighborhood residents. That trust would mean that merchants and residents in the community would let officers know about criminal activities in the area and would support police intervention.

Since then, many large cities have experimented with Community-Oriented Policing (COP) with mixed results. Some have found that police and citizens are grateful for the opportunity to work together. Others have found that unrealistic expectations by citizens and resistance from officers have combined to hinder the effectiveness of COP. It seems possible, therefore, that a good idea may need improvement before it can truly be considered a reform.

15. Community policing has been used in law enforcement since
- **a.** the late 1970s.
- **b.** the early 1980s.
- **c.** the late 1950s.
- **d.** the late 1930s.

16. The phrase *network of trust* in this passage suggests that
- **a.** police officers can rely only each other for support.
- **b.** community members rely on the police to protect them.
- **c.** police and community members rely on each other.
- **d.** community members trust only each other.

17. The best title for this passage would be
- **a.** Community Policing: The Solution to the Drug Problem.
- **b.** Houston Sets the Pace in Community Policing.
- **c.** Communities and Cops: Partners for Peace.
- **d.** Community Policing: An Uncertain Future.

18. The word *touted* in the first sentence of the passage most nearly means
- **a.** praised.
- **b.** denied.
- **c.** exposed.
- **d.** criticized.

Police officers must read suspects their Miranda rights upon taking them into custody. When a suspect who is merely being questioned incriminates himself, he might later claim to have been in custody, and seek to have the case dismissed on the grounds of having been unapprised of his Miranda rights. In such cases, a judge must make a determination as to whether or not a reasonable person would have believed himself to have been in custody, based on certain criteria. The judge must determine whether the suspect was questioned in a threatening manner (for example, if the suspect was seated while both officers remained standing) and whether the suspect was aware that he or she was free to leave at any time. Officers must be aware of these criteria and take care not to give suspects grounds for later claiming they believed themselves to be in custody.

19. According to the passage, when is a suspect not in custody?
- **a.** when free to refuse to answer questions
- **b.** when free to leave the police station
- **c.** when apprised of his or her Miranda rights
- **d.** when not apprised of his or her Miranda rights

20. A police officer questioning a suspect who is not under arrest must
- **a.** read the suspect his Miranda rights.
- **b.** allow the suspect a phone call.
- **c.** advise the suspect of his right to a lawyer.
- **d.** inform the suspect that he is free to leave.

PART TWO: PREPARING WRITTEN MATERIAL

Questions 21–29 consist of four numbered sentences. Choose the sentence order that would result in the best paragraph.

21. 1) Because prisoners remain in a highly emotional state for so long, officers who work on death row often receive special training in dealing with death row inmates. 2) Death row was originally intended as a place where prisoners would live for a short period of time between sentencing and execution. 3) In states that have the death penalty, a section of a prison will be designated as "death row." 4) Today, however, prisoners may remain on death row for ten or twenty years or more.
- **a.** 2, 4, 1, 3
- **b.** 3, 2, 4, 1
- **c.** 4, 1, 3, 2
- **d.** 1, 4, 2, 3

22. 1) No search of a person's home or personal effects may be conducted without a written search warrant issued on probable cause. 2) This means that a neutral judge must approve the factual basis justifying a search before it can be conducted. 3) The Fourth Amendment to the Constitution protects citizens against unreasonable searches and seizures. 4) However, there are exceptions to the Fourth Amendment, such as when evidence is in plain view.
- **a.** 2, 4, 1, 3
- **b.** 1, 4, 2, 3
- **c.** 1, 2, 3, 4
- **d.** 3, 1, 2, 4

23. 1) Sing Sing Correctional Facility takes its name from the village of Sing Sing, New York, which changed its name to Ossining in 1901. 2) He took 100 prisoners from Auburn State Prison to the site, and used them to help build Sing Sing from the ground up using materials from the quarry. 3) Construction of the prison began in 1825, when the New York State legislature appropriated $20,100 to buy a 130-acre site with a quarry. 4) Elam Lynds was the first warden of Sing Sing.
- **a.** 4, 2, 1, 3
- **b.** 2, 4, 3, 1
- **c.** 1, 3, 4, 2
- **d.** 2, 4, 1, 3

24. 1) All of these elements taken together constitute the crime of solicitation. 2) First, the person must have persuaded another person to commit a crime. 3) Second, the person must have been discussing a specific crime and must have had the intention that the act would be done. 4) Police officers may become aware of a person who did not actually commit a crime, but solicited another person to do so.
- **a.** 1, 3, 4, 2
- **b.** 2, 4, 1, 3
- **c.** 4, 2, 1, 3
- **d.** 4, 2, 3, 1

25. 1) Good judgment and the ability to think and act quickly are indispensable. 2) The Occupational Outlook Handbook states that all corrections officer candidates for employment are generally required to meet formal standards of physical fitness, eyesight, and hearing. 3) Therefore, applicants are typically screened for drug abuse, subject to background checks, and required to pass a written examination. 4) In addition, many jurisdictions use standard tests to determine applicant suitability to work in a correctional environment.

   a. 1, 3, 4, 2
   b. 2, 4, 1, 3
   c. 4, 3, 1, 2
   d. 1, 4, 3, 2

26. 1) They tell of cell doors that mysteriously open and close, hearing unexplainable sounds coming from the heart of the prison, and the feeling of being observed by someone or something else 2) The staff say that the areas of Alcatraz that seem to be the most haunted are the old Warden's house, the utility door for cellblock C, and the hospital. 3) Many of the Park Service staff at Alcatraz Island believe that the old prison is haunted. 4) But perhaps the most haunted location of all is the area known as "The Hole," in cellblock D; in fact some of the staff feel uncomfortable going to that area by themselves.

   a. 3, 1, 2, 4
   b. 2, 4, 1, 3
   c. 4, 2, 1, 3
   d. 4, 2, 3, 1

27. 1) Today, there are other major associations for corrections officers as well, such as the International Association of Correctional Officers, and the American Jail Association. 2) It was originally known as the National Prison Association; however, the name was changed in 1954. 3) The oldest association of corrections officers is the American Correctional Association (ACA), founded in 1870. 4) The first president of the National Prison Association was former United States President Rutherford B. Hayes.

   a. 2, 4, 1, 3
   b. 1, 4, 2, 3
   c. 1, 2, 3, 4
   d. 3, 2, 4, 1

28. 1) Visits, especially from family members, can aid in a prisoner's rehabilitation. 2) Usually, this means that a prisoner and his visitors may not have physical contact with each other. 3) Therefore, they are separated by a pane of glass and must talk by phone. 4) However, in order to maintain prison safety, family visits cannot be unrestricted.

   a. 2, 4, 1, 3
   b. 1, 4, 2, 3
   c. 1, 2, 3, 4
   d. 3, 1, 2, 4

29. 1) However, lawyers have received undeserved criticism. 2) Lawyer-bashing is on the increase in the United States. 3) A lawyer is more likely than not to try to dissuade a client from litigation by offering to arbitrate and settle conflict. 4) For example, lawyers are accused of lacking principles, clogging the justice system, and increasing the cost of liability insurance.

   a. 2, 3, 1, 4
   b. 4, 2, 1, 3
   c. 2, 4, 1, 3
   d. 4, 2, 3, 1

For questions 30–33, choose the sentence that best describes the underlined sentence into one.

30. Everyone likes Earl.
I think he is sneaky.
  a. Everyone likes Earl, and I think he is sneaky.
  b. Everyone likes Earl, whereas I think he is sneaky.
  c. Everyone likes Earl, when I think he is sneaky.
  d. Everyone likes Earl, or I think he is sneaky.

31. This area is known as "Death Valley."
We're driving through the hottest, driest, and lowest point in the Western Hemisphere.
  a. This area is known as "Death Valley"; meanwhile, we're driving through the hottest, driest, and lowest point in the Western Hemisphere.
  b. We're driving through the hottest, driest, and lowest point in the Western Hemisphere, but this area is known as "Death Valley."
  c. We're driving through the hottest, driest, and lowest point in the Western Hemisphere; therefore, this area is known as "Death Valley."
  d. We're driving through the hottest, driest, and lowest point in the Western Hemisphere, while this area is known as "Death Valley."

32. All of my siblings are excellent students.
My sister Molly was the valedictorian of her class.
  a. All of my siblings are excellent students; on the contrary, my sister Molly was the valedictorian of her class.
  b. All of my siblings are excellent students; in contrast, my sister Molly was the valedictorian of her class.
  c. All of my siblings are excellent students; rather, my sister Molly was the valedictorian of her class.
  d. All of my siblings are excellent students; for instance, my sister Molly was the valedictorian of her class.

33. I love the weather in Los Angeles.
I sometimes miss the changing of the seasons.
  a. I love the weather in Los Angeles, because I sometimes miss the changing of the seasons.
  b. However I love the weather in Los Angeles; I sometimes miss the changing of the seasons.
  c. Because I love the weather in Los Angeles, I sometimes miss the changing of the seasons.
  d. I love the weather in Los Angeles, but I sometimes miss the changing of the seasons.

In questions 34–40, a portion of the sentence is underlined. Under each section there are four ways of phrasing the underlined option. Choice **a** repeats the original underlined portion; the other three provide alternative choices. Select the choice that best expresses the meaning of the original sentence. If the original sentence is better than any of the alternatives, chose option **a**.

34. His suit had a forlorn odor, as if it had been closed up for a long time in an old trunk.
  a. forlorn
  b. dried-up
  c. musty
  d. decrepit

35. It poured; so I tried to run for cover.
  a. It poured; so I tried to run for cover.
  b. It poured, so I tried to run for cover.
  c. It poured, I tried to run for cover.
  d. It will pour, so I tried to run for cover.

36. Besides its use in jewelry, silver has many uses in photography and electronics.
  a. Besides its use in jewelry,
  b. Beside jewelry,
  c. In addition also to its jewelry applications,
  d. Beside their use in jewelry,

37. Please remember that I am <u>older than him and have</u> more experience in these matters.
a. older than him and have
b. oldest than him and have
c. older than he and have
d. more older than he and have

38. <u>Obvious</u> is a synonym of *outmoded.*
a. Obvious
b. Obsolete
c. Basic
d. Inaugural

39. The <u>enphasis</u> was placed on following proper prison procedure.
a. enphasis
b. emphisis
c. emphasis
d. emfasis

40. It's easy to pet sit for my friend's terrier, Duke; he's a <u>fungible</u> and obedient dog.
a. fungible
b. commonplace
c. meddlesome
d. docile

PART THREE: MATH

Questions 41–50 are followed by four answer choices. Select the choice that best answers the questions.

41. $\frac{4}{5}$ is equal to
a. 0.80.
b. 0.50.
c. 0.90.
d. 0.45.

42. To calculate her overtime pay, Corrections Officer Alvarez uses the expression $30n$, where n is the number of overtime hours worked. What is her overtime pay if she works 3 hours?
a. $33
b. $90
c. $60
d. $27

43. What is six and five hundredths written as a decimal?
a. .065
b. 6.5
c. 6.05
d. 6.005

44. $8^3 \times 8^6 =$
a. 8^3
b. 8^9
c. 16^2
d. 16^3

45. Officer Tate has responded to the scene of a robbery. On the officer's arrival, the victim, Mrs. Lisa Sharma, tells the officer that the following items were taken from her by a man who threatened her with a knife:

- 1 gold watch, valued at $240
- 2 rings, each valued at $150
- 1 ring, valued at $70
- Cash $95

Officer Tate is preparing her report on the robbery. Which one of the following is the total value of the cash and property Mrs. Sharma reported stolen?

a. $545
b. $555
c. $705
d. $785

46. $9,667 - 4,332 + 1,523 =$

a. 6,758
b. 6,858
c. 6,658
d. 6,555

47. Robert works as a cashier at a supermarket. If peaches are on sale for $1.25 per pound, how much will 2.4 pounds cost?

a. $2.00
b. $2.40
c. $3.00
d. $3.25

48. $(25 + 17)(64 - 49) =$

a. 57
b. 63
c. 570
d. 630

49. Juan goes on a trip with $47 in his pocket. During his trip he speeds through a small town and is stopped and fined $5. After that, he is so upset he decides to get a motel room for the night. The room costs $15. After paying for the room, how much money does Juan have left for dinner, beverages, and the rest of his trip?

a. $30
b. $27
c. $25
d. $17

50. Manny is 46 years old, twice as old as Albert. How old is Albert?

a. 30 years old
b. 28 years old
c. 23 years old
d. 18 years old

PART FOUR: MEMORY AND COUNTING

Following is a short reading passage. Study it for five minutes. At the end of five minutes, cover the page and answer the 10 questions without referring back to the study material. You have 2.5 minutes to answer the questions. If you refer back to the study material after five minutes are up, you will be disqualified. When the 2.5 minutes are up, you may continue with the rest of the test.

On Saturday, January 10, 2004, three inmates were assaulted in the 4-East Housing Unit (220 beds) of Rocktown Prison. At approximately 1:30 P.M., four suspects attacked inmates Ojas Hamm, Patrick Favia, and Joseph Tejani with homemade knives. Senior Corrections Officer Martin Thomas recognized that inmate Tejani appeared to have been stabbed in the thigh. He immediately called the medical staff, who treated inmate Tejani overnight in the Medical Unit Building and discharged him the next day. The two other inmates sustained minor injuries, were treated at the scene of the incident, and then instructed to return to their cells in Block 2 of the 4-East Housing Unit. The entire 4-East Housing Unit was then placed on lock-down status.

At approximately 3:00 P.M., the four suspects in the assault were removed from their cells in the 4-East Housing Unit and questioned in the Main Detention Facility about the incident by Corrections Officer Ryan Morton and Captain Ed Buckworth. During the questioning, one suspect, inmate William Dawkins, became unruly and attempted to strike Captain Buckworth in the head with his own head. Inmate Dawkins was restrained, and all four suspects were placed in Disciplinary Unit 1 (20 beds). The incident involving Captain Buckworth is under investigation.

Acting on a tip given to Officer Morton, at approximately 3:45 P.M. inmate Dawkins's cell was searched, yielding 3 homemade weapons, including a homemade knife that Dawkins possibly used to stab inmate Tejani. The search also yielded $348 dollars in cash and approximately a half-ounce of a substance believed to be cocaine. Searches of the cells of the three other suspects in the assault yielded nothing.

At 4:30 P.M., Officer Morton questioned inmate Tejani in the Medical Unit regarding the assault. Inmate Tejani denied that the incident was drug-related and claimed that prior to that afternoon, he had only spoken to inmate Dawkins once before, in passing. Officer Morton then questioned inmates Hamm and Favia in the Main Detention Facility. All statements made by inmates Hamm and Favia closely corroborated with inmate Tejani's statements regarding the assault.

At 9:19 P.M., Corrections Officer Preston Bush was escorting inmate Hamm back to 4-East Housing Unit when inmate Hamm struck Officer Bush in the head with his fist, knocking him unconscious. Inmate Hamm then scaled a perimeter fence surrounding Recreation Unit 3, and escaped. Inmate Hamm then stole a white 1991 Chrysler LeBaron from a nearby shopping center, and was involved in a high-speed pursuit on Route 17 West with New York State Police that ended with his apprehension in Liberty, New York at 11:17 P.M. He was returned to Rocktown Prison by the New York State Police and will face appropriate charges.

51. What day of the week did these incidents occur?
  a. Sunday
  b. Saturday
  c. Monday
  d. Thursday

52. How many beds are in the 4-East Housing Unit?
  a. 100
  b. 20
  c. 200
  d. 220

53. Which inmate was stabbed in the thigh?
  a. inmate Hamm
  b. inmate Favia
  c. inmate Tejani
  d. inmate Dawkins

54. In which block of 4-East Housing Unit are the three assaulted inmates' cells?
  a. Block 2
  b. Block 5
  c. Block 4
  d. Block 6

55. At approximately what time were the four suspects in the assault removed from their cells and questioned about the incident?
  a. 2:30 P.M.
  b. 2:00 P.M.
  c. 3:45 P.M.
  d. 3:00 P.M.

56. Which officer did inmate William Dawkins attempt to strike?
  a. Thomas
  b. Morton
  c. Buckworth
  d. Bush

57. What amount of cash was found in inmate Dawkins's cell?
  a. $328
  b. $338
  c. $348
  d. $438

58. Where were all four suspects placed after they were questioned?
  a. Disciplinary Unit 11
  b. Disciplinary Unit 10
  c. Disciplinary Unit 1
  d. Disciplinary Unit 5

59. At approximately what time did inmate Hamm assault Officer Bush and then escape?
  a. 9:09 P.M.
  b. 9:19 P.M.
  c. 9:29 P.M.
  d. 9:39 P.M.

60. What year and color was the stolen Chrysler LeBaron?
  a. white, 1991
  b. blue, 1992
  c. red, 1992
  d. blue, 1991

You have 1 minute to answer the questions 61–65. When the minute is up, you may continue with the rest of the test.

61. How many 9s are in the following set?
        8 6 3 4 7 3 8 2 7
        3 0 9 7 3 0 9 2 9
        4 8 3 8 4 6 7 7 4
        3 7 4 9 6 3 6 3 4
        6 3 6 3 8 3 3 2 9
  a. 4
  b. 5
  c. 6
  d. 7

62. How many letter *s*'s are there in the following sentence?

> *Corrections Supervisor Baumgarten's many years of experience served him well when the inmates in Dormitory Unit 5 had to be evacuated during the prison fire.*

a. 6
b. 7
c. 8
d. 9

63. How many lower case vowels are there in this set?

D e g d D c d a
N E Q o E o E e
F m f S B F i m
G a a X x T L I
S S e E U h u H

a. 9
b. 10
c. 11
d. 12

64. How many clovers are needed to complete this pattern?

a. 9
b. 10
c. 11
d. 12

65. How many upward arrows (↗) are in the following set?

→ ↘ ↗ → ↗ ↘
↘ ↘ ↗ ↘ → ↘
↗ ↗ ↘ ↘ ↘ ↗
↘ → ↘ ↗ ↘ ↗
↗ → ↗ → ↗ ↘
→ ↗ ↘ ↘ ↘ ↗

a. 12
b. 13
c. 14
d. 15

PART FIVE: SITUATIONAL REASONING

Choose the best answer to the following questions, based on good judgment and common sense.

66. Inmates have access to library materials in order to prepare court documents, but access is a privilege controlled by time schedules, inmate conduct, and prison regulations. Inmate Lucas is in the library conducting research for his case. Other inmates begin complaining because he is yelling across the room to inmate Garcia and refuses to be quiet. What should the officer in charge of the library do?

a. He should remove inmate Garcia, since inmate Lucas is using the library for an important purpose.

b. He should let inmate Lucas take the books he needs back to his cell.

c. He should write inmate Lucas up for causing a disruption, but let him stay to finish the research for his court case.

d. He should cut short inmate Lucas's library privilege and return him to his cell for causing the disruption.

67. "The Hole" is a common term officers use to describe a holding cell where inmates with behavioral problems are placed for disciplinary isolation. Which situation would cause Officer Campbell to consider placing an inmate in The Hole?
   a. Inmate Garvey is tired of standing in line for his haircut. He walks to the front of the line and punches inmate Douglas in the nose before pushing him out of his way.
   b. Inmate Witte is arguing with inmate Alvarez. She tells Inmate Alvarez that she is stupid and then turns and walks away.
   c. A food fight breaks out in the cafeteria, but Officer Campbell cannot ascertain who started it.
   d. A new regulation limiting inmate access to weights in the gym has come out, and inmate Jackson is angry about it. He says he will be filing a grievance with the warden's office.

68. Vehicles entering and leaving prison facilities should be checked thoroughly. Officers on duty at the gates should check the identities of all occupants of the vehicles, and vehicles exiting the area should be checked for possible escapees. Officer Shakley is standing guard at Gate 1. Which situation would cause her to check the vehicle and its occupants particularly carefully?
   a. A solitary man in a two-door convertible drives up to the gate. He presents identification that shows he is an attorney and says he has come to meet with an inmate.
   b. A large delivery van is in the line of cars waiting to exit the facility. The driver, who entered the facility laughing and joking, looks tense and rigid as he approaches the gate.
   c. A corrections officer in uniform approaches the gate on a touring motorcycle.
   d. A prison employee driving a station wagon approaches the gate to exit the facility.

69. Random bed checks during the night are conducted by officers to make sure inmates are where they are supposed to be and to check on the condition and behavior of inmates. Officer Quinton is conducting a bed check and is carefully checking for "living breathing flesh." Which situation below would cause him to check more closely?
   a. When checking one of the cells, he sees a lump under the blanket in the middle of one bunk but does not see a head on the pillow.
   b. In another cell, he sees the inmate lying on his stomach with his face turned away and with one foot hanging off the side of his bed.
   c. In yet another cell, he sees the inmate lying on his back on top of the blanket on his bunk with one arm flung across his face.
   d. In a fourth cell, he sees the inmate lying on the cement floor with his shirt off, snoring loudly.

70. Random searches for possible weapons and contraband are essential for the safety and security of the facility. Inmates know that these searches, often called "shakedowns," of their cells and dormitories are part of prison routine. If an officer expects to get the maximum result from a shakedown, the officer should do which of the following?
   a. Make an announcement at breakfast that shakedowns will occur all that day and ask for inmates to come forward voluntarily with any contraband or weapons.
   b. Schedule a time with each inmate to go through their possessions.
   c. Conduct searches each night one hour before the inmates are locked down for the night.
   d. Conduct searches randomly, at different times, and on different days.

71. Report writing is a critical element of a corrections officer's job. Officers are expected to write detailed reports that tell who, what, when, where, how, and why. Reports are to be written whenever an incident occurs that should be documented, a violation of the rules and/or law occurs, or an official action is taken by a corrections officer. Which situation below would most likely cause an officer to write a report?

a. Every Tuesday the library remains open an extra hour for those inmates who want to conduct research for their court cases. Today it closes early, and several inmates complain loudly as they gather up their materials to leave.

b. Inmate Rossie punches inmate Browder during an argument and starts a fight that lasts a couple of minutes. Inmate Browder tells the investigation officer that it wasn't important and he doesn't want the incident to be investigated.

c. Inmates in the day room are having a heated discussion about who is going to win the World Series this year. Inmate Sebghati pounds the table and shouts.

d. Inmates waiting to use the outdoor recreational yard are told to wait until the rain stops. They grumble among themselves, and inmate Forbes yells to a corrections officer that she wants to go out in the rain.

72. Some corrections officers are required to deal with the public as well as with the inmate population during the course of their work. Officers are expected to treat visitors courteously and respectfully but are required to take action if visitors to the facility behave in a suspicious manner or fail to abide by the rules and regulations. Which situation below should cause an officer to become suspicious of a visitor?

a. A visitor to the facility tries to make a wrong turn when he passes through the first gate. He tells the guard he failed to follow the signs because he can't read.

b. A visitor arrives too late for visitation hours and is angry when officers politely turn him away. He vows to write the warden to complain about his treatment.

c. Inmate Godwin's wife comes for a visit, becomes upset, and asks to leave the facility before her visitation time is up.

d. Cousin Jeremy arrives to see inmate Everson and is seen repeatedly shaking the inmate's hand in the visitor center.

73. It is important for corrections officers to develop a feel for the moods and behaviors of the inmates in their care. Whenever possible, officers should attempt to head off problems rather than wait for them to happen. Officer Riley notices that inmate Napier is edgy and has been arguing with anyone who tries to speak to him. What should Officer Riley do?

a. Take inmate Napier aside and try to find out what is bothering him.

b. Lock down the cellblock until inmate Napier is in a better mood.

c. Take inmate Napier to solitary confinement before any fighting breaks out.

d. Tell the other inmates to stay away from inmate Napier until his behavior improves.

74. Officers are expected to make frequent counts of inmates for the safety and security of the facility. During these counts, inmates are expected to follow the instructions of the officers who are conducting the count. An officer needs to conduct an inmate count on the recreation yard while a basketball game is in progress. How should she handle this situation?

a. She should let the game continue and count the players on the sidelines first and then the other players as they run past.

b. She should wait until the recreation time is over and count inmates as they come in from the yard.

c. She should stop the game, count all the inmates, and then let them resume the game.

d. She should ask each team to count their own players while she is watching.

75. Inmates have been known to befriend officers and then try to convince the officers to perform favors for them. After favors are performed, inmates often try to blackmail officers, knowing that the officers can face disciplinary action if their superiors find out that they performed the favors. Which situation below should Officer Mendoza avoid?

a. Inmate Keiser asks Officer Mendoza to write out a pass for him to get a haircut. Officer Mendoza notices that the inmate's hair is well below his collar.

b. Inmate Mohammed asks Officer Mendoza for permission to go to the library to research court documents.

c. Inmate Saunders asks Officer Mendoza for more socks, because he is wearing his last pair.

d. Inmate Crowley asks Officer Mendoza to call his house once a day to check on his wife for him.

76. Inmates should be watched closely for signs of behavioral changes, because some inmates develop problems that lead to suicide attempts. Officer Bettis knows his inmates well. Which of the following situations should cause him concern?

a. Inmate Fredericks is withdrawn and depressed. He hardly eats and has told other inmates that his wife wrote him a letter telling him she never wants to see him again.

b. Early one morning, inmate Edwards decides he is not hungry and is not going to line up with the other inmates to report for breakfast.

c. Inmates Jardin and Lipscomb argue constantly whenever they are around each other. Inmate Jardin says he thinks Lipscomb is an idiot.

d. Last week, inmate Hass was injured in a fight and now has his jaws wired shut. He sits in his cell and doesn't speak to the other inmates.

77. Sergeant Billings tells Officer Adams that he suspects that small amounts of drugs are being smuggled to prisoners in Cellblock D on visitation day. Officer Adams is standing watch in the visitor's room the next afternoon. Which incident should arouse his suspicion?

a. Inmate Earl is talking with a visitor. The visitor coughs loudly, covering his mouth with his hand, and then stands up immediately and shakes Earl's right hand with the same hand. He then indicates to the officer that he is ready to leave the room. Earl puts his right hand up to his mouth and covers a cough.

b. An elderly woman is sitting at a table talking to inmate Caswell. She starts crying and tells the officer at the door that she has to leave, because she can't bear to see her grandson in prison. She briefly hugs inmate Caswell and leaves the room.

c. Inmate Jessup is nearing the end of his visitation time with his brother, Ely. Ely tells him that he won't be coming back to visit, because he is moving out of state. Inmate Jessup ducks his head and refuses to shake his brother's hand as Ely stands up to leave. Ely quickly pats him on the shoulder as he passes.

d. Greta has arrived to see her husband, inmate Crandall. She has a book with her that she wants to give to her husband as a gift and hands the book to Officer Adams to inspect. Officer Adams checks through the pages and then hands the book back to her. She walks to her husband's table and hands him the book.

78. Faking illness is a popular method inmates use for getting out of work details in prison. An officer often has to decide when an inmate should be given medical attention and when the inmate may be feigning illness. While supervising a voluntary work crew along the highway, Officer Ferris sees an inmate stop working and lie down. He checks and finds that the inmate is nauseated and his skin is cold to the touch, even though the sun is shining and the temperature is hot. What should Officer Ferris do?

a. Tell the inmate he shouldn't volunteer for details if he's not willing to work and then make him stand up and get back to work.

b. Have all the inmates stop for a water break and make sure they do not feel nauseated, too.

c. Radio his supervisor and ask for an appointment with the prison infirmary.

d. Get immediate medical attention for the inmate.

79. Inmate Pollo tells Officer Henry that someone is stealing his socks. He said now he only has two pairs of socks instead of the five pairs allowed by regulations. He said he saw his cellmate, inmate Ireland, stealing them one night, but he's afraid to confront him, because inmate Ireland is bigger and stronger than he is. How should Officer Henry handle this situation?

a. Go immediately to inmate Ireland and tell him inmate Pollo wants his socks back.

b. Conduct a seemingly random search of the men's cell to see if he can catch inmate Ireland with more socks than he is allowed to have.

c. Write inmate Pollo up for not keeping track of prison property.

d. Suggest to inmate Pollo that he wait until inmate Ireland is not in the cell and then take his socks back.

80. Officer Fineman is escorting ten inmates to the exercise yard for their recreation time. Suddenly, six of the inmates turn and jump the other four inmates in one of the long, narrow hallways. The nearest officers to Officer Fineman's location are about 15 yards away around a corner. What should Officer Fineman do?

- **a.** Call for backup and wait until backup arrives before attempting to break up the fight.
- **b.** Try to determine which inmate is the leader and pull that inmate away from the others.
- **c.** Stand back and wait, as the fight will probably last no longer than one or two minutes.
- **d.** Spray the entire group with pepper spray to subdue them all.

PART SIX: APPLYING WRITTEN MATERIAL

Following is a set of rules and procedures for corrections officers. Based on these, answer the questions that follow them. You may refer back to the rules and procedures as often as needed.

An inmate of a prison facility commits a felony if he or she intentionally, knowingly, or recklessly carries a deadly weapon on, or about, his or her person.

Contraband is any item that an inmate is not permitted to have in his or her possession. Officers who discover contraband will confiscate the item(s), investigate the situation, and write a report. Appropriate disciplinary action should be taken based on the results of the investigation.

Pat-down searches of visitors to prison facilities should be performed whenever an officer receives a tip that a visitor might be attempting to smuggle contraband into the facility.

Corrections officers are often responsible for seeing to it that inmates follow personal grooming rules. An officer can direct an inmate to get a haircut. To do so:

1. The officer should approach the inmate and tell the inmate a haircut is needed.

2. The officer should write a pass for the inmate to report to the desk supervisor.
3. The inmate reports to the desk supervisor, who records the inmate's presence in a log and then directs the inmate to wait in line for the haircut.
4. After the haircut, the inmate will report back to the officer who ordered the procedure.

Inmates housed in isolation are to be given the opportunity to shower every other day. The officer in charge of this procedure should document the time, date, and name of the inmate who showered.

Lock down occurs when inmates are sent to their cells and locked inside for a period of time. A lock down may be ordered by an officer whenever order needs to be restored or the safety and security of inmates, officers, and personnel are threatened.

A corrections officer sometimes is required to distribute medications to inmates upon authorization by prison physicians. The officer will:

1. Call out the names of inmates who are authorized to receive medications and have them step forward.
2. Have each inmate sign the medical log to indicate that he or she received the medication.
3. Hand the inmate first a paper cup of water and then the paper cup containing the authorized medication.
4. Watch the inmate put the medication in his or her mouth and drink the water.
5. Have the inmate open his or her mouth and stick out his or her tongue so that a visual inspection can be made to make sure the inmate is not hiding the pills or capsules.
6. Have the inmate go back to his or her cell and then call out the name of the next inmate to step forward to receive medication.

A safety cell is a holding cell equipped with rubber walls and floors where an inmate is placed when the possibility exists that the inmate may harm him or herself.

Inmates are not permitted to pass written notes, otherwise known as "kites," to each other. Kites should be confiscated and reports written detailing the incident.

81. Jewelry is considered contraband in prison environments. Officer Romero conducts a search of inmate Harland's cell and finds a gold ring under his pillow. What should he do?
- **a.** He should confiscate the ring and tell inmate Harland that he can have it back when he is released from prison.
- **b.** He should leave it where it is because inmate Harland might accuse him of planting the ring in his cell.
- **c.** He should confiscate the ring and tell inmate Harland that he won't report it as a violation, but now Inmate Harland "owes him one."
- **d.** He should confiscate the ring, find out how inmate Harland got it, and then write a report detailing the incident.

82. Officer Buckner made inmate Lloyd open his mouth and stick out his tongue after he gave the inmate his blood pressure medication. Inmate Lloyd wants to file a grievance about this procedure. Officer Buckner acted
- **a.** improperly; he should have had the inmate open his mouth, but it is not necessary to have him stick out his tongue.
- **b.** properly; Officer Lloyd should make the inmate open his mouth and stick out his tongue.
- **c.** properly; Officer Lloyd can instruct the inmate to take his medication in whatever manner Officer Lloyd sees fit.
- **d.** improperly; he should have only done so if he suspected the inmate of not swallowing the medication.

83. Inmate Biggs's hair is hanging below the bottom of his collar. Officer Raven orders inmate Biggs to get a haircut. What is the next step for Officer Raven to take?
- **a.** Check inmate Biggs's cellmate to see if he needs a haircut.
- **b.** Call his supervisor to see if he can send inmate Biggs to the barber.
- **c.** Check to see if the barber has an appointment open for inmate Biggs.
- **d.** Write a pass to the desk supervisor for inmate Biggs.

84. Inmate Elia is in isolation for five days for violating a prison rule. On the second day, he will be permitted to take a shower. Officer Simmons, who will supervise the shower, should
- **a.** inspect inmate Elia to make sure his fingernails are clean.
- **b.** record the time, date, and inmate Elia's name in the log.
- **c.** check with the desk boss to see if inmate Elia can leave his cell to shower.
- **d.** take inmate Elia to the showers every day thereafter.

85. Officer Lasher is about to escort inmates to the clothing center. As she is lining them up in the hallway, she notices a bulge in inmate Yang's sock. She finds a shank in the sock, confiscates it, and writes a report charging inmate Yang with a felony for carrying a homemade knife. Officer Lasher acted
   a. properly; she had all the inmates lined up in the hallway.
   b. improperly; she should have completed her escort before she got sidetracked with inmate Yang.
   c. improperly; a homemade knife would not necessarily be classified as a weapon.
   d. properly; for an inmate to carry a weapon is a felony.

86. Officer Lindner is passing out medication to inmates. He calls out inmate Tweedy's name, and the inmate steps forward. He tells Officer Lindner that he knows he needs to take his medication, but he'd rather take it later, and asks if he can put the pill in his pocket. Officer Lindner tells him no. Officer Lindner acted
   a. properly; the inmate's pocket is not a proper, sanitary container for medication.
   b. improperly; the inmate shouldn't be forced to take medication against his will.
   c. properly; the officer in charge of handing out medication must watch the inmate take the medication.
   d. improperly; the officer is only responsible for making sure the inmate is handed the medication.

87. Inmate White just received word that his wife is having an affair with his best friend. He goes berserk in the day room, bashing his head against the wall and throwing himself to the floor. Officer Ratner and Officer Rutledge should
   a. handcuff inmate White and leave him on the floor until he calms down.
   b. restrain inmate White and place him in the holding cell equipped with rubber walls and floors.
   c. lock down the whole cellblock for the other inmates' safety.
   d. tell the other inmates to help inmate White get a grip on himself.

88. It is time for inmate Simon to receive his blood pressure medication. Officer Javier is responsible for passing out the afternoon medications. The first thing Officer Javier should do is
   a. have each inmate show proof that he is to receive medication.
   b. have the inmates open their mouths so that he can make sure nothing else is in their mouths before giving out pills.
   c. call out the names of inmates who are authorized to receive medications and have them step forward one at a time.
   d. send each inmate who is supposed to receive medication to the infirmary.

89. Officer DeSimone is passing out medications to inmates. He calls out the name of the first inmate to receive medication, and the inmate steps forward. What is Officer DeSimone's next step?

a. Hand the inmate a cup of water.

b. Hand the inmate the medication.

c. Have the inmate sign the log to indicate he has received his medication.

d. Tell the inmate to open his mouth for a visual inspection.

90. Officer Mendes gets a tip from inmate Smyth that inmate Jansen's sister will try to smuggle cigarettes into the facility during her next visit. When she shows up, the officer should

a. conduct a pat-down search on this visitor.

b. wait for her to pass on the cigarettes, as the tip might be wrong.

c. watch for any suspicious behavior before taking action.

d. refuse to allow the visitor to see inmate Jansen.

ANSWERS

Use the answers below not only to see how you did but also to understand why the correct answers are correct.

1. a. The overall subject of the passage concerns the criteria for using information about a witness to cast doubt on his or her testimony.

2. d. An accusation of spousal abuse would be prejudicial, but it would not be relevant to the question of the witness's truthfulness.

3. b. The last two sentences state that *police officers should not base an arrest on the testimony of an untruthful or otherwise unreliable witness,* such as a witness with a prior felony conviction, because *a case based on the testimony of a witness with prior felony convictions is vulnerable to dismissal.*

4. c. Petty theft is not a felony; therefore a petty thief would be the least likely of the choices to be vulnerable to having their credibility impeached, according to the criteria set forth in the passage.

5. b. This answer is clearly stated in the second sentence of the paragraph: *The system could be more just if it allowed victims the opportunity to confront the person who has harmed them.* There is no support in the passage for choices **a** or **d**. Although mediation (choice **c**) is mentioned in the paragraph, the statement does not indicate that victims should be the mediators.

6. d. The author of this paragraph most likely has reformist views on the criminal justice system. The very first sentence of the paragraph is your biggest clue to answering this question: *The criminal justice system needs to change.* A man with revolutionary views would certainly believe in change as well, but the word *revolutionary* indicates an extreme or complete change, certainly not what is proposed in this paragraph.

7. d. *They heard yelling coming from inside,* found in the fourth sentence, comes close to confirming choice **d**. The yelling the officers hear coming from inside Mr. Macy's house is most likely Mr. Macy, given all the circumstances described in the passage. The other choices are less certain as they are statements made by Mr. Leary when he was upset, and no witnesses or concrete facts are present to confirm them.

8. c. Dan Leary most likely made the call from his home at 1807 Washington.

9. a. According to the second sentence of the passage, Dan Leary told police he was *kept awake* by the noise coming from Mr. Macy's home.

10. b. Mr. Macy's first words to the police were "It's about time you got here," which indicates he was expecting them.

11. c. The main idea of the passage is summed up in the fourth sentence of the passage: *New violence-prevention programs in urban middle schools help reduce the crime rate . . .* The other choices, though mentioned in the passage, are not the main idea.

12. a. While keeping one's temper is probably an essential aspect of the program, it is not explicitly mentioned in the passage.

13. a. The disproportionate likelihood of adolescents to be victims of violent crime is illustrated in the second sentence of the passage, which states that although adolescents *make up only 14% of the population . . . 30% of all violent crimes . . . were committed against them.*

14. b. The idea that preventing violence against adolescents is a *twofold challenge* is explicitly stated in the fourth sentence: *Adolescents are at risk for becoming both victims and perpetrators of violence.*

15. b. The passage states that *The idea of putting more officers on foot patrol in high crime areas . . . was* *initiated in Houston in 1983 under the leadership of then-Commissioner Lee Brown.*

16. c. The *network of trust* referred to in this passage is between the community and police as you can see from the fourth sentence, where the phrase appears. The key phrase in this question is *in this passage.* You may think that police can rely only on each other, or one of the other choices may seem plausible to you. But your choice of answers must be limited to the one suggested *in this passage.*

17. d. The title should express the main idea. In this passage the main idea comes at the end. The sum of all the details in the passage suggests that community policing is not without its critics and that therefore its future is uncertain. Another key phrase is *mixed results,* which means that some communities haven't had full success with community policing.

18. a. The word *touted* is linked in this passage with the phrase *the best way to reform.* Most people would think that a good way to reform something is praiseworthy. In addition, the next few sentences in the passage describe the benefits of community policing. Criticism or negative response to the passage doesn't come until later in the passage.

19. b. This is implied in the next-to-last sentence: *The judge must determine . . . whether the suspect was aware that he or she was free to leave at any time.*

20. d. Miranda rights are read only when the suspect is taken into custody. The right to call a lawyer (choice **c**) and the right to a phone call (choice **b**) are included in the Miranda rights.

21. b. Sentence 3 is the topic sentence, indicated by the phrase *death row* in quotation marks. Sentence 2 gives the original intention of death row and sentence 4 its current use; the contrast is indicated by the beginning of sentence 4, *Today, however. . . .* Sentence 1 draws on the information in sentence 4 and therefore should follow it.

22. d. Sentence 3 introduces the topic, the Fourth Amendment. Sentence 1 details what the Fourth Amendment protects against; sentence 2 explains what was detailed in sentence 1. Sentence 4, introduced by *However,* tells that there are exceptions to what was stated in the previous three sentences, and gives an example of one of those exceptions.

23. c. Sentence 1 introduces the general topic, Sing Sing Correctional Facility. Sentence 3 introduces the original background details of the construction of Sing Sing. Sentence 4 tells of the first warden of Sing Sing, Elam Lynds; Warden Lynds is the *He* that begins sentence 2, therefore sentence 2 must follow sentence 4.

24. d. Sentence 4 introduces the topic of solicitation and explains how it might come up. Sentence 2 gives the first part of the definition of solicitation; sentence 3 gives the second. Sentence 1 refers to all the elements mentioned in sentences 2 and 3.

25. b. The second sentence is the topic sentence. Sentence 4, introduced by *In addition,* expands upon the topic sentence. Sentences 1 and 3 give of examples the standard tests mentioned in sentence 4; because sentence 3 begins with *Therefore,* it indicates that it should come after sentence 1 and conclude the four sentences.

26. a. Sentence 3 introduces the topic of the haunting of Alcatraz; sentence 1 gives some examples of the haunting. Sentence 2 tells of the different areas of the old prison considered to be haunted; sentence 4 expands upon sentence 2 by detailing the area considered to be most haunted, *The Hole.*

27. d. Sentence 3 introduces the topic, the American Correctional Association. Sentences 2 and 4 both detail the history of the ACA; but sentence 4 should fall after sentence 2 because it refers to the National Prison Association, which sentence 2 first introduced. Sentence 1 concludes the four sentences by detailing two other major corrections officer associations.

28. b. Sentence 1 provides a general rule. Sentence 4, with the word *however*, notes an exception to the general rule. Sentence 2, with the word *usually*, gives an example of the exception. Sentence 3 tells how the example is applied in practice.

29. c. Sentence 2 introduces the topic of lawyer bashing. Sentence 4 begins with *For example*, and proceeds to expand on sentence 2 by giving examples of lawyer bashing. Sentence 1 suggests that perhaps lawyer bashing is unfair; sentence 3 backs up sentence 1 with details.

30. b. The transitional word *whereas* correctly establishes a contrast.

31. c. This answer establishes the causal relationship between the two sentences.

32. d. The transitional phrase *for instance* correctly establishes an example.

33. d. The transitional word *but* correctly establishes a contrast.

34. c. A *musty* odor is one that is stale or moldy. The other choices are not descriptive of an odor.

35. b. The most common way to join two independent clauses is with a comma and a coordinating conjunction. The only sentence that correctly does both is choice **b.** For choice **a** to be correct, the coordinating conjunction *so* needs to be deleted. Choice **c** lacks a proper coordinating conjunction, and has faulty parallelism. Choice **d** contains a verb tense error.

36. a. The word *beside* means *at the side of;* the word *besides* means *other than* or *together with.* Choice **a** also has the correct subject/verb agreement error.

37. c. This is the only choice that contains the correct pronoun and comparative form. The sentence requires the subject pronoun, *he,* not the object pronoun *him.* Because the comparison in this sentence only between two people, the comparative form (*-er*) is required, not the superlative form, (*-est.*) The use of *more* in choice **d** creates a double comparison, and is therefore incorrect.

38. b. Either *obsolete* or *outmoded* could describe something no longer in fashion, in use, or useful.

39. c. *Emphasis* is the correct spelling.

40. d. *Docile* means easily led or managed. This definition best fits the context of the sentence.

41. a. Divide 4 by 5 in order to convert the fraction into a decimal: $0.80 \, 5\overline{)4.00}$.

42. b. Replace *n* with 3. Complete the multiplication ($30 \times 3 = 90$). Her overtime pay is $90.

43. c. This is a mixed decimal. The whole number, 6, is to the left of the decimal point. The hundredths place is the second digit to the right of the decimal point.

44. b. When multiplying the same number with different exponents, keep the number and add the exponents. Therefore: $8^3 \times 8^6$ is 8^9.

45. c. When the values are added together, the amount stolen was $705. (The two rings valued at $150 have a total value of $300, but remember that there is another ring valued at only $70.)

46. b. For this problem, first perform the subtraction on the left side of the equation, and then do the addition. The correct answer is 6,858.

47. c. Multiply the total weight (2.4 lbs) and the sale cost ($1.25) to get the total price. 2.4 lbs × $1.25/lb = $3.00

48. d. Perform the operations within the parentheses first: $25 + 17 = 42$; $64 - 49 = 15$. Then go on to multiply those answers as indicated by the two side-by-side parentheses: $42 \times 15 = 630$.

49. b. To answer this question, set up this equation: $47 - $5 - $15 = ?$, and do the operations in the order presented. The correct answer is $27.

50. c. This is a basic division problem: $46 \div 2 = 23$. Albert is 23 years old.

51. b.
52. d.
53. c.
54. a.
55. d.
56. c.

57. c.

58. c.

59. b.

60. a.

61. a. There are four *9*s in the set:

863473827
30**9**730**9**2**9**
483846774
374**9**63634
636383329

62. c. There are eight letter *s*'s in the sentence: *Corrections Supervisor Baumgarten's many years of experience served him well when the inmates in Dormitory Unit 5 had to be evacuated during the prison fire.*

63. b. There are ten lowercase vowels in the set:

D **e** g d D c d **a**
N E Q **o** E **o** E **e**
F m f S B F **i** m
G **a** **a** X x T L I
S S **e** E U h **u** H

64. d. If the pattern were complete there would be 35 clovers total because there should be seven clovers across and five clovers down. There are only 23 clovers, so twelve are missing.

65. b. There are thirteen upward arrows in the set.

66. d. The fact that inmate Lucas is using the library for an important purpose does not grant him immunity from the usual rules of inmate behavior.

67. a. Inmate Garvey has committed an assault and his behavior is definitely disruptive. Choices **b** and **d** do not warrant that degree of disciplinary intervention. Although some inmates might be sent to solitary for participating in the food fight, choice **a** is a much more obvious choice.

68. b. Vehicles that can easily carry hidden cargo should be searched as a matter of course. Add the fact that the driver is acting oddly and you have a highly suspicious set of circumstances. Of course inmates may be able to hide in the vehicles

mentioned in the other choices, but this is the most suspicious situation.

69. a. If the officer cannot tell for sure that an inmate is physically present in the bunk, he needs to check more closely. In the other choices, there is clearly a living person present.

70. d. If an officer expects to find weapons and contraband, the searches should be done when inmates are not expecting to be searched. Any kind of warning or set pattern gives the inmates time to find better hiding places or give the contraband to other inmates who aren't expected to be searched.

71. b. The fight between the two inmates would require documentation, in case disciplinary action is taken and to create a record of inmate behavior. None of the other choices would involve seriously disruptive behavior that would require an officer to make a written record of what has transpired.

72. d. The frequent handshakes are unusual and might indicate that the visitor is passing drugs or other contraband to the inmate.

73. a. Officer Riley needs to talk to inmate Napier if he is to have a chance at heading off a problem. Taking the actions listed in the other choices would postpone the problem rather than trying to solve it.

74. c. Choices **a** and **d** will most likely not result in an accurate count of inmates. Choice **b** may result in too much of a delay if an inmate has escaped during recreational time.

75. d. Not only is calling an inmate's wife every day not within the scope of a correction officer's duties, but this action could also easily leave the officer open to blackmail. The other situations are normal decisions and requests for officers to consider.

76. a. A person who is depressed is far more likely to commit suicide than someone who is simply not hungry, someone who is arguing, or someone who has been injured and finds it difficult to communicate because of the injury.

77. a. Physical contact is to be expected if people are smuggling drugs, and in choice **a** the physical contact is most suspicious, suggesting the possibility that the inmate has taken a drug palmed to him by his visitor during the handshake. In choice **b**, the physical contact is brief and seems more natural than in choice **a** (a weeping, elderly woman embracing her grandson). Physical contact in choice **c** is also brief and is out in the open, and in choice **d** Officer Adams is able to inspect the gift before it is handed to the inmate.

78. d. Even if you don't know the physical warning signs of heat stroke, it should be apparent that having cold skin on a hot day is not normal. Choice **b** may be a good idea, but it doesn't deal with the inmate's immediate situation, nor does choice **c**. Choice **a** would only be a good one if the officer strongly felt that the inmate was faking, which the information in the question does not support.

79. b. Of the choices listed, choice **b** is the best. Inmate Pollo's safety would be jeopardized if inmate Ireland knew he talked to the officer about the theft. Choice **c** is a poor choice, because it would erode inmate-officer relations, aside from being the wrong thing for the officer to do, and choice **d** would probably lead to inmate Ireland confronting inmate Pollo about the missing socks.

80. a. Backup is not far away and the fight is too large for one officer to try to break up alone (choice **b**), even with pepper spray (choice **d**). Choice **c** is illogical, as there is no way to tell how long any fight will last.

81. d. This is the only choice that properly addresses what an officer should do when contraband is found in an inmate's possession.

82. b. Officer Buckner has properly followed step 5 in the procedure for passing out medication.

83. d. Choices **a**, **b**, and **c** are not listed in the procedures for having an inmate get his or her hair cut. Choice **d** is step 2 in the procedure.

84. b. This is the only procedure mentioned in the policy for showering inmates assigned to solitary confinement.

85. d. The law says that it's a felony for an inmate to carry a weapon. None of the other choices are listed in any rule or procedure.

86. c. Steps 4 and 5 in the procedure for giving medications to inmates are clearly intended to ensure that the officer sees the inmate actually swallow the medication, so Officer Lindner has acted properly.

87. b. Policy states that inmates who may harm themselves should be placed in the holding cell.

88. c. This is the first step listed in the procedure for passing out medications.

89. c. This is the second step in the procedure for handing out medication. The other choices are all things the officer will do, but they come later in the procedure.

90. a. This is the only option that is listed in the policy for dealing with visitors who may be smuggling contraband into the facility. Though choices **b**, **c**, and **d** may appeal to your common sense, they are not options listed in the procedure.

13 ▶ The Physical Ability Test

CHAPTER SUMMARY

This chapter presents an overview of what to expect on the physical ability test that is required in the corrections officer selection process. It describes the different types of tests and offers specific advice about how to prepare for this challenging exam.

Corrections work demands physical fitness, strength, and agility. Corrections officers must be able to sit or stand for long periods of time, restrain and secure offenders, and respond quickly to emergencies, including climbing stairs and ladders to look for escaped offenders or carrying an injured offender or employee to safety. Because of the physical requirements of the job, law enforcement agencies use a physical test to determine if candidates have the strength and stamina for the work. The goal of this chapter is to identify the types of physical assessments you are likely to encounter and to guide your preparations so that you'll be primed for the rigors of the test. Do not arrive at the physical test with the attitude that you'll "just wing it"—the test is too strenuous to go into cold. Advance training, on the other hand, will greatly increase your chances at success.

The kind of test you'll be asked to take, and when you'll be asked to take it during the selection process, is dictated largely by legislation designed to protect against potentially discriminatory hiring practices. The test usually goes by the name Physical Ability Test (PAT), but it may also be called Physical Performance or Physical Agility Test. It is designed to measure your physical ability to be a corrections officer and generally takes one of two forms:

1. Job task simulation
2. Physical fitness

The physical ability test is one area where preparation is guaranteed to pay off. But before you can get started on an effective exercise program, you need to know as much as possible about what kind of physical assessment you will encounter. The tasks and format of the physical ability test varies from employer to employer. Will you face a physical fitness test or one designed to mirror job-related tasks? Some tests focus more on upper-body strength, others on overall fitness. For details about the test, contact the agency office or human resources department to find out how and when the test is conducted and under what conditions. Take advantage of any training sessions or test-course walk-throughs that the agency may offer—this preparation can help you pass the physical test.

Physical fitness tests are widely used and favored for their validity and predictability. A battery of tests measure your physiological parameters, such as body composition, aerobic capacity, muscular strength and endurance, and flexibility. Physical fitness tests also hint at your medical status and, perhaps more importantly, they reveal your ability to perform the potentially hundreds of physical tasks required of a corrections officer.

Job task simulation tests, on the other hand, while they may tax your physiological fitness, are designed for the most part to illustrate your ability in a handful of job tasks. Typically these tests also challenge your motor skills: balance, coordination, power, speed, reaction time, and agility.

Physical Fitness Tests

Physical fitness testing typically takes place in a group setting, most often in a gymnasium, field house, or athletic field—remember, these are "field tests." Attire for a day of testing is usually casual—sweats and sneakers—unless it occurs on the same day as other screening activities, such as a written exam. The time between events and the duration of the test vary according to the number of candidates and the number of test events.

Be prepared for the test. Bring water, nonperishable, easily digested "fuel foods" such as fruits and whole grains (whole wheat bagels or bread), and a change of clothes in the event that locker and shower facilities are available. At least one positive picture identification, a pen, and writing paper should also be in your bag.

Physical fitness test events typically include an aerobic capacity test, which measures your cardiorespiratory system's ability to take in and use oxygen to sustain activity. A field test, such as a one and one-half mile run or a 12-minute run, gives an indication of your ability to participate in sustained activities such as walking a patrol, foot pursuits, and subject control and restraint. The most common standards here are "time to complete the distance" and "distance covered in the allotted time."

Flexibility, the ability to freely use the range of motion available at a given joint in your body, is frequently tested because it impacts upon many movements and activities. Sitting for long periods at a dispatching center or bending over to lift a handcuffed subject—all will affect or be affected by your flexibility. Sit and reach tests to evaluate low back and hamstring flexibility require you to sit with straight legs extended and to reach as far forward as possible. The performance standard for this commonly used test is to touch or to go beyond your toes.

Another staple of fitness tests is muscular strength and endurance measures. Muscular strength, the ability to generate maximum force, is indicative of your potential in a "use-of-force" encounter, subject control, or other emergency situation. Bench press and leg press tests to measure upper- and lower-body strength are commonly used and require you to lift a percentage of your present body weight. A maximum effort is required after a warm-up on the testing machine/apparatus.

Dynamic muscular endurance, on the other hand, is the ability to sustain effort over time. This very common element of fitness tests is related to sitting or standing for long periods of time as well as to the incidence of low back pain and disability. Sit-up and push-up tests are frequently timed events lasting one to two minutes that involve military push-ups and traditional or hands-across-the-chest sit-ups.

Finally, it is not uncommon to encounter a test that estimates the amount of fat compared to lean tissue or total body weight. Body composition is an indication of health risk status, and the results are usually expressed as a percent. Normal ranges for healthy young adults are 18–24% for females and 12–18% for males. A skinfold technique that measures the thickness of the skin and subcutaneous fat at sex-specific sites is the most common field test to estimate overall percentage of body fat.

Job Task Simulation Tests

Job task simulation tests use a small sample of actual or simulated job tasks to evaluate your ability to do the job of a corrections officer. This type of test is used because of its realistic relationship to the job and law enforcement training and because of its defensibility as a fair measure of a candidate's physical abilities.

Because courts of law have found it unreasonable to evaluate skills that require prior training, general job-related skills are tested at the applicant level. It's unlikely that you will be required to demonstrate competency with a firearm or nightstick or knowledge of self-defense movements, for example. But climbing through a window, over barriers, and up stairs in use-of-force situations, such as a takedown or simulated application

of handcuffs, are common tasks. The following are some more examples of the events in a physical ability test:

- Dummy Drag
- Obstacle Course
- Stair Climb
- Run and handcuff
- Lift 45 lbs. and over
- Carry 45 lbs. and over

Simulation tests are often presented as obstacle courses, with the events performed one after another and linked by laps around the gymnasium or athletic field. Frequently, the requirement is to successfully complete the course or each event in a given amount of time. The test may be given on an individual or small group basis. Candidates performing a job task simulation test may have the opportunity to walk through the course or they may be allowed to practice certain events prior to actual testing.

Training Tips

In preparing for a physical fitness test, you must plan ahead, taking into account both the timing and the content of the test. The short-term objective, of course, is to pass the test. But your greater goal is to integrate fitness into your lifestyle so that you can withstand the rigors of the career you want in corrections.

The first order of business is to determine the type of fitness test you'll have to complete. What you have to accomplish on the test will guide your training program. You can tailor your training to simulate the test and to train for the test events.

Following some basic training principles will help you create a safe and effective training program. Steady progress is the name of the game. Remember, you didn't get into or out of shape overnight, so you won't be able to change your condition overnight. To avoid injury while achieving overall fitness, balance in fitness training is essential. Work opposing muscle groups when doing strength or flexibility training and include aerobic conditioning as well as proper nutrition in your total fitness program.

To achieve continued growth in fitness you must overload the body's systems. The body makes progress by adapting to increasing demands. With adaptation, your systems are able to overcome the physical challenge, resulting in a higher level of fitness.

Finally, don't forget rest. It allows the body and the mind to recover from the challenges of training—and to prepare for another day.

12 Weeks to the Test Date

Your primary goal when faced with a short window of preparation is to meet a given standard, either physical fitness or job task simulation. Therefore, "specificity of training"—training for what you will actually be asked to do on the test—is the rule. If you're training for a physical fitness test, then the performance standards are your training goals. You should make every attempt to use or to build up to the standards as the training intensity level. If you are unable to reach the standards right away, approximate them and increase the intensity a little more each week until you achieve them.

If you're training for a pre-academy test, try to determine what the academy's physical training (PT) curriculum entails, use these as your modes of training, and test yourself with the standards every two to three weeks.

On the other hand, if the short-term goal is to meet a job task simulation test standard, particularly one that is used for pre-academy selection, you should determine the content of the PT curriculum and use it as the training model. At the same time, practice the skills required on the test once every two weeks in lieu of a training day.

Six or More Months to Go

A six-month training program is essentially similar to the one described previously. However, the longer time-frame means that your goal can become making permanent, positive changes in your lifestyle rather than simply applying training principles to pass a test. Reasonable and gradual changes in your lifestyle will help to ensure that the behavioral and physical changes are permanent.

This extended timetable also reduces the likelihood of injury and allows for more diversity and balance in your training program and lifestyle. If you're preparing for a physical fitness test, you have the opportunity to set (and meet) performance goals that may be 25–50% greater than the standards themselves. On the other hand, if you have more than six months to prepare for a job task simulation test, you may want to avoid practicing any of the skills required for the first three months to avoid injury. Instead, consider incorporating sports activities into your conditioning routine; this will provide an enjoyable method of training. After three months, you could begin practicing the physical test skills one day every two to four weeks.

Task-Specific Training

If you know that part of your physical exam is a job task simulation test, you may want to integrate some form of task-specific preparation into your general fitness program. Knowing which events will be included in the exam is important to getting ready for the test. Some agencies give candidates the opportunity to do a walk-through or practice on the test course. This can help you understand areas where you need to improve for the PAT.

The following are examples of PAT tasks, in addition to what they test for and how you might prepare for them. Although these descriptions may not represent the exact form of tasks that you will face on the physical exam—be ready to adapt them to your own needs. Contact the hiring agency to find out what specific tasks will be required on your PAT.

Staying "FITT"

FITT stands for Frequency, Intensity, Type, and Time. FITT simplifies your training by helping you plan what to do, how hard, and for how long. Because the four FITT "variables" are interrelated, you need to be careful about how you exercise. For example, intensity and time have an inverse relationship: as the intensity of your effort increases, the length of time you can maintain that effort decreases. A good rule of thumb when adjusting your workout variables to achieve optimum conditioning is to modify one at a time, increasing by 5–10%. Be sure to allow your body to adapt before adjusting up again.

The following presents some FITT guidelines to help you plan your training program.

Frequency
- 3–5 times a week

Intensity
- Aerobic training—60–85% of maximum effort
- Resistance training—8–12 repetitions
- Flexibility training—Just to slight tension

Type
- Aerobic—Bike, walk, jog, swim
- Resistance—Free weights, weight machines, calisthenics
- Flexibility—Static stretching

Time
- Aerobic—20–60 minutes
- Resistance—1–3 sets, 2–4 exercises/body part
- Flexibility—Hold stretched position 8–30 seconds

Dummy Drag

Grab a dummy and drag it over a prescribed distance, such as 100 feet. The weight, distance, and time limit may vary, depending on the hiring agency. For example, the PAT for federal corrections officers requires dragging a 75 lb. dummy a minimum of 694 feet continuously within three minutes.

Tests: agility, leg strength, balance

Tips: Use a good grip, usually behind the shoulders with your arms wrapped around the chest. Lean backward and then use your body and legs to propel yourself backward. Employ your legs more than your upper body, so as not to strain your back.

Practice: Load up a sheet with bulky objects (a tire, bags of sand) to simulate a dummy. Time yourself and measure the distance you are able to cover.

Wall Vault

Vault yourself over a wall of four or six feet. This task may be part of a larger obstacle course.

Tests: balance, coordination

Tips: Try to get both hands on top of the wall. Using two hands you can pull your lower body up and then swing yourself over the wall.

Practice: Uphill sprints of 30 to 50 yards will increase your leg strength, which will help you get the initial power you need to get over the wall. After developing your leg strength, experiment by vaulting over fences of various heights.

Stair Climb

Wear a weight belt, and climb up and down stair steps. The federal-level physical test requires candidates to go up and down 108 steps in 45 seconds wearing a 20-pound weight.

Tests: leg strength and endurance

Tips: Make sure that you understand the task requirements. Some agencies demand that you take each step one by one. Others allow you to take two or three steps at a time.

Practice: Run stair steps, wearing a weight belt or an improvised weight, like a 20-pound backpack. The stairwells of parking structures or the steps at a stadium are good places to practice.

A Sample Exercise Program

All of the information in this chapter about training principles and practices is put into action on the gym floor. A page taken from the academy physical fitness training book will help to get you fit and ready to excel in the physical test.

Physical training begins with a warm-up to increase your core body temperature and to prepare you for the more intense conditioning to follow. Brisk walking or jogging, in place or around a gymnasium, or jumping rope are good start-up options and should be conducted for three to five minutes. This is followed immediately by a period of active head-to-toe stretching to prevent injury.

Basic conditioning in the academy frequently is achieved with calisthenic exercises (cals). Beginners can do sets of ten on a "two count" and those of intermediate or advanced fitness can begin on a "four count" (1, 2, 3, 1; 1, 2, 3, 2; etc.). Running in formation typically follows cals and is done at about a 9–10 minute per mile pace. Marine Corps cadences played on a Walkman may help to put you in the mood for academy runs! For those who are just beginning to prepare for the fitness test, 8–12 minutes of running is a safe start; those more fit may begin with 25 or more minutes. A three- to five-minute cool-down period to recover and some gentle, static stretching from the floor, focusing on the lower legs, will complete your workout.

14 ▶ The Personal History Statement and Background Investigation

CHAPTER SUMMARY

Paperwork tells the tale in corrections—you only get one shot at this document. This chapter will guide you through this critical phase of the application process. It provides useful suggestions for collecting information, choosing personal references, and creating an accurate, error-free document.

The Personal History Statement is exactly that—a detailed personal statement of your life history. You may hear it called by other terms—simply "the application" or the Applicant History Statement. Although the paperwork may go by different names, the purpose of the statement is the same: to provide background investigators with the material for a hiring panel or personnel department to make a sound decision about hiring you. Your Personal History Statement will form the basis of your interview before the oral board—board members who will scrutinize this document and use it, in concert with the results of your background check, to question you and determine whether you are right for corrections work.

You can expect that a high level of detail will be required for your statement. Although not all applications are as comprehensive, some will ask for information as far back as your childhood. Others will require only information from your high-school graduation to the present. This chapter will serve as a guide to help you present an accurate, honest summary of your past and present life. It reviews how to collect essential documentation, select personal references, and present your statement. A clear, well-researched Personal History Statement can help your background check go smoothly and aid in convincing an oral board that you are the person to hire.

Be aware that there are no nationwide standards for the Personal History Statement. Hiring practices depend on the agency and can differ from state to state. Correctional facilities in different areas may not have the same priorities, budgets, or staffing—so, the hiring process may differ as well. If you labored over New Jersey's application last week, do not be surprised that when you pick up the application for New York, it uses a different set of ground rules. As you create your Personal History Statement, be sure to keep copies of your work and important documentation. You will likely be able to re-use portions of it for different applications. Regardless of how various agencies design their application process, their objective remains the same: they all want to learn about your past, present, and potential.

Collecting Information

Before you have even received your applications, you can start gathering important information. With every step in this process, be sure to keep plenty of copies of your work. Collecting information takes effort—keeping copies saves critical time by ensuring that you only have to make the effort once. If you decide to apply to a different agency, you will have all the necessary information on hand. You can begin to develop a personal record, employment history, and driving record by filling out the following lists:

- **Personal addresses** (every residence where you've lived, from birth to the present)
- **Job positions** (list of all of your jobs, including part-time and summer positions)
- **Employer addresses, phone numbers, and names of your supervisors**
- **Driving record** (list of all of your traffic tickets and moving violations)

Do not neglect the last bulleted item listed above: *driving record.* Research your own driving record carefully. You'll be asked by some agencies to list every traffic ticket you've ever received in any state or country,

whether on a military post or on civilian roadways. Some may ask you to list only the moving violations (these include speeding, running red lights, unsafe lane changes), while other agencies want to see moving violations and tickets for things like expired license plates, failure to wear seat belts, and expired automobile insurance.

One agency may ask you to tell them about the tickets you've received in the past five years while others want to know your entire driving history. Do your homework. Create as complete an account as possible. Do not leave off tickets you think investigators won't find out about—you want to be perceived as honest and forthcoming, and you want to prepare yourself to respond to any concerns about your record.

Document Checklist

Your next step is to gather your important documents. Mark off each item as you collect it and make a copy of it. If you don't have certified copies of the following listed documents, start calling or writing the proper authorities now to find out what you need to do to get them. For example, if you've lost your social security card, contact the social security office in your community and arrange to replace it. Legal documents often take anywhere from six to eight weeks for delivery—so begin the process as soon as you can. The following is a list of the important documents you will need. Review the requirements of your application to see if you need to gather additional forms.

- ✔ birth certificate
- ✔ Social Security card
- ✔ DD 214 (if you are a veteran)
- ✔ naturalization papers (if applicable)
- ✔ high school diploma or G.E.D. certificate
- ✔ high school transcripts
- ✔ college transcripts
- ✔ current driver's license(s)
- ✔ current copies of driving record(s)
- ✔ current consumer credit reports

Many agencies have a deadline for filling out and returning the Personal History Statement. If time runs out and you realize you won't be able to turn in the Personal History Statement with all the required documents, contact the agency office or human resources department to see what you should do. Many agencies will tell you to attach a memo to your application outlining your problem and what you have done about it. For example, if you've ordered a copy of your birth certificate but have yet to receive it, attach a letter of explanation to your application detailing when you requested the document, where you asked for the copy to be sent, and when you expect to receive it. If possible, attach a dated copy of the letter you sent requesting your certificate.

Questions to Ask Before You Begin

Before rounding up your important documents, check with the agencies where you are applying to find out the rules for how certain documents are submitted—like college transcripts, for instance. Departmental officials may require you to have the school send the documentation directly to their personnel office instead of to you at home via regular mail. The same goes for credit reports or copies of driving records. Contact the personnel department, explain to them that you are trying to collect all of your documentation, and ask them how they accept these documents so you'll know what to do.

Other questions you need to ask are:

✔ Do you need photocopies or original documents?
✔ Will you return my original if I send it?
✔ How recent does the credit history have to be?
✔ What's the most recent copy you will accept of my college transcript?

The answers to these questions can save you money and time.

▶ Drafting Your Personal History Statement

Once you have made your decision about where you are applying and have received your application, you can begin crafting your Personal History Statement. Do not write directly on the application form—instead, download a blank copy or photocopy the form, and put away the original for now. Use the photocopy as your working draft—this way you can make mistakes without having to request a new application form.

Later when you have transferred your information onto the final form of your Personal History Statement, make a photocopy of the completed version. Make copies of any accompanying documentation as well, and keep them in a safe place. If the personnel office should lose or misplace your application, you will be able to supply them with another copy quickly. It's also essential to have a copy of your Personal History Statement so that you can review it before your interview with the oral board—many of the questions you will face will be based on your statement and your background check. Keeping all of your information on file will also help you complete future applications.

The following is an eight-step checklist to help you draft your Personal History Statement and avoid common applicant pitfalls.

1. **Resume vs. Personal History Statement**
   A formal resume like one you may prepare for a civilian job is usually not much good to a law enforcement agency. Many agencies will simply not accept a resume—they rely on your Personal History Statement to get the details of your life, education, and experience. Although criminal justice instructors in many colleges suggest to their students to have a resume made, it's always best to call and ask a personnel representative whether or not you should.

2. **Read the instructions first.**
   Read the application instructions before you begin filling out the practice copy of the Personal

History Statement. In fact, it's a good idea to read the entire document from first to last page before you tackle this project. Have a note pad next to you and as you read, make notes of everything you do not understand. If your questions aren't answered after you've read the complete document, phone the personnel office. Be sure that you understand each item and what is expected of you. Pay close attention to the instructions and follow them exactly.

3. **Provide thorough and accurate information.**
   While filling out your Personal History Statement, give as much information as you possibly can and make certain the information is accurate. For example, verify phone numbers from your former employers by *calling* the numbers to see if they are correct. If a number is no longer in service and you do not have a forwarding number, make a note of this on your application.

   Never assume that a detail is too trivial for a background investigator to follow up on—give complete and up-to-date information so the investigator can easily verify it. Your Personal History Statement will form a positive impression with the hiring staff if it is correct and detailed. The investigator and the oral board will be looking at the effort you made in filling the application as well as its content.

4. **Do not leave areas blank on your Statement.**
   Many agencies explicitly state in their application instructions that failing to respond to questions or provide requested information will result in disqualification. Other agencies may not disqualify you, but they probably will not consider you a good job candidate. Filling out a Personal History Statement requires planning, efficiency, and attention to detail—demonstrate that you are a strong applicant through your accuracy, thoroughness, and timeliness.

5. **Do your own background research.**
   Do not rely on the background investigator to retrieve hard-to-get information about your history. The Personal History Statement is a prime opportunity for you to showcase your superb organizational skills and professionalism. Demonstrate initiative by tracking down important details. For example, if you worked for a business that is now not in operation, you may need to do some extra leg work to locate the phone number of your former supervisor. If you don't know where she or he works now, but you do have some mutual acquaintances, call them to see if you can get an up-to-date phone number for your supervisor.

6. **Ask questions.**
   If you do not understand a question on the application, do not guess at its meaning—contact the personnel office to clarify it. You may run the risk of being disqualified if you answer an item incorrectly, incompletely, or if you leave it blank. Don't take chances when asking a simple question will clear up the problem.

7. **Be honest.**
   Always give truthful information about your personal history. Avoid lying or presenting an inaccurate picture by giving only half of the information or obscuring the facts. For example, an applicant may not want to admit on his statement that he received a ticket for failing to register his car. He may feel that including this information will make him appear disorganized and irresponsible. However, by not including it, he will appear dishonest. The best strategy is to admit your mistakes and be prepared to explain at your interview what you learned from them and how you corrected them. Your Personal History Statement is a reflection of your character—employers are looking for candidates who are honest and trustworthy.

8. Review and revise.

The hiring staff uses facts, impressions, and sometimes intuition to make hiring decisions. With this in mind, every detail is worth a second look before you call your Personal History Statement complete. Ask yourself:

✔ Is my handwriting as neat as it can be?

✔ Did I leave off answers or skip items?

✔ Do my sentences make sense?

✔ Is my spelling accurate?

✔ Are my dates and times consistent?

How To Read And Answer Questions

Reading questions and instructions carefully is critical to successfully completing the Personal History Statement. Pay close attention to these key words as you read:

- All
- Every
- Any
- Each

If you see these words in a question, you are being asked to include all the information you know. For example, you may see the following set of instructions in your Personal History Statement:

List *any* and *all* pending criminal charges against you.

This agency wants to know about every single criminal charge that may be pending against you no matter what jurisdiction may be handling the case. Do not try to evade the question by offering only partial information. If your fear is that the information looks negative, keep in mind that you will have a chance to explain your actions and describe what you've learned from your experiences at your interview before the oral board. Lying or providing incomplete information on your statement may disqualify you from the job.

Here is another example:

Have you *ever* been arrested or taken into police custody for *any* reason?

Note the use of the key words *ever* and *any*. That means the agency wants you to list any such incidents that have occurred, past and present. If you don't know what is meant by the term *arrested,* then call the personnel office to clarify its meaning. Some applicants may be tempted to justify or deny an arrest by claiming that the police did not put them in handcuffs. Do not interpret key terms in a way that obscures meaning. When in doubt, list any situation you think has falls into the category you are working on.

Here's a request for information that includes several eye-catching words.

List *all* traffic citations you received in the past five (5) years, in this or *any* other state (moving and non-moving) *excluding* parking tickets.

In this example, the agency leaves little doubt that what you should do here is make a complete list of every kind of violation you've been issued a citation for, no matter where you got it and no matter what the traffic violation was for within the past five years. They even let you know the one kind of citation they don't need to know about—parking tickets. If you aren't sure what a moving violation is or what a non-moving violation is, call the agency for an explanation. Keep in mind that when the officer issued you a citation on a single piece of paper, you may have been cited for more than one violation. Most citations have blanks for at least three violations, sometimes more. For example, an applicant was recently pulled over for speeding. The officer discovered that he had no insurance and that his car license plates were expired. She told him that she was writing three tickets for these violations, but handed him only one piece of paper. Did he get one citation or three? The answer is three.

Personal References

The rigor with which your background will be checked depends on the policies of the hiring agency. Some conduct a fairly superficial check, calling your former employers and schools simply to verify that you were there when you say you were there and didn't have any problems during that time. Other departments will investigate you in more depth, asking references how long and how well they knew you and what kind of person they found you to be. For this reason, selecting your personal references is a critical part of your Personal History Statement. Pay close attention to any application guidelines about references: some forms ask you to list at least five people as references, while others only ask for a maximum of three. Some forms specify how long you may know a reference before you list them on your application. For example, some instructions may direct you to list only those individuals whom you've known for a *minimum* of two years.

Choose references who know you well and represent the different areas of your life—school, work, volunteer activities, church, or the military. Good personal references will be able to comment on your personality, ability to interact with others, work style, or outside interests. Do not list a reference that does not know you well or because he or she has impressive credentials. An investigator will know within minutes if a reference knows you—if the reference doesn't know you, the investigator may request another reference. On the other hand, a family relative may know you well, but investigators may not consider him or her to be a reliable source. Personal references who are reluctant to talk with an investigator are not good choices, either—they may do you more harm than good.

Before you list a reference, call the person first to ask if he or she is willing to speak on your behalf. Describe the job position and agency where you are applying. Make sure that the person does not object to being contacted by an investigator as part of a routine background check. If the person agrees to be a reference, verify the phone number where the reference prefers to be contacted. Ask your references to specify the best times to reach them. Some investigators will telephone references, others might make a personal visit.

Let your references know how important it is for them to be open and honest with the investigator. Your references can expect to have a conversation—not an interrogation—with the investigator. The investigator's goal is to create a picture of you from those who know you well.

Preparation is essential to developing the personal reference section of your application—you want to ensure that you provide accurate, up-to-date information. Allow yourself time to complete the process of selecting references, contacting them, and verifying their information.

Finalizing Your Application

You've filled out the practice copy you made of the Personal History Statement, made all your mistakes on that copy, answered every question, and filled in all the appropriate blanks. Now you're ready to make the final copy.

Part of the impression you will make on the hiring staff will come from your application's appearance. Make sure your handwriting is neat and legible. If you do not have enough space on the form for your information, attach an additional sheet of paper instead of writing in the margins. Read your application over carefully—or better yet, have another person proofread it. Did you spell words correctly? Do your sentences make sense to the reader? (A good tip here is to read your answers out loud to yourself. If something doesn't sound right to your ear, then you need to rewrite it.) Here are some items you might find useful as you work on your application:

- a dictionary
- a grammar handbook
- a good pen (or pencil—whatever the directions tell you to use)

Be certain to check your work, check it again, and have someone you trust look over it before you make your final copy.

Every contact you make with the hiring agency makes an impression. The appearance and effort that you put into your Personal History Statement is one that will follow you through the hiring process. The oral board members that you will meet in your interview base their comments and questions on this essential document—and the discrepancies they find in it, if any.

You now have the information you need to make the Personal History Statement a manageable task. This is not a document to take lightly—it is a crucial component to your success in becoming a corrections officer. To review, it's important that you:

- Follow instructions and directions.
- Be honest and open about your past and present.
- Provide accurate information.
- Choose excellent personal references.
- Turn in presentable, error-free documentation.
- Turn in documents on time.

Showing care and interest in the application process will go a long way toward demonstrating that you are right for the job.

15 ▶ The Oral Interview

CHAPTER SUMMARY

This chapter demystifies the interview with a down-to-earth look at the process. It offers tips, suggestions, and scenarios that will help you know what to expect and will increase your effectiveness during the interview. Although you don't know the exact questions you will face, there is a lot you can do to prepare for a successful outcome.

Corrections agencies nationwide depend on some form of interview to help them choose suitable corrections officer candidates. In California, a two-person panel consisting of a Chairperson and a State Services Representative questions state applicants for at least 25 minutes. Applicants in Texas can look forward to a shorter interview, but agencies in other states often question applicants in interviews that last up to one hour.

The interview process for corrections work is unlike any job interview you will ever experience. Most likely you will face a panel of interviewers, and the questions you will be asked may be pointed or personal. Each interviewing board will ask a different set of questions, and their standards for judging your answers may vary. However, each panel focuses on the same objective: to evaluate your character and skills and see whether you have what it takes to do the job well. The information in this chapter will show you how to prepare for the interview so that you can present yourself at your best.

The Oral Board

Most likely you've had at least one experience interviewing for a job. Will an interview conducted by a corrections oral board be similar to a civilian job interview? Yes and no. Both prospective civilian and law enforcement employers are looking for the most qualified person for the job—a reliable, honest man or woman who will work hard. And like any job applicant, you will want to present yourself well by dressing professionally, being on time, and answering questions clearly. However, there are some key differences between a job interview in the civilian work world and an interview for a corrections position.

Unlike most job interviews, an interview for corrections work involves not just one interviewer, but a panel of two, three, four—maybe more—individuals that make up the "oral board." The board members will most likely be experienced personnel specialists trained in hiring corrections applicants. These personnel agencies use the expertise of current and former correction officers to conduct interview sessions and look for the characteristics that will make a successful candidate.

The purpose of the oral board is to get to know you well—through the details of your work experience and your personal life decisions. Instead of relying on a one- or two-page resume, the board will use information you have provided on your application as well as information from your background investigation. Investigators will provide board members with a detailed report about your past and present life history.

In some cases, the board members may ask you questions to which they already know the answer. You may be asked to explain why you've made the decisions you've made in your life—both personal and professional. You may also be asked questions that don't have right or wrong answers, but instead reveal how you deal with difficult situations.

Review Your Personal History Statement

During the interview process, members of the oral board will have a copy of your Personal History Statement and a copy of the investigators' final report on hand. While you are answering questions for the board, some board members will be looking through the pages of your life—checking what you say against what they see on paper. Naturally, you'll want to remember what information you gave them. Make sure that you review—read and reread—the details of your written statement the night before your interview; do not rely on your memory to recall the facts and information you provided. Take the time to go over your application and carefully think about each piece of information you provided in this document. As you review your copy of the Statement, think about the questions such information could generate.

Giving the board an informative, accurate tour of where you've been in your life and who you are will increase your success in the interviewing process. Be ready to address the problem areas of your work and personal history. For example, although you may have written down that you were once fired from a job, and you may have even discussed the incident with a background investigator in an earlier conversation, the board will want to hear your experience and reasoning for themselves. Do not avoid the panel's questions or make excuses about your past. Remember that facing and solving problems can build character. Focus on what you learned from your experiences—both the positive events and the negative ones.

First Impressions

Preparation for the oral interview board begins when you make the decision to apply. From the moment you first make contact with a personnel agency, everything you say and do can later affect your interview. Even walking through the doors of the personnel office to pick up an application, you have the opportunity to make a lasting impression. Remember: you are dealing with professionals who are trained to notice and remember people and details. Dress appropriately each time you make contact with the agency where you want to work.

The same rule applies when you contact an agency by telephone—even if you are just calling an agency to request an application, make a positive impression by speaking directly and clearly. If you have any questions, make a list beforehand. On the phone, listen carefully to each response to your questions. Do not worry about impressing the agency during these first contacts with how much you know. Your opportunity to impress the agency will come later in the appropriate setting—the interview.

Presenting Yourself

How you present yourself at the interview—your first real encounter with your prospective employer—can show how much you want the job. Respect for authority is an important characteristic of a corrections officer, and you should demonstrate this quality through your dress and manner during the interview. One way to show respect for your interviewers is to be on time—preferably 15 to 20 minutes early so that you have time to become comfortable in your surroundings and focus on the task at hand. An early arrival means you planned ahead for emergencies (flat tires, wrong turns, etc.), that you arrived in enough time to prepare yourself mentally, and that you place a value on other people's time as well as your own.

Your appearance is another way to demonstrate that you want the job. You may feel like you don't have much control over what happens to you in during an interview, but this is one area where you do have control. The way you dress sends a signal to the people who are watching you walk into the room. Business suits for men or women, rather than casual wear, are the most appropriate dress for the interview. Whereas casual clothes send the message that you wouldn't mind having the job if someone wouldn't mind giving it to you, business wear tells the board that you want the job and that you take the interview process seriously. If you don't own a suit, consider borrowing one or renting one.

Your posture and body language—how you stand, sit, and carry yourself—can also express your respect for the panel of interviewers. As you answer questions, try not to fidget or slump in your chair. Maintain a polite and interested manner, without being self-conscious or phony. Listen carefully to the board's questions and make eye contact with the questioners.

Be aware that oral boards typically schedule numerous applicants in one day for interviews. That means that little things that can set you apart from other applicants—like dressing appropriately or listening attentively—can take on extra importance.

Developing Self-Awareness

Many of the questions you'll hear from the interview panel are designed to reveal how well you know yourself and how honest you can be about your talents and your shortcomings. Self-awareness—being aware of what you do and why you do it—is important to your success as a job candidate. Just as you should know your strong points, you should be able to list your weaknesses if a board member asks you to identify them. Be sure to also let the board know what you do to correct or compensate for your weaknesses.

Consider any issues from your application that may concern the board. Did the application cover your driving record, drug use, or education? Did you have any problems in these areas? Be honest with yourself about your past experiences. Know your strengths, too. Think about what you have learned from your work and personal history. Some applicants find talking about strengths as difficult as talking about weaknesses. You must be able to do both. The point of learning your flaws and strengths is to develop self-awareness so that you can show how your experience has prepared you for the demanding job of a corrections officer.

Public Speaking 101

Interviews can be nerve-wracking—all the more so if you are facing a panel of interviewers instead of a single questioner. However, you can overcome this common anxiety with practice. Keep in mind some of the following basics behind effective public speaking:

- **Speak clearly and audibly** enough so that the panel does not have to work hard to hear you.

- **Use full sentences,** if possible. Do not use slang.
- **Make eye contact** with your questioners. This will display confidence and help the panel get to know you.
- **Face forward.** When you look away or slump while talking, you will likely mumble and give the impression of being confused or lacking confidence.

Your answering process can also be broken down into simple parts: listen carefully; think first; speak clearly; and stay focused. By taking the time to follow each of these steps, you show the panel not just *what* you think, but *how* you think. If you believe that you may be getting off the subject of the question you were asked, try to get back on track. To do this, you may need to go over the question again—something that you will be able to do if you listened carefully in the first place—and rethink your answer.

Practice is one of the keys to success on an oral board. If you've ever truly practiced something—batting a ball, for instance—you know that once you have the motion down, you can rely on your muscles to "remember" what to do when it comes time to play the game. The same rationale holds true for practicing oral board answers.

Public speaking classes can also go a long way toward polishing the skills needed to ace the interview. These courses can help you develop better listening habits and speaking techniques. They provide you with useful feedback and give you the chance to practice your skills. If speaking in public makes you nervous, strongly consider taking a speech class at a nearby community college or through an adult education center. If you cannot take a class, ask a friend to act as an interviewer and question you. This way you can become comfortable with the interviewing process and work on the areas where you need improvement.

Winning Characteristics

The primary concern of the interviewing panel is to sift through your experiences and responses to see if you can handle the demands of corrections work. Your task in the interview is to convince the board—through your responses to questions—that you can meet the demands of the job. The board is looking to see if you have the following qualities:

- maturity
- common sense
- good judgment
- compassion
- integrity
- honesty
- reliability
- the ability to work without constant supervision

These qualities aren't ranked in order of importance—they are all important to being effective on the job. Corrections officers, probably more than any other law enforcement professionals, depend the on good communication skills. They work in environments where their best tool is their ability to talk men and women into complying with rules and regulations that take away the most basic of human freedoms. Oral board members are looking for the applicants who are good team players, who will be sensitive to the safety and concerns of their fellow officers, and who can follow and give orders at appropriate times.

Demonstrating Maturity

Maturity is a huge concern with corrections agencies. They cannot afford to hire men and women who are unable to take responsibility for their actions or in some cases, the actions of those around them. Although maturity cannot be measured in years, if you are 18 years old and have little work or life experience, agencies will want to see as much proof as possible that you have the necessary maturity for the job. Youth and inexperience will *not* disqualify you from the hiring

Clear, courteous spoken language is important in the interview. Most law enforcement agencies are paramilitary organizations that use a rank structure similar to that of the military. In the military it's customary to address higher-ranking men and women with courtesy and answer questions with "Yes, ma'am" or "yes, sir" or "no, ma'am" or "no, sir." If you have military experience, you will be ahead in this area.

If you are not accustomed to using these terms of courtesy, practice them. Make a conscious effort to use them. It's rarely considered rude to simply respond "yes" or "no" to a question, but you will be on shaky ground if "yeah" or "uh-huh" are your customary responses. Similarly, asking "Could you please repeat the question?" is preferable to uttering "What?"

process, but you may have to put in extra effort to show how well you handle responsibility. If you have a limited job background, consider signing up for volunteer work that you care about. Volunteer work is a great way to gain experience dealing with people, and it can demonstrate your reliability and commitment. If you live at home with parents, consider the ways in which you are responsible around the home. If you are on your own, but living with roommates, talk to the board about how you resolve conflicts that arise in your living situation.

If you do not have a lot of work experience, you may want to work extra hard on your communication skills before going to the board. The more articulate you are, the better you will be able to sell yourself and your potential to the board.

If you have a good deal of work and life experience, you may have some advantages. Oral boards are receptive to men and women who have experience that can be examined and verified. However, you must also be prepared to explain any problematic incidents from your past or present. Carefully review your application and consider the information that the investigator used for your background check. Target areas that you will most likely be asked to explain, and prepare what you are going to say about them.

If you have a longer history, be prepared for a longer session before the oral board. If a board is not required to adhere strictly to time limits, you may stay longer than other applicants because you have more to cover. As with any applicant, self-awareness and confidence in your communication skills will help your interview to go smoothly.

What to Expect

In your interview before the oral board, you will hear all kinds of questions—personal questions about your family life, questions about your likes and dislikes, questions about your temperament, your friends, and even a few designed to make you laugh. Most likely you will *not* encounter many questions that can be answered with a simple "yes" or "no."

Open-Ended Questions

The open-ended question is the one you are most likely to hear. Board members like these questions because it gives them an opportunity to see how articulate you are and it gives them insight into how you think. This is also a way for them to ease into more specific questions. Here is an example of an exchange that begins with an open-ended question:

Board Member: "Mr. Alvarez, can you tell the board about your Friday night bowling league?"

Alvarez: "Yes ma'am. I've been bowling in this league for about two years. We meet every Friday night around 6:00 P.M. and bowl until about 8:30 P.M. I like it because it gives me a chance to see friends who I may not get to see otherwise because everyone is so busy. This also gives me time to spend with my wife. We're in first place right now and I like it that way."

Board Member: "Oh, congratulations. You must be a pretty competitive bowler."

Alvarez: "Yes ma'am, I am. I like to win and I take the game pretty seriously."

Board Member: "How do you react when your team loses, Mr. Alvarez?"

It may seem like small talk, but that one question generates enough information for the board to draw a lot of conclusions about Mr. Alvarez. They can see that he likes to interact with his friends, he values spending time with his wife, and that competition and winning are important to him. Mr. Alvarez' answer opens up an avenue for the board to explore how he reacts to disappointment, and how he is able to articulate his feelings and reactions—from his responses, they'll probably get a good idea of his temperament.

Open-ended questions allow the board to fish around for information, and learn about the real you. Take advantage of these opportunities to open up to the board and give them an idea of who you are and what you value.

Straight-Forward Questions

The oral board will also ask you straight-forward questions—questions to which everyone in the room already knows the answer. Example:

Board Member: "Mr. Alvarez, you were in the military for four years?"

Alvarez: "Yes sir, I was in the Marines from 1982 until 1986."

Board Member: "Why did you get out?"

The straight-forward question is used most often as a way to give the applicant a chance to warm up and to be aware of what area the board is about to explore. It's also a way for the board to check up on the information they have. Board members and background investigators can misread or misunderstand information they receive. Understanding this, board members will usually be careful to confirm details with you during the interview.

"Fishing Expeditions"

When an oral board asks a "fishing expedition" type of question, they are looking for your response to a potentially controversial question. Most likely, you will not know why they are asking the question, and the board isn't giving out any clues. Example:

Board Member: "Mr. Alvarez, in your application you stated that you've never been detained by police. (Usually they will pause a few seconds and then get to the point.) You've *never* been detained?"

In the example above, if the applicant has been detained by police and failed to list this on his application, then he'll be wondering if the board *knows* that this happened. The odds are high that the board already knows the answer. If the applicant has never been detained, he may wonder if someone on his list of references did not tell the truth to the background investigator. Did someone on the board misread his application?

Chances are, the board is simply fishing to see what he'll say. If you encounter this question type, don't let it throw you off balance. Don't try to guess why the board is asking the question, and don't try to answer according to what you think the panel wants to hear. Instead, answer truthfully and openly. Experienced interviewers can detect a false or phony tone, even if your answer isn't a technically a lie. Use this type of question to show your integrity by giving an honest reply.

Situational/Ethics Queries

Board members often present a hypothetical situation to see how an applicant might respond. Some interviews consist almost exclusively of situational or ethics questions. In other interviews, an agency may ask only one situational question and then spend the rest of the time asking you about your past job history. Here is an example of a situational inquiry:

Board Member: "Mr. Alvarez, assume you are a corrections officer and you are alone with 20 inmates. All of a sudden five of them turn on the others and a huge fight breaks out. What do you do?"

Here is an example of an ethics inquiry:

Board Member: "Mr. Alvarez, Imagine that you are a corrections officer and during a routine shakedown of an inmate's cell you discover a small cache of tobacco, which is a contraband substance. The inmate tells you that if you choose to 'look the other way' just this one time, he will give you a very valuable tip regarding another inmate. You are up for a promotion, and it's possible that acting on this tip could increase your chances. What do you do?"

Situational and ethics queries are more difficult to anticipate than questions about your personal or job history. However, your technique for answering them should be the same: preparation, self-awareness, and honesty. Before your interview, consider what your belief system is—what values influence your major decisions and actions? Do not be surprised if the board asks you a round of intense follow-up questions to clarify your choice. Stressful questioning may be part of the point. Because corrections work involves stressful situations, the panel wants to see how you respond under pressure. Expect boards to notice discrepancies in your answers and pick apart some of your comments. However, as with all question types, do not try to guess what the panel wants to hear. Answer truthfully. Ultimately, you need to be able to trust yourself.

Role Play Situations

Role play scenarios take situational questions one step further. As with situational queries, the board will present a hypothetical scene. However, in a role play scenario, board members will not only ask you to respond to a situation, but act it out in some way. They will ask you to pretend that you are a corrections officer and show your verbal or physical responses. *Example:*

Board Member: "Mr. Alvarez, I want you to pretend that you are a corrections officer and I'm an inmate who has just refused to pick up a candy wrapper I've tossed onto the day room floor. I want you to stand up now and tell me to pick up the candy wrapper."

Board members may set up a more elaborate role playing scene for you. Try to enter into these situations with a willingness to participate. Most people are aware that you are not a professional actor or actress so they are not looking for an Academy Award performance. Today, most law enforcement agencies use role play as part of their training, so you can expect to encounter this technique during your career as a corrections professional. Shy, reserved people may have difficulty working up enthusiasm for this kind of interaction. Practice how you'd handle this scene and prepare yourself mentally as best you can.

Personal Information

Applying for a job in public safety places you in a different league than the civilian sector applicant. Whereas federal and state laws may prohibit civilian employers from seeking certain information about their applicants, law enforcement agencies are allowed more freedom of movement within the laws.

For example, you'll rarely find a space for an applicant's birth date on an application for employment in private industry. This is the result of age discrimination litigation. Law enforcement agencies, as well as other agencies dealing with public safety, do not have many of the same restrictions. They need information—like your birth date, race, and sex—to perform thorough background investigations. You are applying for a sensitive public safety job and can expect to provide personal information that relates to your ability to do the job.

In short, agencies can ask you any question that bears on your mental stability, your ability to do the physical tasks common to corrections work, your integrity, honesty, character, and reputation in the community. You may be asked how you will cope with the working conditions of a corrections officer, or about your ability to function during a night shift. Agencies may ask you questions about your attitude toward diverse populations—such as coworkers and prisoners who may come from different racial, ethnic, religious, or cultural backgrounds than yourself. The best strategy to answering these questions is to be honest and direct.

Strategies for Answering Questions

The answers the board wants to hear are the ones only you can give. They want your opinion, your reasons, your personal experiences, and they want to know what you would do under certain circumstances. During the interview, no one else matters but you and how you present yourself. If you try to say what you think the board wants to hear, you will likely give them unsatisfying responses. Board members will often overlook answers they don't agree with if you show that you have a good reason for your response and that you are being honest.

The following are some suggestions for what works—and what doesn't work—when you are answering questions before an oral board.

- **Listen carefully.** Listen to the entire question. This shows your attentiveness and will help you focus your response. If you don't understand a question, ask the board member to clarify it.
- **Think first.** Don't answer impulsively. Take a moment to consider if any of your preparation relates to the question. Can you think of any specific examples that help answer the question?
- **Be direct.** Do not try to evade questions or put a spin on negative information. Give an answer that demonstrates that you've examined your actions and learned from your experience.
- **Stay focused.** Try to avoid long answers that wander off-track. If you lose your train of thought, take a moment to refocus. Keep your answers short, but give enough information to fully answer the question.

Giving thoughtful answers that are specific and brief is a good strategy for your interview. Here's an example of three responses to the common interview question, "Why do you want to be a corrections officer?"

- **Answer #1:** "The hours are good for me."
- **Answer #2:** "Corrections work is good, honest work."
- **Answer #3:** "I like the variety of duties and working with different people. I like the challenge of trying to figure out what's really going on in a given situation."

Answer #1 does not give a satisfying response to the question. It makes the applicant sound as if he or she is not interested in *performing* the job, and is only interested in a convenient work schedule. Although board members may want to know if a work schedule will suit you, it is not an adequate reason for why you want the job. Answer #2 is a positive answer, but it is too general. It does not show that the applicant knows about the nature of the job, nor does it reveal much about the applicant's goals. Answer #3 is the best of the three: it offers specific reasons why the applicant is interested in corrections work and reveals something about the applicant's skills.

Here are three responses to another common interview question: "Now that we know about some of the things you are good at, tell us something about yourself that you'd like to improve."

- **Answer #1:** "I'm really good with people. People like me and find it easy to talk to me for some reason."
- **Answer #2:** "I'm good with people, but my shortcoming is writing. I've always had trouble in that area."
- **Answer #3:** "Writing doesn't come easy to me. I'm better at saying things than writing them down. This is something I've worked hard on in my job as a security guard, in keeping daily records and writing up any incidents."

Answer #1 simply does not address the question. The applicant's response gives the impression that she did not listen carefully or has another reason for not being forthcoming. Answer #2 begins well—the applicant targets one of her weaknesses, but she does not offer any examples of how she has tried to correct the issue. Answer #3 is the best answer—the applicant is clearly aware of her weakness and has worked to remedy it.

Answering questions about problems or sensitive areas from your work or personal history may be challenging. However, the same answering strategies apply for these type of questions: think about the question before you answer, be honest, and stay focused. Here's an example of an exchange that tackles a difficult subject from the applicant's past:

Board Member: "Mr. Alvarez, I see you've been arrested once for public intoxication while you were in college? Is that true?"

Alvarez: "No, sir."

Board Member: "Really? That's odd. It says here on page seven that you were arrested and spent the night in the city jail."

Alvarez: "Yes, well, I wasn't exactly arrested because the officer didn't put handcuffs on me."

In this case, the applicant is playing word games with the board member instead of giving a direct reply. He knows that the board is aware of his arrest record but he's trying to downplay the incident by trying to duck the question. If you feel defensive about a particular aspect of your past, evaluate your feelings and reasons before the interview. This will help you overcome some of the emotional responses you might feel about the topic, so that you can answer questions clearly and openly.

Likewise, avoid giving brief answers that do not provide adequate information. For example:

Board Member: "Mr. Alvarez, tell the board why you left the job you held at Tread Lightly Tire Shop."

Alvarez: "I was fired."

Board Member: "Why were you fired?"

Alvarez: "Because the boss told me not to come back."

Board Member: "Why did the boss tell you not to come back?"

Alvarez: "Because I was fired."

Board Member: "What happened to cause you to be fired?"

Alvarez: "I was rude."

Board Member: "Rude to whom and under what circumstances?"

This question could have been answered fully when the Board Member asked Alvarez why he left the tire shop job. This answering technique would wear a board member's patience. Provide board members with full information, while at the same time staying focused so as not to offer a mix of emotional responses that sound like excuses.

By now, you should have a good idea of what an oral board is looking for and how you can do your best at your first interview. Read the following scenarios, trying to put yourself in the shoes of the oral board member who is asking the questions.

Scenario #1
Rosie Kramer is sitting before the oral interview board. She is wearing a pair of black pants, loafers, and a short-sleeve cotton blouse. As the board asks questions, she taps her foot against the table.

Board Member: "Ms. Kramer, can you give the board an example of how you've handled a disagreement with a coworker in the past?"

Kramer: "Nope. I get along with everybody. Everyone likes me."

Board Member: "I see. So, you've never had a disagreement or difference of opinion with anyone you've ever worked with."

Kramer: "That's right."

Board Member: "Well, I see by your application that you were once written up by a supervisor for yelling at a fellow employee. Can you tell us about that situation?"

Kramer: "That's different. It was his fault. He started talking with a customer who I was I was supposed to be waiting on."

Now read the second situation.

Scenario #2
Rosie Kramer is sitting before the oral interview board dressed in a gray suit. She is sitting still, with her hands folded in her lap and is looking directly at the person asking her a question.

Board Member: "Ms. Kramer, can you give the board an example of how you've handled a disagreement with a coworker in the past?"

Kramer: "Yes sir. I can think of an example. When I was working at "Pools by Polly," I had an argument with a coworker over which one of us was supposed to wait on a customer. I lost my cool and yelled at him. My boss wrote me up because of how I handled the situation."

Board Member: "I see. How do you think you should have handled the situation?"

Kramer: "If I had it to do again, I'd take James, my coworker, aside and talk to him about it in private. If I couldn't work something out with him I would ask my supervisor to help out."

Board Member: "What have you done to keep this sort of thing from happening again?"

Kramer: "I've learned to stop and think before I speak and I've learned that there is a time and place to work out differences when they come up. I haven't had a problem since this incident."

Although these scenarios seem somewhat exaggerated, they highlight some common pitfalls during interviews. In scenario #1, the applicant presents a nervous demeanor through her body language. Although her clothing is not offensive, it does not demonstrate her respect for the board or for the job. She also makes several key errors in her responses. She shows that she is unwilling to accept responsibility for her actions and that she hasn't learned from her past experiences. In addition, she isn't honest with herself or the board members when she said everyone liked her and she's never had disagreements with coworkers.

On the other hand, in scenario #2, the applicant shows her interest in the job by her dress and manner. She is able to admit her mistakes and take responsibility for her part in the incident. Although she may have wished she could present herself in a better light, she illustrates maturity by being honest, open, and straightforward in talking about the disagreement.

The Lie Detector Test

Some departments require a polygraph test (better known as a lie detector test) as part of the background investigation and interview process, although the polygraph, if required, is typically one of the last steps you will go through. A polygraph test is usually given after you've had the oral board interview.

There really is no such thing as a lie detector. What the polygraph detects are changes in heart and respiratory rates, blood pressure, and galvanic skin resistance (basically a measure of how much you are perspiring). A cuff like the one your doctor uses to take your blood pressure will be wrapped around your arm. Rubber tubes around your trunk will measure your breathing, and clips on your fingers or palm will measure skin response. The theory is that people who are consciously lying get nervous, and their involuntary bodily responses give them away.

Don't worry about being betrayed by being nervous in the first place. Everyone's a little nervous when confronting a new technology. The polygraph examiner will explain the whole process to you. More importantly, the examiner will ask you a series of questions to establish a baseline both for when you're telling the truth and for when you are not. For instance, the examiner might tell you to answer "No" to every question and then ask you whether your name is George (if it isn't) and whether you drove to the examination today (if you did).

All questions for a polygraph exam have to be in yes-or-no format. You should be told in advance what every question will be. Some will be easy lobs like whether you're wearing sneakers. The questions that really count will be ones that relate to your fitness to be a corrections officer: whether you've committed a crime, or whether you've been arrested. You will probably have been over any problematic areas with the background investigator or other interviewers before, so just tell the truth and try to relax.

▶ Pulling It All Together

The interview is a major factor in the hiring process for corrections work. The interview is your chance to show the board who you are and how much you want the job. You may not know what questions the board will ask you, but there is a lot you can do to get ready and improve your chances of success. Before you step into the interview room, review the guidelines and scenarios in this chapter and do some background research about the duties of corrections work. If you are short on job experience or education, look into volunteer work, job opportunities, or courses that will increase your knowledge and skill level. Be sure to do some research about yourself as well—review your strengths, shortcomings, beliefs, and your work and personal history. As you gain self-awareness, you will also gain confidence in your ability to effectively answer the questions of the oral board.

16▶

Psychological Assessment and Medical Exam

CHAPTER SUMMARY

Some states and correctional facilities require a psychological interview and testing as part of the application process, and all require a medical examination. This chapter highlights the basics of psychological testing—test types and formats as well as the characteristics the test is looking for in a candidate. You'll also learn what to expect when you go in for your medical exam.

Because corrections work is safety-sensitive, high-stress, and demands a great deal of responsibility, some law enforcement agencies use psychological testing to screen applicants during the hiring process. Agencies use psychological testing—along with a lengthy application, background check, and one or more interviews—to complete the picture of a candidate. Because interviews before the oral board may be subjective—dependent on the differing opinions of board members—an agency may use testing to provide a uniform measure with which to compare job applicants. They may also be looking for specific factors that make an applicant a good fit for corrections work. Its purpose is to make sure you have the emotional and mental health to do the job. Psychological tests can assess qualities such as your:

- work style
- leadership abilities
- style of interacting with people
- unique stress factors and ways of coping
- approach to conflict resolution

- likelihood of mature, responsible behavior
- response to supervision

If you've never taken a psychological test before, the prospect of completing one may make you anxious. Knowing what you can expect will help calm your nerves and increase your confidence during the process.

What does testing involve? Although the type of psychological testing you encounter may vary depending on the law enforcement agency, it often consists of a two-step process. The first phase is a pencil-and-paper test—applicants are asked to answer multiple-choice questions or complete another kind of written format. Testing can take less than an hour, or several hours. The second phase of the assessment is a personal interview with a psychologist. For example, the sheriff's department in Pima County, Arizona, which serves the seventh largest county in the nation, requires a battery of psychological tests for corrections officer positions. The testing takes about three hours to complete and is followed by a psychological interview.

What will the psychologist ask you? Questions may concern your work or personal history, but they must relate to your ability to perform the corrections work. You may be asked about your family relationships, your former jobs, or your military or school experiences. Difficulties or problems in your past that come to light during the interview are not necessarily seen as negative factors. During your assessment it may be helpful to remember that psychologists recognize that everyone makes mistakes and that overcoming difficulties does not necessarily impair your ability to do the job. More likely, the psychologist will be interested in how you handle difficulties and problems—for example, how do you cope with conflict? How do you deal with others? What have you learned from your experiences?

Movies and television shows that depict psychologists often give the impression that psychologists have special powers to read minds or "look into your soul."

The objective of psychological testing is not to read your mind—nor is it to criticize you. Rather the goal is to look at your personality characteristics and behavioral patterns to see if you are a good match with the job demands of being a corrections officer. The psychological assessment is a tool to help select the right candidate for the job.

▶ Psychological Testing

Testing is often the first part of the assessment process. A common test used by law enforcement agencies is some form of the Minnesota Multiphasic Personality Inventory (MMPI). This personality test consists of 560 true/false questions and takes from 60–90 minutes to complete. The test is designed to produce a general psychological profile and to detect possible problem areas in attitude and behavior. The results may or may not be explained to you, depending on the policies of the department. If the test results raise any questions, your interview with the psychologist will enable you to answer them face-to-face.

Another type of test that law enforcement agencies use to screen job candidates is called an integrity test. This kind of assessment is designed to evaluate an applicant's specific job-related behaviors. It looks at a candidate's dependability and trustworthiness as well as an applicant's potential for problematic behavior on the job, like drug use or workplace violence.

You cannot study for a psychological test—but you can prepare for it. The following strategies will ease pretest jitters and make you more comfortable in the test setting.

- **Learn the details.** Know the testing location, the test format and duration, and find out what you need to bring with you (like ID or a pencil). The more you know about what to expect, the less anxious you will feel.

- **Stay as relaxed as possible.** Remember that the psychological test is only one part of the hiring process. If you feel tense or find it difficult to concentrate on the questions, pause and take a few deep breaths.
- **Don't try to figure out the "right" answer** or guess at what each question is getting at. The tests are designed to make this difficult. Trying to psych out the assessment will only confuse the results.
- **Answer questions honestly.** If you fake your answers, your assessment will be skewed. You want to give a true picture of yourself.

▶ The Psychological Interview

It's important to show up for your interview on time and be neatly dressed. The psychologist (or psychologists—some departments use a team) may spend a few initial moments breaking the ice, but the rest of the 60–90 minutes will be focused and businesslike.

The psychologist, who may be either on the hiring agency's staff or an independent contractor, will have the results from your psychological assessment. He or she may follow up on areas highlighted by the test or ask for additional information. You may be asked questions about your family background or work experiences as they relate to your ability to be effective as a corrections officer. Questions may cover aspects of your upbringing, relationships or marriage(s), and military and high school experiences. Expect questions about the job supervisors you liked or didn't like in your work history; this will give the psychologist some insight into how you deal with authority. If some aspects of your work life are areas of concern, like if you've moved around from job to job, be ready to explain your reasons if asked. And, as in your interview with the oral board, be prepared to answer why you want to be a corrections officer. The psychologist may

be as interested in the way in which you answer questions—whether you come across as forthcoming and honest—as in the content of the answers themselves.

Respond politely to the psychologist's questions—give full answers without over-elaborating. At the same time, avoid being evasive or defensive when answering questions. The same strategies that are useful during your interview before the oral board will aid you in the psychological interview: listen carefully to questions, think first before you answer, be direct, and stay focused.

It's okay to be nervous—psychologists expect job candidates to display nervousness. You can even admit that you are nervous—this shows that you are being upfront. However, you don't need to try hard to sell yourself. The point of the assessment is to get an accurate picture of you—your personality, attitudes, and experiences—to see if you are a good match to fit the duties and responsibilities of a corrections officer.

▶ The Medical Examination

At some point in the application process, every candidate must undergo a mandatory medical exam. The medical exam is similar to any other thorough physical exam. The doctor may be on the staff of the department, or, in some smaller departments, an outside physician with his or her own practice on contract with the department. The physician will measure your blood pressure, temperature, and weight; listen to your heart and lungs; and examine your limbs, eyes, ears, nose, and mouth. You will also be asked to supply some blood and some urine for testing. It may take a few weeks for the test results to be complete—you will be notified of the results of the physical exam at that time.

Before passage of the Americans with Disabilities Act (ADA), most corrections departments conducted a medical examination early in the process, before the physical ability test. Now, the ADA says it is illegal to do any examinations or ask any questions that could reveal an applicant's disability until after a conditional offer of employment has been made. That means that in most cases, you will get a conditional offer before you are asked to submit to a medical exam. Indeed, you may get such an offer before the polygraph examination, the psychological examination, or, in a few cases, before the background investigation, because all these components could reveal a disability.

Drug Testing

Note, however, that a test for use of illegal drugs can be administered before a conditional offer of employment. If the test comes back positive because of an applicant's use of prescription drugs, the department can ask about and verify the prescription drug use. However, it cannot use the condition for which the drugs are prescribed to reject an applicant.

Being drug-free is an occupational qualification for a corrections officer—many agencies have a "zero tolerance" policy about drug use by officers.

Physical Disabilities and the ADA

After the conditional offer of employment, applicants can be rejected for disabilities revealed in the medical or psychological exam, according to the ADA, as long as the disabilities are related to essential job functions and no reasonable accommodations exist that would make it possible for the applicant to function in the job. For instance, a potential corrections officer with a heart condition can reasonably be rejected on the basis of that disability. While officers don't often need to run down inmates, they may have to do so at a moment's notice, and the department can't accommodate someone who can't safely run a prison hallway and still get the job done.

If you've gotten this far, you don't have any obvious or seriously disabling conditions. You got through the written exam, physical ability test, psychological evaluation, and interview. Any other conditions that you reveal at this point or that come up in the medical exam will be dealt with on a case-by-case basis. Even conditions such as diabetes or epilepsy need not disqualify you, if your condition is controlled so that you are able to fulfill essential job functions.

NOTES

NOTES

NOTES

NOTES

NOTES

NOTES

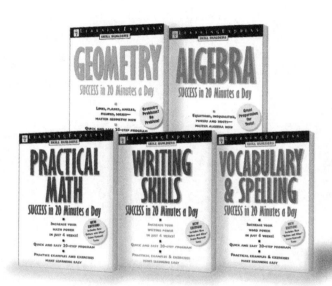